D1132887

t 15 —

Kel⁻
was+   SB3153

The Romance of
Bible Scripts and Scholars

The Romance
of
Bible Scripts
and
Scholars:

Chapters in the History of Bible Transmission

and Translation

John H. P. Reumann

Prentice-Hall, Inc.
Englewood Cliffs, N. J.

The Romance of Bible Scripts and Scholars
by John H. P. Reumann

© 1965 by Prentice-Hall, Inc., Englewood Cliffs, N.J. All rights reserved including the right to reproduce this book, or any portions thereof, in any form except for the inclusion of brief quotations in a review.

Library of Congress Catalog Card Number: 65–21174

Printed in the United States of America

T 78294

PRENTICE-HALL INTERNATIONAL, INC., *London*
PRENTICE-HALL OF AUSTRALIA, PTY., LTD., *Sydney*
PRENTICE-HALL OF CANADA, LTD., *Toronto*
PRENTICE-HALL OF INDIA (PRIVATE) LTD., *New Delhi*
PRENTICE-HALL OF JAPAN, INC., *Tokyo*

To My Parents

Abbreviations

K.J.V. The King James Version of the Bible, 1611
E.R.V. The English Revised Version, 1881–85
R.S.V. The Revised Standard Version, 1946–52
N.E.B. The New English Bible, New Testament 1961

Contents

Introduction

ROMANCE IS NOT A WORD WHICH PEOPLE INSTINCTIVELY AS-
sociate with old manuscripts and erudite scholars. Yet there
is drama in the pages of the Bible—Walt Whitman spoke of its
verses as "thick-studded with human emotion." The story of
how these Scriptures, Jewish and Christian, have been transmitted through the centuries to us is likewise studded with
emotion and drama. And "romantic" is the word to describe
some of the experiences of those learned men who have translated
Scripture.

We seldom think about the long centuries through which the
Bible has been handed down to us. What vicissitudes has it
suffered? Who played heroic roles? The importance of "transmission history," from the time a biblical document was finished
until we read it in translation today, has grown on me in preparing these chapters.

Translation is likewise an art and science which we may take
too much for granted. Any translator is faced with an enormous
challenge in transferring words and thoughts from one language
and age to another. In the case of the Bible, he is taking up the
most intensely studied body of literature in history, the world's
most frequently translated book—over 1,215 languages and

dialects currently. He handles the sacred books of Jews (of varying shades of thought) and of Christians (who are of even more
diverse views denominationally). He must make decisions and
put them down tersely in black and white about matters fraught
with centuries of dispute.

Feelings can run high about a Bible rendering. A new translation is likely to be "glouted upon by every evil eye" and "gored
by every sharp tongue"—the Preface to the King James Version
of the Bible used these very words in 1611 to describe the experience of its translators. "He that meddleth with men's religion in
any part, meddleth with their custom, nay with their freehold."
Hence the outcry. What these Jacobean scholars discovered in the
seventeenth century has held true at other times. A Jewish
proverb recorded in the Babylonian Talmud (*Kiddushin* 49a)
sums up the translator's dilemma. "He lies who renders a verse as
it reads, with strict literalness; he blasphemes who makes additions." Literalness is wrong because it doesn't really transfer the
thought of the original; paraphrase is wrong because it reads in
other meanings. "Damned if you do, damned if you don't," is
the translator's fate. Jerome, who put the Bible into Latin about
A.D. 400, complained that if he had been a basketweaver, no one
would have cared about his work, but since he obeyed the Lord's
precept to prepare "the bread which perishes not," men have ac-
cused him of falsifying the sacred text if he corrects errors and
of disseminating them if he does not. It's small wonder that a
scholar in our own day, Ronald Knox, entitled a book about his
experiences *Trials of a Translator!*

There are, of course, a number of good books about the
broad sweep of the history of Bible translation, but usually these
surveys must cover so much ground that they cannot go into detail about some of the more fascinating chapters in transmission
and translation. In writing such a general account, *Four Centuries of the English Bible* (Philadelphia: Muhlenberg Press,
1961), I found myself concentrating almost exclusively on the
two "great centuries" of translation work—the period from

1515 to 1615, culminating in the King James Version; and the century beginning about 1880 and continuing to the present—only on the big names, at that, within each century. Even the definitive *Cambridge History of the Bible*, now appearing, has but a page or so for men like Ronald Knox and Charles Thomson or for that diverse group of laymen behind *The Twentieth Century New Testament*. Hence one aim in this collection of stories is to enrich the broad outline of how the Bible has come to us, by recounting certain chapters which deserve to be better known.

A second aim will also appear. In retelling certain tales, I have used these stories to discuss *why, what,* and *how* men translate. Chapter One deals with the story of the Septuagint in order to help answer the question of motives in translation. Chapter Two relates incidents from the second century A.D. to enable us to see the problem which every translator faces, about what text is to be followed. Chapter Three takes up the question of *how* Bible translation should be done, by narrating the efforts of Luther and the other Reformation translators when the "how" of translation was quite sharply posed. The other chapters deal with the "who" of translation, and answer the question of who shall translate by reminding us of some of the men and women who have already translated Scripture. An Epilogue ventures to predict something about the why and what and how of future translations.

Within this framework, I have chosen the episodes, in some cases, because the handbooks must ignore them or because the information is buried away from the wider public in archives and learned journals; in other cases, because it is worth looking at a familiar tale from a fresh angle or in light of recent discoveries; at times, simply because the story is so good that it deserves retelling. I am also conscious, as I watch the list of reprints and paperback editions, that some of these translations from the past are again available in bookshops today, and readers may want to know more of their backgrounds. It remains

true that whether we champion some older translation or pre-
fer a single new one or revel in the variety of renderings available, it behooves us to know as much as possible about our
favorite renderings and the alternatives possible. Then we can
judge—and appreciate—results in the ongoing drama of Bible
transmission and translation.

To several of my colleagues, Professors Russell D. Snyder and
Theodore G. Tappert; to Dr. Robert Kraft, of the University of
Pennsylvania; and to Dr. J. Carter Swaim, now pastor at the
Church of the Covenant, New York, I appreciatively record my
thanks for reading portions of the manuscript. The assistance
of the staffs at the Krauth Memorial Library of the Lutheran
Theological Seminary, Westminster Theological Seminary, the
Historical Society of Pennsylvania, the American Philosophical
Society, and the Presbyterian Historical Society, all in Philadel-
phia, and the John Rylands Library, Manchester, is likewise a
joy to record.

The quotations of the Knox Bible in Chapter Eight are from
The New Testament in the translation of Monsignor Ronald
Knox, Copyright 1944, Sheed & Ward, Inc., New York, and,
for Psalm 22, from *The Old Testament* Volume II, in the translation of Monsignor Knox, Copyright 1950, Sheed & Ward,
Inc., New York, with the kind permission of the Archbishop of
Westminster. The lines from Knox's poem "Absolute and Abitofhell" are quoted with the permission of his literary executor,
Mr. Evelyn Waugh. A briefer version of Chapter Six appeared
in *The Lutheran* (Philadelphia), 44, 19–20 (Feb. 14, 21, 1962),
pp. 16–18 and 16–19.

One

The "Committee of Seventy" and Its Work, The Septuagint:

Bible Translation in the Ancient World

W HY TRANSLATE THE BIBLE—OR, FOR THAT MATTER, ANY book?

Obviously, translations exist in order to help us read what an author has written in some other language. Translation helps us get clearly and rapidly the drift of what he says. But a little thought reminds us that translations are really never wholly accurate. They filter one man's thought through another man's words, then to us. They vary among themselves. That is why one translator always must try to improve on the work of the other. Each rendering is but an echo of the original, so that we need several, sometimes many of them, if we are to get the "meat" and sense. Thus a translation, and better, translations will come into being in order that we may get not only the broad idea of what someone once wrote years ago or far away, but also in order that we may have, even through variations and different ways of putting things, a deeper understanding of that writer. We want to get the "feel" of his style, his mind, his view of life. If we can't read the original (and sometimes even if we can), we want translations to help us understand more fully, to enable us to "stand under" the man we read and grow kindred with him.

With sacred writings the matter is somewhat different. In

5

scriptures we are interested in more than understanding points in an argument, in more than the surface sense and even than the "feel" of a composition. The translator here deals not just with literature but with *religious* literature, the documents of a faith, whether Judaism, Christianity, Islam, or Hinduism are involved. Emotions, sentiment, tradition, and convictions rise to the surface. The words are words of power, not just for entertainment, but for the living of life. And with the Bible, the Holy Scripture of Jews and Christians, a special situation exists for those who believe, as is evidenced by the various ideas of inspiration men have held and hold about this book. God's Holy Spirit is felt to be at work creatively, both in the making of the words of witness in the Bible and in their proclamation afresh today, even in a translated tongue. Here in the words of ancient witnesses the Word of God is held to speak anew, again, to men who heed, so that, in Karl Barth's terms, Paul's Epistle to the Romans is "God's special delivery letter to the twentieth century," and Moses, Jeremiah, Peter, John, though dead for centuries, yet speak. Thus the translator of biblical documents is confronted with two further factors: he deals with *sacred* writings, and they are sacred to a *community* or church, to whom the very words he translates speak as Word of God.

Why translate? Accustomed to translations as we are, we find we use them to get the sense and meet the author and his world. Even on this literary level we seldom think how hard the task is and we shy away from the harsh realism of the Italian proverb, *traduttore traditore,* "translator, traitor"—the translator seldom brings across the sense fully and precisely and thus betrays his author. And on the level of religious writings we find the harried translator must work not just for accurate meaning well expressed, but also with material to be used devotionally and inspirationally, both in private and public. He deals with documents of the church which will be used especially by and for the religious community.

Recent writers about the Bible have emphasized this last point admirably. The Bible is the church's book. The story of how the Bible came to be put into English must be told from its setting within the church's life. Thus F. C. Grant's account, *Translating the Bible*, insists that "chiefly, the Bible is the book used in worship"; its presence at public worship, on the lectern of church or synagogue, stands in the forefront.[1] "The most natural setting for the Bible is liturgical," and the history of its translation gains perspective when seen from this vantage point. But it is worth noting that while we live in a period when church groups and councils of churches are actively promoting Bible translation, such was not always the case. As the Reformation broke in England, William Tyndale had to proceed with his translation plans contrary to ecclesiastical officials. Fifty years ago we went through a period when individuals like Weymouth, Moffatt, and Goodspeed (whose very names became household words for Bibles) wrote new chapters in translation annals by working on their own, not under churchly auspices or toward versions to be used liturgically. Therefore, although today much emphasis is being put on church translations and the Bible's use in worship, it is worth asking *why* in the course of history men have translated Scripture, for there are a variety of reasons and factors.

No better place to ask "Why translate?" exists than the very first attempt, by Jews, to render the Old Testament from Hebrew into a more universal language. Analysis of this so-called Septuagint, the work of a "Committee of Seventy," in the ancient world will show us a variety of reasons for translating, motives which hold good down to our own day and parallel contemporary motives in part, e.g., the arguments for producing the New English Bible. Our study of the Septuagint—that first giant step in the romantic story of Bible translation—need be no academic exercise in dry-as-dust history (though it is forbiddingly complicated), for here we see some answers to the question "Why translate?"—and here we are brought face to face with the Bible of the early Christians. This Septuagint poses problems, but it also offers insights for Bible students today; though little known, it deserves wider attention.

The oldest account which has come down to us from antiquity concerning how a Bible translation was made is *The Letter of Aristeas*. As the document unfolds its tale, Aristeas, the author, is seen to be a Greek, probably from the island of Cyprus. He is an official at the Greek court of Ptolemy Philadelphus, the king of Egypt in the third century B.C. The events described seem to fall into a period between 278 and 270 B.C. Aristeas is writing to his brother, Philocrates, a man who loves learning and encourages Aristeas to record his travels and experiences in the royal service.

Actually, *The Letter of Aristeas* deals more with a trip to Jerusalem and with the table-talk at a banquet in Alexandria than with Bible translation. Its story about how the Pentateuch —the Law or Torah of the Jews, the five Old Testament books of Genesis to Deuteronomy—was put into Greek is something of a closing appendage, comprising less than a tenth of the whole document. But the lengthy travelog and the banquet scene all serve to enhance this climactic account of the translation of the Jewish Law into the Greek language.

Aristeas begins by telling how, one day, he heard the learned Demetrius, from Phalerum in Greece, in charge of the king's library, relate his plans for expanding the library's 200,000 books so as to acquire "the rest," a goal of half a million books. (The figures are not completely fantastic. Some estimates assure us that the famous Alexandrian Library eventually did reach a total of 500,000–700,000 scrolls!) Demetrius reports that he had heard that the laws of the Jews are worth transcribing, but first they need to be translated. The king, perhaps aware that his subjects include a sizable Jewish population, offers to write to the High Priest in Jerusalem for aid. At this point Aristeas petitions the king for what he has long desired, namely, the release from slavery of some hundred thousand Jews who had been captured in a recent campaign against the Seleucids in Palestine. As a gesture of good will, Ptolemy magnanimously agrees. Surely his "emancipation proclamation" would do no harm in persuading the High Priest to help in getting a Pentateuch translation for the royal library! Aristeas, appropriately, is then chosen (along with Andreas, the chief of the Bodyguard) to head the delegation to Jerusalem and put the matter before the High Priest, Eleazer.

The *Letter* at this point seems to go into excruciating detail. The Ptolemy's proclamation freeing the Jewish slaves is quoted in full. So is his letter to the High Priest, as is Eleazer's reply. There is a full description of the gifts which the king sends to the High Priest: a table of "massive gold" adorned with precious stones for use at the Temple, twenty golden and thirty silver cups, five bowls, and golden vials—all so lavish and beautiful that Aristeas despairs of describing them adequately. There is, moreover, a detailed picture of Jerusalem—of the Temple (not neglecting even its water supply), the ministry of the priests, the citadel and the rest of the city, and the surrounding country-side. One might fear that the thread of the story is forgotten, but ancient readers reveled in such travel accounts of wonders in other lands, and we may recall that the messengers in Greek tragedy always seem to give the most involved narrations about trivia before they come to their news.

Eleazer indicates that he will grant the unusual request conveyed by Aristeas, and will send manuscripts and translators to Alexandria. Six learned elders from each of the twelve tribes are appointed, and they are named by name. (Only seventy-one of the seventy-two names are preserved in our manuscripts.) Aristeas calls attention to their character, culture, and linguistic ability. At last the plot begins to move again, as the seventy-two bid farewell to Eleazer and leave for Alexandria and their work, but even here Aristeas pauses again to record for his brother a lengthy defense by Eleazer of the Law of the Jews. This defense, which strikes Aristeas as excellent at all points, is almost as lengthy as the description of Jerusalem.

Then, in a single sentence, the seventy-two translators, together with their magnificent parchments written in gold, accompanied by Aristeas, arrive in Alexandria. But they cannot go to work as yet, for the Ptolemy himself is anxious to see them. He waives the usual five-day waiting period for foreign envoys and immediately welcomes them himself. He reverences their scrolls, bowing deeply seven times, and both thanks them for coming and thanks the God "whose holy words these are." When they cry, "God save the king!" he weeps for joy. That very day, which also happens to be the anniversary of an Egyptian naval victory, he insists they must dine with him, and so a banquet scene follows for several pages more, before the actual translation work begins. It is not so much the sumptuous fare of the banquet which is featured (Aristeas carefully points out that the *kosher* customs of the Jewish guests were respected), as the dialog which goes on during the seven days of banqueting. Each day, during a pause in the menu, King Philadelphus addresses a series of questions to the scholars from Jerusalem, one after another, ten each day and eleven on the sixth and seventh days, so that each of the seventy-two distinguishes himself with a wise and philosophical answer. The king is delighted at their learning and practical wisdom, and Menedemus, a Socratic philosopher from Euboea, joins in praising them. All the banqueters applaud at the end of this intellectual tour de force, and Aristeas himself is especially impressed at the way these Jews give perfect answers on the spur of the moment to questions which the philosophical mind has long pondered. Perhaps he is aware that his narrative is a bit forced, for he comments, "I imagine that to all those who read the account in the future, it will seem incredible." As a matter of fact, many later scholars have felt that *The Letter of Aristeas* is here drawing on a Hellenistic handbook of "Moral Sayings," for the sentiments expressed in the answers are duplicated in proverbs and philosophy all over the Greek world—some as far away as India. Even if we allow that the Jerusalem priesthood in the third and second centuries B.C. was consid-

erably secularized at times, it does seem incongruous for priests
from the Temple to be answering questions like "What is philosophy?" in definitions commonplace among Greek Socratics,
or to be claiming that a man should occupy his hours of recrea-
tion watching plays.

At last, three days later, the seventy-two learned translators
are escorted along the sea wall of Alexandria's harbor, four-fifths
of a mile along the Heptastadion, the "Seven Stades," a mole
built by Alexander the Great connecting the island of Pharos
with the mainland. To the west was a harbor called "The Haven
of Happy Return." To the east, protected by its own breakwater,
was the even larger Great Harbor. Further to the east lay the
Jewish Quarter of Alexandria, surrounded by its own walls and
gates. Closer by, across the Great Harbor, was the palace of the
Ptolemies and the great Library and Museum of Alexandria. On
the "island" of Pharos at the easternmost tip stood the great
Lighthouse, one of the wonders of the ancient world. Over three
hundred feet in height—some claim five hundred—it towered,
crowned by a statue of Poseidon, god of the sea. Its four stories
contrasted pleasantly in design. The first was square, the second
hexagonal, the third circular, and in the fourth stood the lantern
and a "mirror" (either a metal reflector or a telescope). It had
only just been dedicated, in 279 B.C., and was destined to stand
intact as a landmark for mariners until the Arab Conquest nine
centuries later. Somewhere in the shadow of this lighthouse, on
the northern shore of Pharos, in a house "seated upon much
quietness," a house prepared with everything translators might
need, the seventy-two go to work.

The Letter of Aristeas tells us disappointingly little about their
actual methods of work—a point which unfortunately holds true
for most Bible translations down to the present; seldom are we
left accounts describing how a translator works. We are told in
this case that each morning the elders appear at court to salute
the king before starting work. Later accounts have them ferried
back and forth across the Great Harbor two by two in thirty-

six skiffs. Then, following Jewish custom, the translators wash
their hands (in the sea) and pray to God before starting work,
just as a pious scribe at Qumran might have done, or the Pharisees in Jesus' day (cf. Mark 7:3–4). The translators, we are told,
labor until three P.M., after which time they are free to attend
to personal needs and to relax. It is emphasized that they arrive
at a harmonious rendering by comparing their work and making
details agree; there is no emphasis on miraculous inspiration, only
laborious work. Once a translation is agreed upon, it is copied
down under the direction of Demetrius the librarian. It turns out,
Aristeas adds, that the seventy-two translators completed their
job in exactly seventy-two days.

The report from Aristeas concludes by describing the reactions
to the translation. The Jewish community at Alexandria ap-
proves it as "accurate in every respect" and enjoins a curse on
anyone who should add, omit, or change a word of this Greek
Pentateuch, just as Deuteronomy 4:2 commands, and as the
author of the book of Revelation was to do in Christian times
(Rev. 22:18f.). The king rejoices, especially when he hears the
contents of the Jewish Law read to him, and he wonders why
such a magnificent achievement had never been referred to by
the poets or historians. Demetrius explains that Theopompus, a
historian who had a craving for the sensational and sought out
exotic, foreign tales, from as far away as India, once had tried
to insert excerpts from the Pentateuch in one of his histories,
and that Theodectes, a dramatist who was a friend of Aristotle,
had attempted to adopt some of the incidents in a play of his.
But both men were smitten by God because they were transmitting things divine to ordinary men just out of a sense of med-
dling curiosity. For that reason, Theopompus lost his mind and
Theodectes was afflicted with cataracts, until they repented and
desisted from their rash actions.

Aristeas' *Letter* lets the curtain fall with the seventy-two
scholarly heroes on their way back to Jerusalem, laden with
gifts. "And you, Philocrates," he concludes, "you have your

story in full. You who are devoted to study of what improves the mind, you will find these books, I think, will delight you more than those of the Greek myth-writers."

How has this tale of Aristeas fared down through the years? It is, we said, the oldest account of Bible translation. It depicts no translators individually (even though the seventy-two are named), for Aristeas, Ptolemy Philadelphus, and even Demetrius are bystanders, not translators. We must wait another three or four centuries until individual personalities emerge in the second century A.D. But there is a decided tendency to play up the learning, piety, and wisdom of the men who first put the Torah into Greek from Hebrew.

From the number of scholars mentioned by Aristeas as engaged in the project has come the name by which their work has subsequently been known. For a time, later writers referred to their achievement simply as "the interpretation of the elders" or "of the seventy-two men," but at least since the fourth century A.D. the number seventy-two has been rounded off to seventy. For what reason, we cannot tell. Manuscripts of ancient writings, it is true, frequently vacillate between the numbers seventy and seventy-two (e.g., Luke 10:1). And Aristeas' figure —twelve tribes times six equals seventy-two—was awkward for his pattern of ten questions at the seven banquets. Somehow, for some reason, in time, his number came to be rounded off at seventy (which is a popular and significant number in Scripture; cf. Exodus 24:1 and 9, for example). The translation became known as "the work of the seventy." Since the Latin word for "seventy" is *septuaginta*, the translation got the name of "Septuagint," i.e., that of the seventy elders. Frequently this was further abbreviated to the symbol "LXX," the number seventy in Roman numerals, and "LXX" has been its designation ever since.

After Aristeas' day, the story of the LXX was frequently retold. Philo, the Jewish philosopher in Alexandria, in recounting it about A.D. 40, introduced a new note, when he emphasized the inspiration of the translators. They were, he says, "as if possessed, speaking forth not some one thing, some another, but they all employed the very same Greek terms and words, as if there were a prompter invisibly dictating to each one." Later in the first century, Josephus, the Jewish historian who had been a general in the revolt against Rome, made the story of the Septuagint a part of his *Antiquities of the Jewish People,* and then the Fathers in the Christian church took up the tale.

The accounts grow curiously more elaborate. The seventy-two translators are said to have worked in pairs, each pair isolated from the other pairs even at night, sleeping in thirty-six separate chambers; nonetheless, their thirty-six separate translations, when finally compared, are said to have agreed miraculously. Gone is the picture in *Aristeas* of a team of scholars working together to harmonize details in the most accurate way possible; Philo's Hellenistic concept of inspiration (his word is in Greek *enthousiōntes,* to be "enthused," to be "full of the god") has won the day, and the wondrous, almost the magical, is stressed. Most significantly, the later writers extend the name "LXX" and the miraculous story of its translation to cover *all* the books of the Old Testament, instead of just the five books of the Pentateuch to which it had been limited in Aristeas' account. The term "Septuagint" is now applied to a very diverse collection of books in Greek, including not only the canon of twenty-four books recognized by Judaism (the sixty-six books of the Protestant Bible), but also the so-called Apocrypha (accounted canonical by Roman Catholics), and beyond that sometimes including III or IV Maccabees, books found in no later Bible, Jewish, Protestant, or Catholic.

Critical scholarship, however, has come to question much in the accounts. Already about the year A.D. 400, Jerome protested, "I do not know who was the first author to construct seventy cells at Alexandria with his lie," for Jerome knew that the notion of separate cells was not in *The Letter of Aristeas. Aristeas* itself

was challenged in the Renaissance. The most thorough demoli-
tion came in a book by the Reverend Humphry Hody, Regius
Professor of Greek at Oxford, in 1684. Hody demonstrated to
the satisfaction of most subsequent readers that parts of *Aristeas*
are legend, not history. The figure seventy-two, for example, for
both the number of translators and the number of days involved,
is suspicious. So is a reference to the twelve tribes almost five centuries after ten of them disappeared from recorded history. The
names of the translators seem sheer invention, and several times
the author of *Aristeas* nods in his references to historical persons
or events. Most glaring of all is the fact that a Greek in the
Ptolemaic court has penned what is an obvious defense and glori-
fication of Judaism, its Bible and Holy City. More likely, it has
been concluded, *The Letter of Aristeas* is a piece of propaganda
by a Jew to enlighten non-Jews about his people and their
faith. His device, of having "Aristeas" write an "objective" account to a fellow-Greek, his brother "Philocrates," is precisely
that—a device.

Even though most modern investigators thus feel that *The
Letter of Aristeas* is unhistorical in its pose and in certain details,
many are willing to grant that a basically true story about Bible
translation is at the core of the document. They allow, for instance, that Alexandria, with its large Jewish population and
great Greek cultural heritage, was the natural place for the first
translation of the Pentateuch into Greek. They allow that Hebrew texts for the purpose could have been brought from Jerusalem, and even that a copy of the translation could have found
its way into the royal Library, and that the translation effort
could have begun as early as the third century B.C. But they
doubt that the king commissioned the undertaking or welcomed
the translation so warmly—that is propaganda. More likely, the
endeavor originated within the Jewish community at Alexandria.

Some critics are even more radical, however. They would date
The Letter of Aristeas not at about 270 B.C., when it claims to
have been written, but as late as 40 B.C. One of the most in-

triguing theories is that of the late Professor Paul Kahle, a re-
nowned Semitics scholar (1875–1964), who argued that there
never was any LXX, at least until Christian times, and that our
Letter of Aristeas is propaganda for a *revision* of the Greek
Bible which was made in Alexandria. Kahle claimed that there
were no "official" translation undertakings in Judaism such as
Aristeas suggests, but rather a number of local attempts—in
Alexandria, in Ephesus, in any town with a sizable group of
Greek-speaking Jews. These translations naturally differed in
quality, and there was no standardization. But about 130 B.C.,
the theory continues, Jews in Alexandria revised the competing,
ragged renderings which were circulating in their area of Egypt,
and put out a sort of "Revised Standard Version," intended to be
the norm thereafter. *The Letter of Aristeas* was an attempt to
give this revision authority by cloaking it with antiquity. Hence
also the curse on anyone who would change a word of it. But
even this attempt at standardization, Kahle thought, did not
bring about order from the chaos. Different Greek renderings
continued to circulate. And so, when Christians (who increasingly after the year A.D. 50 were Greeks who knew little or no
Hebrew) employed the Old Testament, they inevitably borrowed from these varied Jewish Greek translations—the Pentateuch as it had been revised at Alexandria, the book of Daniel as
it had been translated at Ephesus, and so forth—until they put
together an Old Testament in Greek, complete now, which they
called the "Septuagint," after the title from the Aristeas legend.
On this reading of the evidence, the LXX is a Christian compilation, and *The Letter of Aristeas* is a fiction designed to further
the use of a revision in Alexandria about 130 B.C.

Professor Kahle's theory has its enthusiastic supporters. However, perhaps a majority of those concerned with the intricate
problems still hold to the traditional view in some form, especially as that view was developed in the nineteenth century by
Professor Paul Anton de Lagarde of Göttingen—viz., that
Aristeas correctly reflects the fact that Jews in Alexandria had

translated the Pentateuch into Greek as early as the third century B.C., that by the late second century B.C. the rest of the Old Testament had been translated, and thus there was a LXX Bible prior to the Christian era. We may further note that even though experts once tried to dismiss *Aristeas* completely as any sort of history, researches into the papyri recovered from the trash heaps of Egypt in the late nineteenth century have vindicated *Aristeas* on certain details once questioned. A fair summary of the evidence would be that *The Letter of Aristeas* is to be dated about 130 B.C. and, while propaganda-like in tone, reflects the tradition of a translation made some time previously.

Why translate? What can be gleaned as to *motives* for this initial translation of Scripture reported by Aristeas?

It is obvious that the Greek translation of the Pentateuch came into existence to meet certain needs within the Jewish community at Alexandria. Jews, after several generations there, did not fully comprehend the Hebrew of their sacred books any longer, and needed the Law (and eventually the Prophets and Writings) in the "common" Greek dialect which they spoke daily. It is also obvious that the Jews themselves were the ones who saw the needs and undertook the translation, for no one will be concerned about religious literature in the same way as the group of believers to whom it is Holy Writ. But granting all this, what *are* the needs within the community, what are its concerns, which cause some of its members to take up the translator's task? In *The Letter of Aristeas* at least four reasons appear, all of which are reflected throughout the later history of Bible translation. Rather strikingly, the reasons which we can see in Egypt prior to Christ continue to come to the fore in our own day as precisely the motives behind the New English Bible and other modern translations.

The *liturgical* factor has already been mentioned. People translate the Bible for use in worship, at public services and for private devotions. Curiously *The Letter of Aristeas* makes little

of this reason, at least compared to the weight which modern investigators might give to it. It is true that the High Priest, in a
lengthy speech, defends the Law which guides the life and worship of the Jews, and the closing scene has the Jewish community
warmly accepting the translation for itself, but nothing directly
is said about how the LXX would be used Sabbath after Sabbath
in synagogue worship in the Jewish Quarter. We may safely
infer, however, that the Jews of Alexandria read the LXX in their
synagogal services and pondered its phrases in their study, as
Philo did so minutely.

When we thus view the Bible on the lectern, however, we
must be careful not to impute worship practices of later ages or
of other places. The synagogue was basically a house of prayer
and of Bible study, not a temple with sacrifices or priests. Only
in Jerusalem was there a bona fide Temple, with ritual and
priests and animal sacrifices (all of which Aristeas rather fully
describes). Jews throughout the rest of the world, and even in
Jerusalem, gathered on the Sabbath in their rather plain, un-
adorned synagogues to hear a call to worship from Deuteronomy
6:4, to join in prayers, and then to listen to lessons read and expounded from the Law and the Prophets, after which the bene-
diction (Numbers 6:24–26) was pronounced. For such services,
a Bible in the language which the people spoke became increasingly a necessity. It may be that the switch to Greek in worship
in a place like Alexandria began, as some scholars think, with the
Hebrew Scriptures being written out in Greek letters (much as
we might write out a Greek phrase like "Kyrie, eleison" in English letters). Then attempts might have been made to put just
the Sabbath lessons into Greek. A key step was the translation
of the entire Pentateuch, such as Aristeas describes. Finally came
translation of the other Old Testament books, which might be
read liturgically or studied in private.

Needless to say, many subsequent Bible translations have been
motivated, at least in part, by such needs of public worship.
Luther had an eye on the Bible's use in the liturgical services he

was reshaping as he made his German translation. The King James Version was "appointed to be read in the churches." The Revised Standard Version is expressly designed "for use in public and private worship." The New English Bible may not put as much emphasis on this liturgical usage, but the memorandum to the translators from the General Director, Professor C. H. Dodd, hopes that the N. E. B. "may prove worthy to be read occasionally" in church, "even at public worship"—a hope which has often proved reality.

However, the liturgical is not the only purpose in view in Bible translation. The *literary* aim must also be taken into account. Again, this motivation is a rather modern one. No one in antiquity would have dreamed of publishing *The Bible as Literature,* for the ancients saw books as things of power and sacred books as vehicles for the deity, not just as "literature." Nonetheless, what we have come to appreciate as the literary side of Scripture was not unknown to men centuries ago, and from time to time the element of literary style and concern for it and pride in good expression do appear in biblical translation. *The Letter of Aristeas* has a rather heavy emphasis on this point. No less a literary critic than Demetrius, the head of the Alexandrian Library, is said to have insisted that "the laws of the Jews are worth transcribing" for the greatest library in the world. Ptolemy himself expressed wonder at their content. Aristeas goes to great lengths to show how skilled in philosophy and how learned the translators were, and if he does not cite passages from the LXX to indicate its literary style (which is in fact often quite rough), Aristeas does stress how they pondered and compared each phrase so that a suitable translation might emerge. Philo and later writers attribute the style of the LXX to nothing less than divine inspiration. The tradition about a curse on anyone who changes a word of the LXX may be taken to indicate satisfaction with the translation and as the equivalent of a modern copyright to prevent tampering.

It is rather obvious that many subsequent translators have

been concerned about literary style. Luther spent hours seeking the phrases which would speak best to the Germans of his day. The King James revisers adopted that famous principle that a Greek or Hebrew word should not always be translated by the same English word each time, but its rendering should be determined in each case by the nearby context. Perhaps the N. E. B. has been boldest at this point. It deliberately seeks to avoid "Bible English" and all the phrases carried over from Hebrew and Greek. It seeks to express in fresh English what the original author said in his own tongue, and tries to catch the peculiarities of style in each of the biblical authors. Only that sort of attention to literary features will evoke in our minds the sort of response which the verse aroused in hearers then.

Liturgical and literary aims scarcely exhaust the motives for translating the Bible, however. There is, thirdly, the *educational* aim. Men translate the Scriptures in order to use them in instructing and edifying those who read and hear. At public services, in private study, by means of literary excellence, the endeavor is to build up men in faith and to present the message of the Bible for their lives. *The Letter of Aristeas* suggests this educational function for Scripture when it portrays Demetrius as seeking a Greek rendering of the Law of the Jews "because the view of life therein is marked by a certain holiness and sanctity." The High Priest explains that the Law was drawn up by a lawgiver "especially endowed by God" and that it is laid down as truth and with regard to right reason. The seventy-two translators are able to answer the king's questions so skillfully because they have made the God who gave the Law the starting-point of their words. And the entire pose—a Greek, Aristeas, speaking so enthusiastically about these Jewish writings and commending them to his brother Philocrates—has as its purpose to encourage men to take up and read the LXX. What Aristeas hints at is, of course, only a partial picture. We can imagine Jews in their synagogues using these Greek Scriptures not only in worship but also for instruction. Indeed, the dividing line between the liturgical and the educational, between the devotional and the hortatory, is a very thin one. And, in fact, this educational function of the synagogue made such an impression on Gentiles that the synagogue service reminded them of nothing quite so much as the school of a Greek philosopher: here was wisdom and the law of the universe. Old Testament books like Proverbs or Ecclesiastes would have little place in liturgy but great appeal educationally. The aim of Ecclesiasticus, a book preserved in the Apocrypha, is to instruct "those who love learning" on how to "make even greater progress in living according to the Law."

The instructional, didactic purpose in Bible translation appears regularly throughout later centuries. The Luther Bible sought to anchor believers in the scriptural word as a guide for life. So did the Geneva Bible of 1560. Particularly since the advent of the Sunday School movement, the role of the Bible in religious education has been recognized as a necessary consideration in translation. Most modern renderings pay some attention to this instructional usage, perhaps even more attention than to the literary and liturgical qualities. For it is likely that, even in a liturgical church, the Bible will be used more frequently in the lap of the church-school teacher than on the lectern. The R. S. V. deliberately included experts in religious education on its committees. Plans for the N. E. B. took note of the fact that in the British Isles, Bible instruction may be given in the school system as well as in the church, and so a translation which can provide the meaning of the ancient text for school pupils is imperative.

Even the liturgical, literary, and educational aspects do not exhaust the reasons for Bible translation. Frequently Bible renderings have an *evangelistic* aim: they seek to convert men to the message of this Bible. Perhaps that aim does not stand out so clearly in what Aristeas says, but the motivation is behind what his Jewish author writes, and the missionary motive seems to have been an element in the preparation of the LXX.

We do not always realize today that Judaism in the period when the LXX was translated was a missionary religion, seeking converts and finding them. Matthew 23:15 reflects this situation when it quotes Jesus' sharp rebuke against the scribes and Pharisees who "constantly go about land and sea to make a single proselyte." Paul, who, some think, may once have been a missionary for Judaism before he became a missionary for Jesus Christ, pays tribute to Judaism's missionary zeal at Romans 10:2. This missionary movement, to bring men to Moses and the Law, seems to have enjoyed great success in the centuries B.C. Harnack once estimated that the world Jewish population rose from under one million in 440 B.C. to perhaps four or five million in the first century A.D., and Harnack was inclined to count conversions to Judaism as a chief factor in this increase. The missionary impulse continued even after the fall of Jerusalem in A.D. 70, and some think it still existed in the period after the Bar-Cocheba revolt was crushed in A.D. 135. Among the reminders to us of this concern among Jews to be "a light to the nations" and win Gentiles to Yahweh and his Law, are certain references in the New Testament and some literary remains. Every time the book of Acts refers to "proselytes" and "God-fearers," we have an allusion to pagans who had been attracted to the Jew's faith in the One God and his austere but highly ethical way of life. A number of documents survive which are part of what must have been an extensive Jewish missionary literature in Greek. Among these must be reckoned fragments of plays, poetry, philosophical tracts, and *The Letter of Aristeas* itself. This *Letter*, with its elaborate pose, seeks not merely to earn good will for Judaism in an anti-Semitic world, but actually to convince Gentiles that they should look into the Scriptures, way of life, and practices of Israel and find true wisdom. The reaction of any fair-minded reader, like Philocrates, must be that he owes it to himself to examine the LXX. Aristeas does not carry the missionary motive as far as later writers do, but the very use to which the LXX may be put —to attract, interest, and instruct "inquirers" from the Gentile world—points toward the aim of conversion through a translated Bible.

It is no secret that many subsequent Bible translations have been made with evangelism in mind. The initial translators into languages like Gothic or Armenian were churchmen who wanted the Bible in the tongue of a people they were laboring to convert. In modern times the missionary movement has been responsible for multiplying the Scriptures into many new tongues and dialects. A Luther or a Tyndale must always be regarded as translating with a missionary purpose. Even the N. E. B. may be said to have an evangelistic purpose. The original purposal in the Church of Scotland memorandum which led to this translation faced quite frankly the fact that many people in today's world no longer understand the language of the seventeenth century, and if they are to hear the Gospel in terms relevant for them, they must hear it in the language of today. Further, many church people who hear standard translations read no longer bother to seek for the meaning, because the words are too familiar. Therefore, within the churches and outside, there must be a translation which speaks to men so that they hear what they have never heard before, the scriptural message, and may be turned to God. Such an aim ranked high in the minds of the N. E. B. translators.

Motives in Bible translation, then, may be liturgical, literary, educational, evangelistic, or some combination thereof, as the story of the LXX makes clear.

The LXX became the Bible of the early church. Most New Testament quotations of the Old seem to come from the LXX, not the Hebrew; the amount runs 60 to 70 percent, and in some books, like Hebrews, all quotations are from the LXX. Sometimes the point of the Old Testament citation can be understood only on the basis of the LXX and is impossible on the basis of the Hebrew text, e.g., Matthew 1:21, Acts 7:43 and 15:12–18, and Hebrews 10:5–7.

Thus the LXX, the world's first translation, looms large as the Bible of the early church. It continues to be the normal Old

Testament among the Greek Orthodox to this day. This LXX was revised or retranslated, however, at least three times in the second century A.D., and three or four attempts were later made to straighten out the readings from these various revisions, which were hopelessly mixed together in the manuscripts. The most heroic effort along these lines was that of a brilliant but controversial Christian scholar named Origen about A.D. 230–40. It is also of some interest to know that the LXX has twice been translated into English, and that one of these renderings is by Charles Thomson, a devoted patriot leader in the American Revolution. The work of each of these men, Origen and Charles Thomson (and of others like them), is a story in itself and deserves its own retelling.

Two

The Crucial Second Century after Christ:
Bible Transmission from the Ancient World to Us

WHAT SHALL WE TRANSLATE? WHY, THE BIBLE TEXT, OF course, common sense replies. But *whose* Bible? which text? what comprises the Bible? These are questions we scarcely trouble about as we read the King James Version or N.E.B. or Phillips or Ronald Knox—though they may dawn on us if we look at these Bibles side by side. But they are problems the translator must wrestle with before he puts a single word on paper.

Of course, the easiest answer would be, "Translate the original." But the autographs, the original manuscripts which Jeremiah or Paul wrote (or properly, which their scribes wrote, at their dictation), were lost long ago. What we have are copies, of copies, of copies—copies penned hundreds of years after the originals.

The student who has had a bit of work with the original languages may answer that we should base a translation on the recognized critical editions. But all such editions rest on the opinions of modern editors and ultimately on the evidence of a variety of ancient manuscripts and versions. Again the problem: "Whose edition? Which manuscripts?"

The historian might reply, "Translate the standard text." But when was the standard text attained, which of the various standards shall be followed? For the Old Testament, is it the rabbinic edition printed by Jacob Ben Chayim in 1524–25, "standard" as a printed text until recent times? Or is it the Ben Asher Text, standardized by a family of Jewish scholars at Tiberias of Galilee between A.D. 780 and 930? Or should we regard as normative the consonantal Hebrew text established by the time of Rabbi Akiba, about A.D. 130? Or should we press back to the Hebrew underlying the Septuagint of a century or two before, or even, more conjecturally, to the Hebrew as it was written in the older Phoenician alphabet prior to the fifth century B.C.? In the case of the New Testament, do we rest content with the *Textus Receptus* (or "text as it has been received"), as printed by Erasmus in 1516, based on some twenty-five medieval manuscripts? Or do we use the great manuscript discoveries like Sinaiticus (see Chapter Six) to gain a Greek text such as was circulating in the fourth century after the Council of Nicaea? Do we press back to the second century by means of recent papyrus finds, or behind all manuscripts to what presumably Paul or Jesus said, prior to any textual corruptions?

Involved constantly with this question of text is the matter of the canon. What books are Scripture? As far as the New Testament is concerned, there was a gradually developing consensus as to what writings were authoritative, though there were many exceptions, and though it was not until A.D. 367 that the twenty-seven books eventually accepted were listed together, those twenty-seven, no more and no less. Today, however, all of Western Christendom and most of the East, Protestants and Catholics alike, agree on this New Testament canon.

The Old Testament is more complicated as to canon. The LXX, we saw, encompassed a longer list of books than any religious group, Jewish or Christian, later accepted. In Jesus' day there was widespread agreement on the Law, the Prophets, and the Sacred Writings as authoritative, with the Law most significant by far. Doubtless in groups like the Covenanters at Qumran other books might be counted within the circle of Scripture, too.

It was about A.D. 90, however, that the rabbis at Jamnia (or Yabneh) on the seacoast of Palestine determined on the final canon of the Hebrew Bible. This canon—the one subsequently transmitted in Hebrew—was the one followed by Luther and the other Reformers, so that the Holy Scriptures as published today by the Jewish Publication Society and the Old Testament of Protestants agree on canon.

The "extra" books from the LXX, which, after Jamnia, Christians had continued to use somewhat, especially in the Middle Ages, were included by Luther in his German translation, but as "Apocrypha," books historically instructive to read, but no guide for doctrine or life. The Roman Catholic Church, as part of its Counter-Reformation program, decreed at the Council of Trent in 1546 that its Bible should include these books of the Apocrypha, and also that the Latin Vulgate translation should be authoritative. Thus—and here canon and the question of a standard text come home to roost—a Roman Catholic Bible will include what for Jews and Protestants is the Apocrypha and will be based (at least until recently) on the Latin, not the Greek or Hebrew, as definitive. In this way, decisions made long ago as to canon and text determine what goes into a Bible translated today. But even here the Roman Catholic translator will have to decide "What Latin text?" For there is a long, involved history of text transmission for the Vulgate too, let alone for the Old Latin which preceded it.

In short, any translator, even when he has settled the questions of canon and the language from which he will translate, is often faced with a problem of which readings, out of the hundreds of thousands which have accumulated over the centuries, he will choose. Twenty or thirty centuries is a long time, and many things have happened to the text with which the translator works today. But no more crucial period can be imagined for both the Old and New Testaments than the second century A.D. It was a time when the canon was taking shape, when texts were often free in form but in some cases were being standardized. It was a time of danger, threatening even the survival of the biblical text. For the historian it is a time of shadows. But it is also a time when the first individual names begin to appear in the story of transmission and translation, the first faces whose features we can make out.

The second century is thus probably the most decisive time in the long history of transmission for both the Hebrew testament and the Greek one. Unfortunately it is a period which Jews and Christians have all too often ignored. It falls into a "no-man's land" between biblical studies and church history, obscured by a dearth of sources and by the fact that what sources we have from rabbis, Church Fathers, and heretics are difficult to use. The century is like a tunnel, dark and unexplored, through which the road of Bible transmission passes. Yet within this period one particular Hebrew text type was made normative, its consonants fixed irrevocably, errors and all. During this time the oldest scraps of evidence we possess for the New Testament were copied, the Pauline *corpus* circulated, and the fourfold gospel canon was settled. What emerges from the second century has become standard for us; what happened prior to this time, we can only guess at with difficulty.

The profile of this century can be described in a few words. For the Roman Empire it was a time of prosperity and calm, new progress, new practices, and able rulers from the provinces. More than one historian has mused that of all the centuries in which to be alive, none would be more satisfying than this period. For Christians it was a not impossible time, though there might be local outbreaks against them. For Jews it was far more difficult than we ordinarily suppose. Anti-Semitism, Jew-baiting, and pogroms were common in antiquity, and there must have been "bad blood" in every city which had a large Jewish population. More important were the Jewish revolts. The result of the first such rebellion was that Jerusalem was burned in A.D. 70, and in a sense this tragedy set the tone for the next hundred years. There were further revolts by the Jews in A.D. 115–17 in Cyrenaica and Egypt, and again in 132–35 in Palestine, when Simon Bar-Cocheba, "Prince of Israel," defied Hadrian's legions for two years. Then the Romans prevailed. Hadrian, who had the honor of finishing the great temple of Zeus in Athens which Antiochus Epiphanes had begun over three hundred years before, now carried to completion another project which Antiochus had tried but at which he had failed: the conversion of the Temple at Jerusalem into a shrine of Olympian Zeus (see II Maccabees 6:2). Hadrian not only erected his altar and an equestrian statue of himself at the Temple site, he also renamed Jerusalem *Colonia Aelia Capitolina* and excluded all Jews from it, permitting them to enter the city only on the ninth of Ab, to lament its fall. Much of the population of the land perished in the revolt, learned rabbis as well as fighting men. "No bird was seen flying in Palestine for fifty years," the Talmud says.

Recent archeological finds along the Dead Sea, in the caves at Murabba'at and further south, pinpoint dramatically how these freedom fighters made their last stand in the most rugged terrain imaginable, and then perished, often to a man. In the "Cave of Dread," as the discoverers named it, at Naḥal Hever, a thousand feet above the floor of the ravine below and over two hundred and fifty feet beneath the edge of a precipice above, the skeletons were found of more than forty men, women, and children who chose thirst and starvation rather than surrender to the Romans who encamped on the plateau above and in the valley below. A few of those who died earliest were given a pathetic sort of burial; the names of some were inscribed on pottery sherds: "Saul the son of Saul—*shalom,* peace." Remnants of clothing, baskets, weapons, and tools lay strewn about. A few coins bore the inscription "for the freedom of Jerusalem." Here and there were fragments of the Scriptures, in Hebrew or in Greek, the sacred Law for which these people had died. In such an age, how could the biblical text survive and be passed on?

Not every Jew in Palestine fell in such revolts, of course. There were also large Jewish communities in Persia which would

have preserved the sacred text in one form or another, regardless
of what happened in Palestine. But ultimately, in Palestine and
elsewhere, survival of the Bible in Hebrew depended on Jewish
scholars and their devotion to the Scriptures. Their dedication
to learning and to the words from God is what enabled them to
transmit the text even through this most difficult of periods.
They were clear that the future of their faith, especially after
A.D. 70 and absolutely after 135, depended on study rather than
ritual. For them, the Torah ranked ahead even of Temple or
worship. "Study is greater than doing." Johanan ben Zakkai
told his pupils, "Study is the purpose of your creation." Such
absolute devotion to the study of the sacred text is what preserved the Hebrew Bible through the turmoil of the time.

Three figures stand forth as especially vivid for the roles they
played in transmitting the biblical text. These men have stories
almost unparalleled in the romance of biblical scripts and
scholars.

THE MAN WHO "DIED" THAT THE LAW MIGHT LIVE

The aged rabbi Johanan ben Zakkai, more than any other man
after the debacle of A.D. 70, saved the biblical text and preserved
the tradition of study surrounding it. He achieved this by
choosing peace over war, by feigning death, and by training up
students who would transmit his teachings and build the structure of rabbinic Judaism.

A contemporary of the apostles, born about the same time as
Saul of Tarsus, Johanan was for a time a tradesman in some urban
business. He studied in the school of Hillel and then settled as a
teacher for some eighteen years (c. A.D. 20–40) in the village of
Arav, in Galilee, determined to teach the provincials something
of the glory of the Law. But discovering, to his disappointment,
that Galileans had little interest in the pronouncements of the
sages of the Pharisees and hated the Torah, Johanan moved to
Jerusalem. There he achieved renown both as a teacher of Torah

in an academy and as a public lecturer in a forum series which attracted such crowds that sessions had to be held in the Temple porticoes. Study was Johanan's constant theme. To a priestly family, he said that sacrifices and offerings would not save its sons, but "Go, and study Torah, and live."

Revered and honored in Jerusalem, the learned Johanan became a member of the Sanhedrin and leader of the Hillelite wing of the Pharisaic party. His famed debates with the Sadducees need not detain us here, but his position as leader of the "peace party" within Judaism is of importance. Johanan shunned extremism and found no attraction in the widespread Jewish nationalism and messianic claimants of the day. His hope for the future was the development of Jewish learning, and he maintained that study of the Law was no less possible in a Roman than in a Jewish state. Therefore, though no sycophant of Rome, he counseled constantly against acts of defiance or revolt against Caesar, e.g., in the great crisis of A.D. 40. The mad emperor Caligula had commanded that his statue be placed in the Temple at Jerusalem. The proconsul Petronius, fearing a popular uprising, delayed carrying out the order until the crisis suddenly ended with the assassination of Caligula. During this time Jews at Jamnia tore down a brick altar erected by pagans. Amid such a crisis Johanan advised, "Do not destroy their altars, so that you do not have to rebuild them with your own hands." Later, in the swift-moving events of A.D. 66, when Jewish arms were winning some success against the Romans and the fanatics were fanning a war fever, the aged rabbi—tradition says he was over one hundred years old—spoke out against coercing men into the army, fearing lest the cities of Israel should become graveyards. Even though Johanan was respected by all parties, such advice went unheeded, and the revolt grew.

At first some revolutionists thought that unrest throughout the Empire might swell into a force that would push Nero from his throne. But this never happened. By autumn of 67 Vespasian had subdued most of the land, and by the spring of 68 he had surrounded Jerusalem from Emmaus on the west to Jericho on the east. But Vespasian did not press his attack. He seems to have been well informed by spies as to what was going on within Jerusalem, and he determined, for the time being, simply to keep an ever-tightening blockade, while Jewish factions inside the city bickered and fought among themselves. During the winter of 67–68 the moderates in Jerusalem lost control, there was a bloody purge, and the radical Zealots took over. Johanan could foresee the inevitable: siege, famine, thirst, the final assault, plunder-hungry soldiers let loose on the survivors, the Temple in flames. Alas for the Torah then!

But what to do? Secretly he summoned his closest friends and hit upon a plan to preserve the Law and thus provide a future for the Jews. There are two separate lines of tradition reporting what was done, and they differ in certain details. But the gist of the plan was that Johanan ben Zakkai was to pretend to be ill; his death would be announced, and then two of his most trusted disciples would carry him in an open coffin past the guards, outside the city, through Roman lines, to Vespasian himself. Then Johanan would ask the boon of permission to set up a rabbinical academy in some provincial city already under Roman control. There the study of the blessed Law might go on.

The plan was set in motion. No one was surprised at the death of one so aged. A great crowd of mourners gathered. Johanan, scarcely daring to breathe, was placed on a bier and covered with death clothes. To provide the smell of death, a piece of animal meat was inserted beneath the shroud. At the gate, the guards wanted to stab the corpse to make sure of death, but Ben Betiah, Johanan's nephew, dissuaded them, lest the people reproach them for violating the body of so great a rabbi. At last he was outside the city and soon inside the lines of the Romans, who doubtless knew that Johanan had held a viewpoint favorable to their aims. In the interview with Vespasian, Johanan received permission from the general to go to Jamnia and set up his school and also, apparently, permission to have several illustrious rabbis like Gamaliel II and Zadok evacuated from Jerusalem and spared the fate of the rest in the city. At some point, all accounts agree, Johanan also predicted Vespasian's victory on the basis of Isaiah 10:34 and hailed him as a future emperor—just as Josephus had done when captured by the Romans earlier in the war. It has been argued that what Johanan went to was really a sort of internment camp in Jamnia where he lectured to fellow-prisoners, but it is much more likely that the Roman general found that Johanan's request fitted precisely into his plans. How could stability better be achieved after the war in Palestine than by the influence of Pharisees like this man who would quietly go on with study while practicing and preaching peace?

So it was that Johanan ben Zakkai went to Jamnia and set up his academy in a vineyard. It remained there for only sixty years, until the second revolt of A.D. 132–35, but in that time the "Vineyard of Yabneh" became famous among Jews. It amounted to a new Sanhedrin, guiding their religious life. Here the Mishnah began to take shape and a faith was restructured to meet new times. Johanan was a sort of "living manuscript" when he was smuggled out of Jerusalem, and from his immense learning and that of colleagues who gathered in the school he had had the foresight to set up, the Hebrew text and the traditions surrounding it could continue and be transmitted to future generations. It is fitting that Johanan died a peaceful death in bed, c. A.D. 80, surrounded by his students who would carry on his way of life centered in the sacred text.

RABBI AKIBA, RELUCTANT REVOLUTIONIST

Of all the later students at Jamnia, none casts a longer shadow than Akiba, who, while he may have helped lead Israel disastrously along the path of revolt again, surely set his stamp upon the biblical text and the pattern of Judaism for all time to come.

Akiba ben Joseph was born on the fertile coastal plain of

southwest Palestine shortly before A.D. 50. He was of peasant
stock, of the sort of "worthless people of the land," utterly un-
instructed in the Law, whom the Pharisees hated. Akiba's kind
returned the compliment. "When I was an *am ha-arez* ["people
of the land," a rustic]," he later said, "I used to say, 'Give me a
scholar in my hands, I should bite him like an ass!' " It was his
wife Rachel who rescued him from all this. An amazing woman,
she persuaded him to forsake his herds of sheep and goats and
take up study. She encouraged and supported him financially.
To buy food, she once sold her hair, and for seven years she lived
apart from him so that he might study and she might support
the family by working. But to a grown man accustomed to labor
in the fields, reading and writing came hard, and it was really
only in trying to teach their son that Akiba mastered letters
himself. Later in life than most men, he completed his studies
and was ordained. For a time he taught in Galilee, but soon he
returned to Jamnia where he absorbed the teachings of one
master after another and began to make a name for himself,
thanks to his brilliant pronouncements. In time, tradition says,
he had a following of 24,000 pupils, but success came only with
hardships—tradition also says that he was flogged five times,
apparently for violating some of the many, minute rules of the
academy. Eventually, however, he became its acknowledged
leader and fixed the Hillelite views forever in rabbinic Judaism.

In general, Akiba followed the policies of Johanan ben Zakkai:
concentrate on expounding the biblical text and eschew politics.
But once again, there were problems with the Roman rulers to
plague the man who would have preferred to devote all his
energies to study of the Law. Sometime early in the second
century, Trajan offered to permit restoration of Jerusalem, full
reconstruction of the Temple, and even official sacrifices there,
with a Greek named Aquila, a disciple of Akiba, in charge. Most
Jews rejoiced, the account runs, and Akiba advised acceptance
of the offer. Impressed by Roman good will, he even began to
reproach Johanan ben Zakkai's conduct; he might have saved

the Temple at Jerusalem when he settled for an academy at Jamnia! But other groups, including Jewish nationalists, Samaritans, and the Christians, protested the plan. Negotiations dragged. Eventually Rome withdrew the offer of a new temple. Akiba was disappointed, but encouraged the people not to lose hope. When the Jewish revolt in A.D. 115 and Rome's repressive measures fanned new hatred against the emperor, Akiba continued to advise patience. After all, he himself had an open door for conversations with a friendly governor, Tineius Rufus, even though tension and fanaticism grew apace. The edicts of Hadrian at about A.D. 125—prohibiting circumcision and certain other ceremonies and practices—were still not enough to shake Akiba from his basic position. Observance of the Law might be sacrificed, he reasoned, if only study of it could go on and keep the Law alive for a better time in the future. But gradually even this compromise was eroded away. Other Jews became more openly rebellious. The underground stockpiled supplies in hideouts. Hadrian's decision to rebuild the Temple but to dedicate it to Jupiter Capitoline seemed the last straw. Even at this point Akiba made a personal plea to Hadrian, but he got nowhere when they met face to face. The die was cast. "Prepare for suffering," Akiba advised at the graves of two rabbis martyred for publicly engaging in their faith.

Many Jews, however, prepared for war instead. Simon Bar-Cocheba (or Kosebah; the name has been subject to various explanations and spellings) was the man who galvanized the people into action. A giant of a man physically, he was also something of a statesman. He coordinated the guerilla forces which sprang up and created a state which lasted for almost three years against the might of Rome. In the maelstrom of events, Akiba, like others, looked on Bar-Cocheba as a deliverer, indeed as the Messiah. His birthplace was a village called Cosiba, and in a word play Akiba applied to this son of Cosiba the prophecy of Numbers 24:17: "A star [cochab] shall come forth out of Jacob." The man from Cosiba, the star, has stepped forth out of Jacob.

"This is the Messianic king," Akiba said. After the revolt failed, rabbinic tradition began calling Bar-Cocheba Bar-Coziba, "son of deceit." But his meteoric career is now being clarified by letters signed in his own hand, found in Dead Sea caves.

Akiba had placed his approval on Bar-Cocheba, but did not live to see his final downfall. Apparently Akiba had not been an active participant in the revolt, and so the Romans let him go unmolested as they pinned down the hardpressed Bar-Cocheba for his last stand. However, as fighting dragged to a close, the Romans issued a command in A.D. 134 that led to Akiba's death. They forbade study of the Torah. All that he had hoped to preserve by compromise and later by endorsing Bar-Cocheba was threatened. Even study was outlawed. Now, finally, reluctantly, he rebelled. He would be like a fish out of water without the scriptural text. He defied the ban and lectured. Arrested, condemned to death, he died with his flesh being torn by iron combs. During his tortures, as dawn broke, Akiba's voice spoke out the words of the Shema, as was the custom at that hour of the day, ". . . the Lord is One, and thou shalt love the Lord thy God. . . ." He died repeating the verse, happy in the thought that "now I know that I love Him with all my life."

What this man did in his eighty-five and more years was to rehabilitate and refurbish the faith of Israel. The oral traditions surrounding Scripture, passed down in such a fragile but tenacious way, were now collected, codified, and gradually recorded. The *masora* or tradition became, in Akiba's words, a fence or hedge around the Law for Jews. It was during his years at Jamnia that the decision about the canon was made. And for all who read the Hebrew Bible, Akiba helped fix its text. The Masoretic Text, which was coming into dominance in this period, was not invented by Akiba and his contemporaries, but inherited by them —he speaks of getting the tradition from his teacher, Nahum of Gimzo, and he from Hillel, and so on—and thence it was passed on, even more carefully edited than before, for posterity.

In all this process of scriptural transmission and interpretation

Akiba seems the single greatest influence. The theory of Professor Paul de Lagarde, that all our subsequent Hebrew manuscripts stem from just one archetype established in Akiba's day *c.* 130, may be an exaggeration. But at the least, Akiba and his school left their stamp on the Bible we read today through the text they passed on. It is small wonder that in Jewish estimates Akiba ranks as a second Moses.

AQUILA, THE WORLD'S MOST UNUSUAL TRANSLATOR

An entire school of scholars worked with Akiba and were influenced by him. One has already been mentioned who deserves a word, the convert Aquila, who was at one time, in Hadrian's planning, to be in charge of a restored Temple. He was also one of the oddest Bible translators the world has ever known, producing a translation which reads unlike anything else ever written in Greek, yet operating with a methodology that was clear and distinct.

Aquila, or "eagle" as his name means in Latin, came from Sinope on the shores of the Black Sea. He was born a pagan. In the first quarter of the second century he turned up at Jerusalem where a relative was in charge of Roman building operations. A man of some wealth and education, Aquila was first converted to Christianity, only to be excommunicated for practicing astrology, according to later Christian writers. Aquila than was drawn to Judaism. He learned Hebrew and underwent circumcision. When we consider the situation of the Jews in the eastern Roman Empire in these years from 115 to 130, the conversion is a tremendous tribute to the prowess of Akiba and the other rabbis under whom Aquila studied.

Since Aquila's native tongue was Greek, he conceived the project of translating the Hebrew Scriptures into his own language. There existed, of course, the Septuagint and probably a variety of other renderings and revisions in Greek. But increasingly the LXX had become the Bible of the Christian church, repudiated by the synagogue. Aquila wanted a translation which would give no grounds for the "proof texts" which Christians had found, such as the use of "virgin" at Isaiah 7:14 in the LXX, which Matthew quoted in describing Jesus' mother (Matt. 1:23). He further wanted a translation which would agree with the Masoretic Hebrew text emerging then as standard in the school of Akiba. (Aquila was probably unaware that alternate Hebrew recensions had once existed, such as the LXX was based upon.) Above all, he wanted a translation which would enable the Greek reader to get out of the Bible all the wondrous teachings an Akiba found in the Hebrew.

It is not always appreciated that Akiba's school not only established a text and fixed the canon but also developed a method of interpretation. In actuality, a hermeneutics, or art and science of interpreting, always goes along with textual work, and a set of rules for such matters was articulated by Akiba as never had been before. It is true that Akiba did not invent these rules. He plainly admits receiving many of them from his teachers. But he worked them out more fully and applied them systematically. Akiba's method of interpretation centers round the thesis that every word in Scripture, every letter, has significance. The principle came from a rather obscure predecessor, Nahum of Gimzo, and it led to attempts to find hidden meanings even in the little Hebrew word *'ēth*, which serves as the sign for direct objects. (Hebrew nouns do not have a complete set of case endings as do Latin and Greek, and so this device of using *'ēth* had to be employed to distinguish objects from subjects.) It was Akiba who at one point saved this system of exegesis from discard. Nahum of Gimzo, the story runs, was ready to abandon his whole method because he didn't know what to do with an *'ēth* at Deuteronomy 6:13. The text read, "You shall fear the Lord your God, *'eth-Yahweh*," and according to the system this *'ēth* should denote someone else alongside God who ought also be feared. But to posit that would deny the very monotheism which Akiba died confessing, that God is one. Especially there was the danger that Christians would gleefully pounce on the point as a refer-

ence to the Messiah as God's equal. Just when Nahum was ready
to abandon his whole system to prevent such consequences,
Akiba came up with an explanation which provided a way out.
"The *'ēth* in this verse refers to the scholars," he said, "who must
be paid as much reverence as God himself!"

Such was the exegetical system that Aquila determined to
follow in his Greek translation. Every peculiarity of the Hebrew
must be followed in the Greek. The same Hebrew word must
always be rendered by the same Greek term, preferably one of the
same length. All words derived from a given Hebrew root must
be equated with forms from a single Greek root, even if this
meant inventing Greek forms never used before or since. Of
course important details like *'ēth* must find reflection too. Greek
normally would put a direct object in the accusative case, with
a distinctive ending, and did not require any other "sign of the
accusative." But for Aquila that would not suffice. An equivalent
for *'ēth* must be found. Since the Hebrew term could sometimes
mean "with," Aquila adopted the Greek word for "with" to
represent *'ēth*. Unfortunately this Greek word regularly should
be followed by a dative case, and so the bizarre result was an
utterly impossible construction, the word "with" followed by the
accusative case! It was impossible in Greek, but for Aquila's
purpose, of showing (in his own system) what stood in the
Hebrew, the device was ideal.

Aquila's Greek is not always as bad as this sounds. His ways of
expressing Hebrew direct objects were even more intricate and
subtle than this one example suggests. And when he wanted to,
he could write perfectly normal Greek. What needs to be
remembered is that Aquila was trying to follow an exegetical
system that was in vogue among the rabbis of his day. On that
basis his rendering deserves high commendation. It is for exegetical literalness that the literary has been sacrificed. Bible study
has taken precedence over beauty of form desirable for public
reading. Concern for petty detail has triumphed over sense. Few
subsequent translators have followed Aquila's path. Perhaps the

English Revised Version of 1881–85 and the Jehovah's Witnesses translation share something of this desire to render consistently the same Hebrew or Greek word with the same English
term. But no one has followed Aquila to his extremes. However,
he does raise, in sharpest form, the problem of how we shall
translate. This scion of Akiba challenges us to think about hermeneutics and the method of translation. It is to be lamented that
only fragments of his work remain today, recovered from here
and there. The most interesting bits of Aquila are perhaps
portions of his rendering of I and II Kings, transcribed in the
fifth century and rediscovered in 1897 in the *geniza* or storage
room of a synagogue in Old Cairo. These fragments suggest that
Aquila's translation was prized and used by Greek-speaking
Jews in Egypt for some centuries.

Still other translators who put the Hebrew testament into
Greek appeared in the second century. Theodotion was another
convert to Judaism, Symmachus probably a Jewish-Christian
theologian. They with Aquila begin a long parade of translators
who start to emerge in these hundred years. But Johanan ben
Zakkai and Aquila—without them and other studious rabbis
and scribes, often unknown to us by name, there would be no
Hebrew Bible for later translators to use, certainly not the text
which has become most familiar.

TATIAN AND HIS GOSPEL HARMONY

The fortunes of the New Testament text in the second century are in no way marked by such dramatic tales. The trans-
mitters are, for the most part, anonymous and faceless. In many
ways we do not know precisely what was happening. There is
an ominous silence in manuscript evidence for this century. What
is more, there was no tradition of textual work as in Judaism, no
temple archives, no academy at Jamnia, no schools in Persia, to
preserve manuscripts. Text transmission in primitive Christianity
must have been a rather hit-and-miss affair.

Unlike Jews, however, Christians in this period did not face waves of persecution. It was only the later violent persecutions by Decius and then by Diocletian in the fourth century which deliberately sought to destroy the books of the Christians, as if these writings were the jugular vein of Christianity. But early Christian transmission of the text in the second century did suffer from preoccupation with the Second Coming. The expectation that Jesus might appear at any time on the clouds of heaven was a deterrent to careful handling of a text for posterity. Why slave over manuscripts when the Lord himself might, at any moment, bring an end to ordinary history? The Old Testament too was a factor retarding development of a New Testament scriptural text. As long as the Greek Old Testament was recognized as *the* Bible exclusively, writings by Christians might be treated with a certain casualness.

With such factors at work, it is no surprise that the text of the New Testament books took a variety of forms—a "Western Text," an Egyptian Text, Caesarean and Syrian Texts. It is possible that each geographical area had its own particular variety of text. Further, our oldest manuscripts are often "mixed" in their text types. Thus our "tunnel period" marked a time when the New Testament text was making its way through a labyrinth, to change the metaphor, along a variety of tracks which sometimes switched from one line to another.

Theologically, though there was a central Gospel, a rigid orthodoxy was scarcely defined as yet and the dividing line was thin between what were to prove normative interpretations and heterodox views. Therefore quasi-heretical movements were quite possibly an influence on the emerging text and canon. It is from the ranks of those judged unorthodox that we take two men as examples of what was happening with the New Testament text between A.D. 100 and 200.

About the middle of the second century a Syrian named Tatian was converted to Christianity. He had been born of pagan parents in Mesopotamia, then on the fringes of the Empire, and educated in the Greek learning of the day. He explored various philosophies and was even initiated into one of the mystery cults. Spiritually still unsatisfied and seeking truth, he then came across the Old Testament, either in its LXX or Hebrew form, of which he speaks as "certain barbaric writings, too old to be compared with the opinions of the Greeks, and too divine to be compared with their errors." Struck by the unpretentious language but exalted monotheism, high ethics, and prophetic insight of the contents, "I was led to put faith in these writings," Tatian said, and he became a Christian.

Tatian became a Christian with a zeal that often characterizes converts. He listened eagerly to lectures at the school of Justin, the future martyr, in Rome. He renounced with a vengeance all the Greek philosophy and culture in which he had previously been trained. His break with philosophy was sharp and much like Karl Barth's in 1918 with the spirit of his age— against philosophy, in favor of the Bible. He left Rome and became a missionary in the East. But Tatian's extremism carried him far beyond the Christian norms. Like many gnostics of the day, he identified physical matter with evil. Hence, meat, wine, and even the marriage relationship were regarded as wrong. Abstinence became the key word, and Tatian ended in one of the many little groups of Encratites or "Abstainers," whose monastic-like outlook increasingly characterized late second-century Christianity. Already while he was in Rome, Tatian's tendencies were denounced as heretical, but he seems not to have been under any special stigma in the East during his lifetime.

Tatian wrote many treatises—one of them survives, an *Address to the Greeks*—but it is his work on the Scriptures he so fiercely championed which catches our eye. He is said to have composed a book on *Bible Problems* that dealt with obscure, unclear passages and to have done an edition of Paul's epistles, but these are lost. It is his *Diatessaron*, dated usually about A.D. 170, which is his most important work. Tatian hit upon the scheme of combining the four gospels into a continuous life of Christ. Perhaps others also thought of this—Bishop Theophilus of Antioch is reputed to have compiled a harmony *c.* 180—but we have no evidence of anyone doing so prior to Tatian. His work was named the *Diatessaron* to describe its contents, for the term means "one account 'through four.' " Whether he composed it first in Greek or Syriac is uncertain. There was a Greek version, we know, because a tiny fragment of it, dating from about A.D. 220, turned up in the ruins of Dura-Europos, in Tatian's native Mesopotamia. That was the form in which the gospels were being read in that outpost. The Syriac version had amazingly wide circulation and was used especially in liturgy, something which is not surprising, since liturgy loves to conflate biblical passages anyway, as for example in "the Words of Institution," or the Passion Narrative and the "Seven Last Words" of Christ. Only in the fifth century was Tatian's harmony replaced in Syriac by the more customary four "separated" gospels. The *Diatessaron* was also translated into a great number of other languages, and even today it is reflected in Arabic, Persian, Latin, Medieval German, Dutch, Italian, and Middle English evidence. The surviving Middle English harmony was once part of the library of no less a literary light than Samuel Pepys.

But Tatian's pervasive *Diatessaron* definitely served at times as a vehicle for some of his theological peculiarities. His Encratite leanings seem to have inserted themselves with regard to marriage, for example. At Matthew 1:19, the description of Joseph as Mary's "husband, a just man," was rephrased to eliminate any marital reference. Luke 2:36 gave similar offense to those ascetically-minded when it described the prophetess Anna as "having lived with her husband seven years from her virginity": the Tatianic harmonies cut this to read, "seven days she had been with a husband," or rewrote it along completely "celibate" lines, "She remained seven years a virgin with her husband." Tatian's ideas enjoyed considerable reception, however, before their heretical features were denounced in the East and his *Diatessaron* was hunted down and destroyed. It was in the time of Bishop Rabbula of Edessa (d. 435), under whose leadership the Peshitta translation grew up which contained the four separated gospels, that the *Diatessaron* was especially ferreted out. One contemporary alone, Bishop Theodoret of Cyrrhus, destroyed some two hundred copies in his diocese. So thorough were the ecclesiastical officials that not a single copy of Tatian's *Diatessaron* survives in Syriac or Greek. However, Tatian's careful weaving together of phrases from the four gospels was not without influence. His work probably accounts for certain harmonizations which took place in manuscripts of the gospels in several languages. Exactly how much effect such second-century harmonizations had on later manuscripts is something which scholars still debate. But Tatian's work in the century prior to the time from which our manuscripts begin to appear has made it more difficult to separate the original phraseology of one evangelist from another, and his example of constructing a harmony has been much imitated.

MARCION, HERO AND HERETIC

A man of genius, pioneer at many things, but perverse in certain of his views, Marcion provides a story which exemplifies another type of textual manipulation in the second century. More information is available about this theologian and Bible editor than about Tatian. He came from Sinope, Aquila's home, where his father, according to later accounts, was bishop of the local church. Later orthodox writers also claim that Marcion's father excommunicated him for seducing a virgin, but this may be simply an attempt to blacken the character of a hated heretic. Evidently wealthy from the shipping business, Marcion appeared in Rome about A.D. 140 and ingratiated himself with a donation of some thirty thousand dollars to the church—money which, we are told, was returned to him as his unorthodox views became known. He was excommunicated in July of 144. Meanwhile he had begun to build up his own following. Marcion shared many characteristics with gnostics of the day, Christian and otherwise, but unlike them he organized, not just a school or academy in which to teach, but a church, with bishops, priests, and liturgy, and above all a theology and a distinct canon of Scripture. Indeed, in all these areas he may well have accelerated orthodox development as a response to the Marcionite threat. For Marcion's church spread widely and competed with the orthodox faith for several centuries. Its golden age was between 150 and 250, and it survived in a few eastern regions till the Middle Ages dawned.

The doctrinal emphases of the Marcionite church—a gospel of sheer love revealed in Jesus Christ, in sharp antithesis to the god of law found in the Old Testament; a docetic Christology, and a rigorous morality—need no discussion here, but their relation to the Scriptures in the second century is noteworthy. Marcion sought, in the Bible he employed, to return to the gospel of Christ and Paul. Accordingly, and quite contrary to all those Christians for whom the Old Testament was the Holy Scripture, Marcion rejected the Old Testament completely, in the Hebrew, Septuagintal, or any other form. The captious, wrathful god revealed in those books, Marcion said, was a mere creator-god, a demiurge, who has nothing in common with the Supreme God revealed by Christ. Gleefully Marcion listed all the inconsistencies of a god who claimed omniscience but had to ask, "Adam, where art thou?" (Gen. 3:9), or who made man with a foreskin and then commanded him to cut it off. The mission of Jesus had been precisely to expose and overthrow this god of law, who didn't even recognize the Stranger he crucified—until it was too late and the risen Christ appeared before him to put him in his place.

Having thus solved the problem of the text and canon of the Old Testament by excluding it, Marcion went on to frame a canon of his own which would reflect the gospel as he understood it. Of all the New Testament writers, only Paul, he felt, really grasped what a new thing had come about in Jesus Christ. All the others had been blinded in one way or another by Jewish influences. Marcion's canon therefore comes very close to being "Paul alone," for he headed his Scriptures with ten epistles by the apostle. The Pastorals were excluded, Ephesians was listed

under the title of "Laodiceans" (cf. Col. 4:16), and even those
letters accepted were subject to careful pruning to exclude any
"Jewish taints." Whole sections of Romans were left out, and
Galatians 1:1, for example, was probably read by Marcion so as
to omit any reference alongside Jesus Christ to "God the father
who had raised him from the dead"—Marcion seems to have
had, "Jesus Christ who raised himself from the dead." So vigorously did Marcion champion Paul that Paul almost did not survive his embrace. The Marcionite affection for Paul could have
proved a kiss of death. Some orthodox Christians must have shied
away from the Pauline epistles when they saw how Marcion in-
terpreted them. Adolf Harnack's famous judgment in the 1911
edition of the *Britannica* is still worth quoting: "in the second
century only one Christian—Marcion—took the trouble to
understand Paul; but it must be added that he misunderstood
him."[1]

Alongside the Apostle, Marcion canonized one gospel. Why
have four, or try to harmonize them? The single gospel which
Marcion chose, because it suited his purposes best, was Luke—
not Luke as we know it, but in an edited form. This "Gospel of
Marcion" lacked the two opening chapters containing the na-
tivity stories we are familiar with, which are so full of Jewish
and Old Testament allusions. Instead his gospel began with a
combination of 3:1*a* and 4:31–37, the most striking opening
sentence in any gospel: "In the fifteenth year of Tiberius, Jesus
Christ [or perhaps Marcion read "God"] came down to Caper-
naum, a city of Galilee, and taught in a synagogue." At least a
quarter, perhaps 40 percent of the verses in our canonical Luke
were absent in Marcion's edition. Thanks to his work, though, a
rigorously edited version of Luke was circulating in the second
century.

How much effect this Marcionite recension had on our later
manuscripts is a topic still under discussion. The usual view is
that Marcion chopped up a finished gospel which had been completed fifty years before, and that the Marcionite version was

generally forgotten in later years. But other theories have been proposed. At the very time that Marcion was editing a Lucan Gospel, the so-called Western Text is known to have emerged. This Western Text is marked by a series of omissions and additions in Luke unparalleled in any other text types. And often Marcion agrees with the Western Text in these variants. Verses like Luke 24:12 and 40, for example, are omitted precisely by Western manuscripts and by Marcion. One wonders what was happening to the text of Luke during this "tunnel period," where we can see influences at work but cannot ascertain the exact connections. A bolder hypothesis has been advanced from time to time claiming that the gospel which Marcion edited was really some earlier form of Luke, and that our canonical Luke was constructed only *after* Marcion prepared his recension. In this case, it is not so much a matter that Marcion omitted passages as that a later second-century editor inserted them.

Current theories here fall far short of proof, and the most we can say with surety is that several editions of a Lucan Gospel were circulating in the second century—a Western form and a non-Western one, Marcion's version, a Luke that had been blended into a harmony by Tatian, Luke in a fourfold collection with the other three gospels, and perhaps a Luke as the author originally had envisioned it, as Volume I, along with Acts, in a two-part "Beginnings of Christianity." This fact is enough, however, to make us realize that prior to our oldest manuscripts of Luke there were already different editions.

Together with the Apostle and a gospel, Marcion placed in his canon a writing of his own, for after all he felt he possessed revealed truth from God just as Jesus and Paul had. Marcion's book was entitled *Antitheses*, and it set forth his sharp distinctions between the two gods of law and gospel. Some scholars think they have detected a warning against this book at I Timothy 6:20, where Timothy is urged to avoid "the contradictions of what is falsely called knowledge"; the Greek is, literally, "the *antitheses* of *gnosis* falsely so-called"—though this reference requires a very late date for the Pastorals or for this final verse in I Timothy. Marcion also developed a system of exegesis to go along with his canon and his text; among other things, it completely rejected allegory as an approach to Scripture. His disciples wrote for each of the Pauline epistles a prologue, which, strangely, got into many good manuscripts of the Latin Vulgate, the Bible of the Western Catholic Church. Marcionites at Rome were also probably the ones responsible for the earliest Old Latin translations of the Pauline epistles.

Thus in Marcion and under his aegis there developed a theology, a canon, textual work, expository writings, and translation endeavors, all in the setting of a distinct confessional community. We ought make no mistake: Marcion's text was based not on a desire to find the original readings, but on theological convictions. His work raises again the question of how one's understanding of religion and of God colors work even on the text and in translating. But before giving an answer in Marcion's case, we ought, for each passage, at least examine the possibility that what look to us like "Marcionite changes" from the text we know, might be primitive readings which he inherited and which other more orthodox editors saw fit to change.

CORRUPTION EXEMPLIFIED

Is it possible that changes made in the second century A.D. affect the Bibles we read today? The text critic von Soden thought so, holding that Tatian and Marcion had corrupted all subsequent Greek, Latin, and Syriac New Testaments. Some verses can be noted where such corruption is a possibility.

At I Corinthians 1:12 Paul refers to four competing groups, "It has been reported to me . . . that there is quarreling among you, my brethren. What I mean is that each of you says, 'I belong to Paul,' or 'I belong to Apollos,' or 'I belong to Cephas,' or 'I belong to Christ.' " The first three groupings are reasonably clear. The "Paul party" consisted of those who had been converted by that apostle and were loyal to him. The "Apollos party" was made up of Corinthians swayed by the eloquence of Apollos, an erudite preacher from Alexandria (*See* Acts 18:24–28), and baptized by him. The "Cephas party" was a Jewish-Christian group making its appeal to Simon Peter and seeking a path between traditional Judaism and new Gentile Christian practices.

But what of a "Christ party"? Would a similar party group have arisen around Jesus of Nazareth? Were not all the groups invoking the name of Christ? A gnostic party of this name is unlikely. Paul would scarcely have let a group get away with exclusive use of the slogan, "I belong to Christ." His very next sentence (1:13) seems to contrast Jesus Christ with *all* party-spirit at Corinth, even that of his own supporters: "Is Christ divided? Was Paul crucified for you?" I Corinthians 3:21 seems to exclude any "Christ party" with its majestic statement, "All things are yours, whether *Paul* or *Apollos* or *Cephas* . . . and you are Christ's. . . ." There are three party groups here, but all of them belong to Christ. Most strikingly, the oldest outside evidence we possess, a letter from Clement of Rome to Corinth about A.D. 96, refers to three groups only. Clement says, Paul wrote "to you concerning himself and Cephas and Apollos, because of the fact that even then you were given to factions" (I Clement 47:3).

If only three parties were mentioned in Paul's original letter, how has the reference to Christ gotten into our text? The most likely answer in the judgment of several commentators is that the words, "but I, of Christ," are the insertion of some indignant copyist in the second century. As he wrote out Paul's letter and came across these references to men of sectarian spirit who labeled themselves as Paulinists or claimed "I belong to Apollos," or "I am of Cephas," this scribe was moved to write piously in the margin, "But as for me, I belong to Christ." The next copyist then inserted these words in the text, and there they have been ever since, as a part of Paul's letter. Some would trace this insertion all the way back to Paul's original scribe, Sosthenes. If one wishes, he can, of course, attribute the words to Paul himself, as a devout aside, as he dictated the letter. English translations regularly include the words for the simple reason that all our manuscripts have them. The point is that any alteration which may have taken place here, must have occurred prior to the time of our manuscripts, possibly in the second-century "tunnel period."

Another passage in I Corinthians where we have to resort to some sort of conjecture to ascertain what Paul means is 4:6. In rebuking the party spirit at Corinth, Paul has emphasized the task of every Christian to work faithfully and humbly as a steward of God. He had used a series of illustrations at 3:4–9 to show how he and Apollos have labored together under God for the good of the church. Now at 4:6 he goes on, according to the King James Version, "These things, brethren, I have in a figure transferred to myself and to Apollos for your sake; that you might learn in us not to think *of men* above that which is written, that no one of you be puffed up for one against another." The opening and closing parts of the verse are clear. Paul's illustrations are to teach the Corinthians not to be proud in behalf of one teacher and scorn others within the community. But the middle clause, and especially the words translated by the King James Version as "not . . . above that which is written," have caused headaches for all commentators. The verb "to think" is a late addition, attested only in inferior manuscripts. The words *"of men"* are an addition by the King James translators themselves (which they put in italics to show that they added something found in no manuscript), to pad out the sense.

The crux then is what to make of the phrase "not . . . above that which is written." Elsewhere when Paul speaks of "what is written" he means the Old Testament. The R.S.V. seems to have this in mind in its translation, ". . . Learn by us to live according to scripture." The problem is, however, that no specific passage can be turned up in the Old Testament which says exactly what we have here. Some have sensed a reference to a Greek proverb like "Nothing too much" or to an assumed maxim

of the rabbis, "Keep to the written word, not a step beyond."
Some such interpretation is assumed by the rendering in the
New English Bible, ". . . learn to 'keep within the rules', as
they say." In all these cases, we are conjecturing what Paul
might have meant, and there are arguments against each interpretation. Our confidence in any such solution is not increased
when we learn that the words have been taken in diametrically
opposite ways, as expressing either (a) Paul's protest against a
literalist, biblicistic group at Corinth which criticized his daring
uses of the Old Testament (to whom he says, ". . . learn from
Apollos and me, with regard to the slogan, 'Not beyond the strict
letter,' that no one among you should get puffed up for one type
of teaching against the other"), or (b) his protest against the
criticism that he is too narrowly biblical and not mystical and
speculative enough (in reply to which he writes, ". . . learn
from us the sound principle of 'Never go beyond the scriptural
text'"). When we know even a little about the problems behind
this verse, we can feel nothing but sympathy for the translator
who must commit himself to one definite (or indefinite) interpretation and express it in a very few words. We can appreciate
why J. B. Phillips chose to paraphrase, ". . . learn from what I
have said about us not to assess man above his value in God's
sight," and why James Moffatt wrote that "in the Greek five or
six words are inserted whose meaning lies beyond recovery"[2]
and left a gap in his translation: "Now I have applied what has
been said above to myself and Apollos, to teach you . . . that
you are not to be puffed up with rivalry over one teacher as
against another."

There is just one other possible solution which has been advanced. It depends on the assumption of scribal errors in the
"tunnel period." The verse contains two clauses both beginning
with the word "that" (in Greek, *hina*):

> that ye might learn in us not [to think] above
> > that which is written,
> that no one of you be puffed up for one against an-
> > other.

The latter clause begins in Greek,

> *hina mē heis* . . . , "that no one. . . ."

The conjecture of a Dutch scholar, Baljon, in 1884 was that an early copyist accidentally left out the negative word *mē* in this clause. When he saw his omission, he inserted it above the line, to be precise above the last letter of the preceding Greek word, *hina,* something like this:

mē

HINA HEIS. . . .

To call attention to this insertion, a second scribe put a note in the margin, "The [word] *mē* is written above the [letter] *a.*" In Greek, *to mē hyper a gegraptai.* Unfortunately a later copyist did not understand this and inserted the marginal note into the previous clause,

> that ye might learn in us *to mē hyper a gegraptai.*

This Greek could now be rendered, with one breathing mark altered, as "not beyond what is written." In order to make sense of the words now in the text, the later scribes added the verb, "to think" and the King James translators inserted "of men." On this hypothesis, what Paul wrote originally was,

> that ye might learn in us
> that no one of you be puffed up for one against an-
> other.

Subsequent hands corrupted it into what we have in the 1611 translation. The work of the third copyist must have been done before the end of the second century, for no manuscript exists minus the words "not above what is written" or with them in the margin. But ever since that gloss got into the text, copyists and translators have made all sorts of insertions and interpretations to make sense of a verse corrupted, apparently, in the "tunnel period." It is only fair to add, however, that our conjectured "solution" has been rejected by more than one scholar as "too clever," and no standard English translation has fully adopted it.

In each of the cases in I Corinthians there is no manuscript evidence at all for the solution proposed. In a final example, at John 19:29, there is a noteworthy reading supported by just one late manuscript, but the assumption of the New English Bible translators is that this lone manuscript is correct and that all other witnesses are wrong—because of a corruption in the second century or so. John 19:29, which has to do with a detail in the crucifixion scene, reads in R.S.V., "they put a sponge full of vinegar on hyssop and held it to his mouth." The K.J.V., many other translations, and virtually all manuscripts agree on the word "hyssop," in the Greek *HYSSŌPŌ*. Commentators recognize the difficulty that the hyssop plant, a shrub of some sort, perhaps like thyme or marjoram, is a rather frail reed on which to raise a sponge, but most of them assume that John was concerned more about symbolism than about camera-like detail. Hyssop was used in Passover rites (see Exodus 12:22), and John probably has in mind the symbol of Christ-crucified as a Paschal lamb.

Not all readers have been satisfied with this explanation, however, and in the sixteenth century Joachim Camerarius, a German classicist who was a close friend of Philip Melanchthon and who had a hand in creating the Augsburg Confession and later translated it into Greek, suggested an emendation for John 19:29. Instead of *HYSSŌPŌ*, he proposed *HYSSŌ* as the original reading; this would mean "on a spear" or "javelin." This easy change makes excellent sense, and a javelin is just what one would expect a soldier at the cross to use. Later a manuscript copied in the eleventh century (manuscript No. 476) came to light which contained the very reading Camerarius had conjectured. No other manuscript contains the word *HYSSŌ* here, and so one must decide whether this eleventh-century copy, alone out of all the five thousand Greek witnesses to the New Testament, has preserved the true reading. The contention is not impossible, but the corruption would have had to take place at an early date—at least before A.D. 200—so that the true reading was obliterated in all other witnesses. A good many recent translators have accepted the reading of this single manuscript. Goodspeed has "pike," Moffatt and J. B. Phillips "a spear," and Charles Kingsley Williams allowed it as the only place in his translation where a meaning was "guessed." The New English Bible has followed them and reads "on a javelin," but with the frank footnote, "*So one witness; the others read* on marjoram." This assumption, that an original Greek reading, *HYSSŌPERITHENTES* ("having put it on a spear"), was corrupted into *HYSSŌPŌPERITHENTES* ("having put it on hyssop") by the addition of two Greek letters, in all save one manuscript, has not, however, been accepted by every scholar. C. K. Barrett, in his extensive commentary on John, doubts that the Fourth Evangelist was concerned, the way modern critics are, about whether one can put a sponge on a hyssop stalk, and G. D. Kilpatrick, an Oxford text critic, wonders if the type of weapon called a "javelin" here would really have been long enough for the height required. Manuscript 476 may be a coincidental corruption, not an original reading. Perhaps a final decision depends on one's feeling about whether John is more concerned with historical details or symbolic allusions. At this point the translator must take a stand concerning the theology of the evangelist.

What a translator translates, therefore, the text he employs does in many cases make a difference. He and we are at this end of a long chain of transmission, some links of which we can examine in detail, some of which are quite obscure. Probably no segment in this chain is more exciting and significant than the second century A.D. Barring further discoveries of manuscripts, we can for the New Testament scarcely expect to get behind the period, though for the Old Testament we have been vaulted over it to earlier days by the Dead Sea Scrolls. Any translator today must rest heavily on the results of work done in the second century, and we who read ought to be grateful for the labors of those men, good and otherwise, known and unknown, in this exciting period.

Three

Luther's Legions:
The Protestant Reformation and Bible Translation

M ARTIN LUTHER, SO AN OFTEN-TOLD STORY RUNS, ONCE stood before the pope's special representative in Germany. For three days the Cardinal legate had tried to dissuade this "son of iniquity" from his views, first by fatherly counsel, then by argument and by threats. Unable to get Luther to say the single, necessary word, "*Revoco,* I recant," the Cardinal finally thundered at him, "The Pope's little finger is stronger than all Germany. Do you expect your princes to take up arms to defend you—a wretched worm like you? I tell you, No! And where will you be then? Tell me that—where will you be then?"

"Then, as now," Luther replied, "in the hands of Almighty God!"

The story may well be apocryphal, more popular with preachers as an illustration than substantiated by historians as "gospel truth." But the scene is true to life in the way it asserts Luther's habit of seeing everything in relation to God and in the way it raises the question of what Luther did have going for him—save his firm faith in God—in the years when the Reformation movement was gathering force. Could he expect princes like Frederick, Elector of Saxony, to take up arms to defend his views? Who would contend on Luther's side? In later times, it was Napoleon,

55

was it not, who flung the taunt, "How many legions has the pope?" That question has often been raised by realists about men of religion, whether they are popes or reformers. So in Luther's case: how many legions did he have which would take up the defense of his gospel? What forces would fight for him?

Various answers have been given as to why the Reformation succeeded to the extent it did. Political, economic, and social factors were all involved. Likewise Luther's personal magnetism must be reckoned with, a personality that still attracts the biographer, psychologist, and the playwright today. But to this list of factors one must also add the religious element. Luther's "new theology" sounded a clarion call of return to the Gospel of Jesus Christ, with a freshness which cut across the centuries of tradition and did away with much of the philosophical structure so carefully built up by the medieval doctors of the church. There was also in Luther a certain common-sense directness which defied the "establishment" of the day and went to the heart of what mattered most and to the underlying question of authority. Thus any analysis of the elements promoting Luther's cause must not overlook his work as Bible translator. Regardless of the role assigned to the other factors, and all those mentioned had a part to play, Luther's contribution through his study and translation of the Holy Scriptures is of inestimable import.

There is, of course, always the danger that in treating in isolation his story as a biblical scholar, we shall make Luther too much a biblicist or lose the overall context of his work. That is why certain details must be noted which, strictly speaking, are auxiliary to the translation of the Bible. But these admissions made, that Luther's story as translator must be seen in its context and in light of his total work, there is a sense in which it can be said that "Luther's legions" consisted precisely in the Bible translations he made and inspired and let loose upon the lands of Europe. As auxiliary forces there were his Prefaces and commentaries to the biblical books, and the sermons that he preached. As armor and artillery there were the hymns, the theological essays, and the confessional writings. All these—legions, auxiliaries, armor, and artillery—were used concertedly in one vast striking force that wrought the work of reformation. To sing "A Mighty Fortress" brought much the same experience as to read Psalm 46 in Luther's German Bible. To ponder his rendering of Romans or Galatians or to read his introduction to James or comments on Genesis was nothing less than to receive a capsule course in Luther's theology. The Bible translation is thus inseparably intertwined with everything else Luther ever did, or, if you wish, his whole theology and life-experience finds expression in his Bible translation.

It has with truth been said that the Luther Bible was the device which in many German-speaking parts of Europe prepared a way for the Reformation and solidified its gains. Luther's followers in other lands translated the Bible into their native languages, with much the same approach as Luther himself employed and with similar results. In Scandinavia, central Europe, the Low Countries, and even in the islands west of the Continent like Iceland and England, these vernacular translations helped win Reformation victories too. The Lutheran Bible translations—those in German and other languages, inspired and influenced by Luther—were spread and multiplied by the power of the printing press. They circulated far and wide. They conquered in the name of the Doctor of Wittenberg and the Evangelical Confession of Augsburg. They spread "Lutheran" influence even where they did not ultimately prevail. They even infiltrated the lines of the opponents and left some imprint on Roman Catholic biblical study. Such were the legions which Luther unleashed, the forces in which he trusted as exponents of the power of the Word.

But *how* did Luther translate? What precisely did he do which others, his many predecessors and successors, did not? That is a larger question which demands attention. To set Luther in proper perspective, we must realize that he was not so completely a pioneer with the Bible as friends have often made him appear. After all, there had been printed Bibles in Latin before Luther was born. Gutenberg's first printed book was a Vulgate, c. 1455 at Mainz. There had been German translations, many of them, decades and centuries previously. Ulfilas had put the Bible into Gothic before he died in A.D. 383, thus providing the oldest literary monument in a Germanic language. There are fragments preserved of a Frankish translation of Matthew, dated A.D. 738. Some unknown "German Tatian" provided a harmony of the gospels through a ninth-century translation. By the end of the Middle Ages, German manuscripts of the Bible numbered in the thousands. What is more, there were also German translations in print before Luther's day. The first printed Bible in any modern European language was the German version from the press of Johann Mentelin of Strassburg in 1466, and that translation went back to the fourteenth century. In all, four Low German translations and fourteen in High German had appeared in print before Luther ever began his work. Eight to ten thousand vernacular copies were on the market, each costing the equivalent of a town house or fourteen oxen.

Of course, judged by the standards on which a translation always must be measured, such as the text followed and the clarity and accuracy of expression, these pre-Luther German Bibles left much to be desired. The textual base was regularly the Latin Vulgate, and sometimes in a corrupted form at that. Thus these translations of the Vulgate translation usually included in their New Testament the "Epistle to the Laodiceans," a fourth-century forgery attributed to Paul. The poor quality of the textual foundation was not improved by men who were often rather weak in Latin or unidiomatic in German. The question at Matthew 22:42, "What think ye of Christ?"—in Latin, *"Quid vobis videtur de Christo?"*—was rather woodenly brought over by one of these German translators as *"Was ist euch gesehen von Christo?"*; literally, "What is seen for you of Christ?" The familiar Latin idiom *gratias agere*, to "give thanks," was totally missed by a translator at Mark 8:6, for he makes it, quite mechanically, to "work grace" (*"Gnade wirken"*). As exegetes, such men can scarcely be commended. Their outlook was often limited to the beliefs and piety of the day. Two of these German translators left the Song of Solomon in Latin, so that young people might not be corrupted by reading such love poetry!

There was therefore in many ways a great gulf between the work of these earlier translators and what Luther was to do, but by 1515, when Luther appeared on the scene, Bible translation into German was at least under way. There was a desire for vernacular Bibles, which some within the church manifestly encouraged. There existed also a tradition of book manufacture as an art, with such features developed in Bible-making as use of woodcuts, red letters, and chapter summaries. While Luther's work was to be different in many ways, it had this heritage upon which to draw. To make the point emphatic: German Bibles existed before Luther. They were not suppressed as much as they were overlaid with the whole structure of scholastic theology. The difference was to be not *that* Luther translated the Bible, but *how* he did and the place he gave to Holy Scripture in the unified whole of theology and life. Luther's contribution was that he went about the task of translation with a perspective different from that of his predecessors in Germany.

Luther unleashed the Scriptures from the ecclesiastical subservience of the day. He freed the Bible from the churchly framework of philosophy and patristic theology then dominant. We must even say that Luther set it free from the bondage in which current worship had imprisoned the scriptural message. "When I was twenty years old," Luther once wrote, describing the period when he was a university student, "I had not yet seen a [whole] Bible. I believed there to be no more to it than the gospel and epistle pericopes" which were read in church. These traditional pericopes, or selections for public reading on Sunday and at festivals, are often a rather poor guide to what is central in Scripture. Here the liturgical use of the Bible, in the Mass, played false with what Luther found to be the biblical message. Luther's work was to wrench the Bible from even this context

and from most other current settings, in an endeavor to let the
Word of God speak for itself. It was not simply a matter of
exalting the Bible, however, to the disparagement of all else;
rather it was, in the context of a profound awareness of the
Christian community, of history, and of the world round about,
a matter of the exaltation of the Word of God—something
Luther saw as related to, but not flatly identical with, the Holy
Book. Mid all the currents of the Renaissance and Reformation,
in a Europe which was "coming of age," Luther set out to
translate the Scriptures as part and parcel of his total theological
program.

Therefore, perhaps more acutely than any other translator,
Luther raises the question of *how* one should go about the task
of rendering the Bible. This question had surely been raised by
the work of Aquila, for he followed a method that derived from
the hermeneutics of Akiba. Aquila translated every syllable with
an exegetical system in mind and with the theology of rabbinic
Judaism firmly implanted in his thought. Tatian and Marcion
likewise posed the problem of the "how" in translation, for in
each case the theology of the man influenced his text, his canon,
and his renderings. Indeed, every translator, whether he realizes
it or not, is faced by the problem of theological context for his
work. To pose this question with regard to the age of the
Reformation and in connection with so controversial a figure as
Luther is not without its hazards. But the Reformation is precisely the proper period in which to ask our question, because in
the sixteenth century the Bible was coming to the fore as it had
not for centuries previously. So also was real scholarship, the first
stirrings of the historical-critical method, as part of the Renaissance's search for truth. So too was theology, for this was an age
when men died for their convictions about the church or for
their beliefs concerning the proper mode of baptism or over the
right interpretation of bread and wine. In an age when the
emphases were, as never before, on historical study, biblical re-
vival, and new confessional assertions, how did Luther translate?

The Translator Who Shook Germany

Certain external facts about Luther as translator and the series of Bibles for which he was responsible are quite clear. There is the matter of his preparation, for one thing. Educated at the Cathedral School at Magdeburg, then at Eisenach, and finally in the University of Erfurt (1501–05), Luther aimed originally at becoming a lawyer. But all study in those days was so heavily weighted with philosophy, theology, and, of course, Latin, that there was really no problem of "academic background" when, on a July day in 1505, during a thunderstorm near the village of Stotternheim, Luther made his vow to become a monk. In fact, his previous study fitted him for special work in his new life. In 1508, three years after he had entered the order of the Augustinian Hermits at Erfurt and a year after he had been ordained a priest, Luther was sent by his superiors to study further and to lecture in philosophy at the recently established University at Wittenberg. Then, in September, 1511, John Staupitz, vicar of the order, suggested to Luther, in a meeting under a pear tree in the garden of the Black Cloister, that he should prepare himself to become preacher to the convent there and a Doctor of Theology. It is probably significant for Luther's development that the two offices of preacher and teacher intertwined, and within a year Luther had been confirmed in both. It was on October 19, 1512, at seven in the morning, that Luther was promoted to the doctoral rank. He was immediately given a chair in the theological faculty at Wittenberg. His title, *Doctor in Biblia,* is virtually the equivalent of "biblical theologian" today, and the opinion is probably correct that in a modern faculty Luther would occupy, not the chair of systematic theology, but a post in the biblical department, probably as Professor of Old Testament. He began his lectures exactly one week later, again at seven A.M. (the academic schedule was more rigorous then). Most likely his first lectures were on Genesis. Thus by training and in the position to which he was appointed, Luther was being prepared for the task of Bible translation.

In his years as university teacher, Luther made strides which further equipped him for his future translation work. He knew Latin well and was learning Greek and Hebrew. It is to his credit that he made use of some of the significant new texts and tools currently coming from the press. In March, 1516, the Greek New Testament was available in printed form for the first time, as edited by Erasmus, from the publishing firm of Johann Froben in Basel. By August, Luther had a copy and began using it immediately in his lectures on Romans, from chapter nine on. In 1517–18 he was citing the Hebrew in his lectures on the Old Testament, taking advantage of the Bibles which Jews had printed in Italy, and was absorbing the grammars of Reuchlin and others. Luther's debt to the biblical humanists in the years 1512–20 is immense. At first his knowledge of Greek and Hebrew was quite sparse. It has been estimated that he took up Greek seriously only in 1514. By 1518 he had matured in knowledge of it, and by 1520 the results of his study plainly could be seen in what he wrote.[1] Two years later he was translating the New Testament, and by 1523 publishing portions of the Old Testament from the Hebrew.

Luther not only thus improved his knowledge of the sacred texts, but in these years he was also developing his German style, the language into which he would translate—facility in which is the other absolute requirement for any translator. Germany was then a land of many dialects. Luther's travels acquainted him with some of them. His preaching taught him to be forceful in expression so that the people might understand clearly. Normally his teaching would be of little help here, for all university lecturing was then in Latin. But Luther had the habit of inserting German expressions into his lectures to drive home a point, and is said to have been the first German professor to lecture in his native tongue. He was developing a flair for expression which would cause him to be called "the German Cicero." In terms of content he was also now mastering the biblical material in a way that would aid his translational activity. It is the man who knows the Bible best, its ins and outs, who can often best grasp its "feel" and get the right nuances. Luther in the years between 1512 and 1517 was lecturing on Genesis, Psalms, Romans, and Galatians, we know. What is more, he was trying his hand at preliminary translations which were published. Between 1517 and 1521, Luther's renderings of the seven Penitential Psalms, plus Psalms 37, 68, 110, and 118, the Lord's Prayer, the Magnificat, Solomon's prayer in I Kings 8, and certain Sunday gospels were published. In such ways the translator was being prepared.

Theologically Luther was developing too, though we cannot take time here to pinpoint all the changes and events of these crowded years as his split with the papal hierarchy grew wider. It suffices to say that many of Luther's positions related directly to discoveries he was making in his biblical study. The Ninety-Five Theses, posted on the door of Wittenberg's Castle Church on October 31, 1517, arose originally out of protest against the hawking of indulgences which promised plenary remission of sins in exchange for money which would help build the new basilica of St. Peter, then under construction in Rome. But ultimately Luther's position in these theses was influenced by his current lecturing on Paul. Thesis 1 really sums up the lot when it insists, "Our Lord and Master Jesus Christ, in saying 'Repent ye, etc.,' meant the whole life of the believer to be an act of repentance." The next theses reinforce this theme like hammer blows: not outward mechanics matter, but a change of heart that lasts for life. By 1518, when Luther came to publish *Resolutions,* expanding his views on the Ninety-Five Theses, he had discovered from his study of the Erasmus New Testament that Jesus' words in Greek are literally *"Be* penitent," not *"Do* penance" as in the Vulgate Latin (*poenitentiam agite,* Matt. 4:17). This was for Luther a "glowing" discovery and a case where his theology took shape around insights from biblical study.

Over the Ninety-Five Theses fierce debate arose throughout

Germany. In 1519 came the disputation with Eck at Leipzig. In
June, 1520, a papal bull declared forty-one of the theses heretical. Luther's answer was to burn the pope's decree, and in January, 1521, he was excommunicated. Then came the famous
hearing before the emperor at the Diet of Worms, with Luther's
well-known words, ". . . Unless I am convinced by Scripture
and plain reason . . . my conscience is captive to the Word of
God. I cannot and will not recant . . . ," with, perhaps, the
addition that is even more famous, "Here I stand, I cannot do
otherwise." Luther had entered Worms under a promise of
safe-conduct from the emperor, and he left under the same terms
on April 26, 1521. But friends, fearing that this promise would
not be honored, took matters into their own hands. The Elector
of Saxony fathered a plot, details of which were not known even
to Luther. The route homeward took Luther through the Thuringian Forest, near Eisenach, where he paused to visit relatives
on May second. Next morning he preached in a village church,
and then, accompanied by two friends and a driver, set out in a
wagon. Relatives also traveled with them until nearly nightfall.
As soon as these relatives turned back, four or five horsemen
ambushed the wagon. A fellow-monk jumped from it and ran
away. The other companion was assured by Luther, "We are
among friends," but the companion's reactions seemed so real
that even the driver never guessed the plot was prearranged.
With feigned roughness Luther was dragged away by the horsemen who disappeared into the night. It was about eleven P.M.
when they rudely dumped him into a cell at the Wartburg, a
castle in the Thuringian hills. Even the guards there were not
told who the "prisoner" was. Luther stayed under cover till he
grew a beard, and long hair replaced his monk's tonsure. For the
next ten months he became Junker Joerg, "Knight George,"
while Europe buzzed with rumors about his disappearance. During this time and under these unusual circumstances, Luther was
to translate the New Testament.

In the Wartburg, which Luther, comparing himself to the

author of the book of Revelation, called "my Patmos," Junker Joerg occupied a room about fifteen by twenty feet in size. It towered high above the ground and looked out over the hills and forests of Thuringia. The height and trees made it seem like "the land of the birds." Luther could take walks through the countryside. Once he tried hunting but found it a "bitter-sweet pleasure." Most of his time he stayed alone, with his Lord, in the room. The legend that the devil once appeared and that Luther threw an inkwell at him, marking the wall, if not spattering Satan, is only a legend, the type that grows up about the shrine of some religious man. No writing by Luther refers to any such incident. The story seems to have originated in the imagination of a sixteenth-century biographer, and as with many other similar stories it is also told of rooms in three other towns where Luther stayed. There were many more important things to be done than inkwell-tossing. At first Luther busied himself with expository writings. Then he turned out a variety of pamphlets. He was also occupied in correspondence with the Wittenberg faculty over problems of all sorts. Carlstadt was insisting, for example, on the basis of I Timothy 3:2, not merely that priests could marry, but that they *must* be married. There was rioting in Wittenberg against relics and the Mass. The "Zwickau Prophets," a sort of Pentecostal group, set themselves up in Wittenberg about Christmastime of 1521. Once in that month Junker Joerg went back to the city, incognito, disguised by his beard and rough clothes, and then returned to his Wartburg aerie. It was amid these happenings, fightings without and fears within, "danger in the city, danger in the wilderness, . . . danger from false brethren; in toil and hardship, through many a sleepless night, . . . the daily pressure . . . of anxiety for all the churches" (II Cor. 11:26–28)—in a spirit not unlike Paul's in his apostolic ministry—that Luther took pen in hand to translate.

Why Luther decided to turn translator at this time, when seemingly there were so many other things to do and when he was cut off from colleagues and library facilities, is not precisely known. There was, of course, a pressing need for a German Bible which spoke fervently in the way in which Luther had experienced its message. He now had enforced leisure. Certainly his friends encouraged an already existing desire to translate. Luther later stated that Philip Melanchthon, Professor of Greek at Wittenberg, whom Luther had been responsible for bringing to the university, was instrumental in persuading him to translate. During the incognito visit to Wittenberg on December 3–4, he had probably seen Melanchthon and discussed the project. Earlier during his "exile" Luther had had books sent to the Wartburg. From a letter dated December 18, 1521, we know that Luther then expected to stay in his hiding place until Easter and that in the meantime he planned to translate the New Testament into German. That is exactly what he did, in two and a half months. On March 6 Luther returned to Wittenberg with his manuscript. There was revision with Melanchthon. By May printing was under way, in secret, using three presses, and by at least September 21 the Luther New Testament was on sale, the "September Testament" as it was called. The three thousand copies sold well at a price variously reported as a half or one gulden (perhaps depending on which type of gulden was involved), and variously estimated as the equivalent of fifteen dollars or as "the weekly wage of a journeyman carpenter" in Luther's day,[2] a good figure at present standards.

Translation of the Old Testament began with just as much rapidity. Genesis and Exodus were finished by November, the rest of the Pentateuch by December, 1522. Luther worked from the Hebrew Bible published at Brescia, Italy, in 1494, by Gerson Ben Moscheh. The Pentateuch was published in the summer of 1523. The historical and poetical books, Joshua to the Song of Solomon, plus the Psalter, came out in 1524. Then the pace slackened, and the rest of the work was to drag out over a ten-year period. Jonah and Habakkuk were published in 1526 and Zechariah in 1527, in each case with an accompanying commentary.

Isaiah was in print the next year, and so on, until all the prophets were completed by 1532. The Apocrypha was the last section to be tackled, and it was the autumn of 1534 before those extra-canonical books appeared as part of a complete Bible. Accordingly the decision had been a wise one to publish the Old Testament in sections, as completed.

It is rather amazing that Luther could keep so doggedly at the task of translation over all these years. Other activities and demands must have sorely tempted him to lay such an arduous task aside. In 1525 had come the Peasants' Revolt, the death of Frederick, and Luther's marriage to Katherine von Bora. In 1529 there was the Marburg Colloquy with Zwingli, over the theological exegesis of words of Jesus in the Upper Room, whether they mean "This *is* . . ." or "This *means* my body." The year 1530 saw the presentation of the Augsburg Confession. Most of these events meant the publication of essays and "tracts for the times" by Luther. In addition he continued to lecture and preach with regularity and carried on a considerable correspondence.

One explanation as to how Luther managed to continue his translation work is that he doubled up on things and did it in connection with his current teaching program, as many a subsequent professor has done—what he lectures on one year is next year's book. Thus during the years 1524–26 it was the Minor Prophets that were the subject of his courses, and this material was subsequently published. Luther also tended to take up certain Old Testament books in the order which current interests dictated. Thus the Turkish menace, which in 1529 penetrated far into Austria and laid siege to Vienna, led Luther to treat the book of Daniel, because of its apocalyptic visions of "the beast" in the "last times." (Melanchthon saw in the vision a reference to the Turks.) Sometimes physical circumstances compelled what Luther tackled. When he was ill in 1527, for example, he translated the Wisdom of Solomon which was extant only in Greek and demanded no use of the more difficult Hebrew. Similar personal circumstances played a part in determining what he did in the period around 1528 when the university was temporarily removed to Jena and Luther was deprived of Melanchthon and other faculty members as consultants. These months were a poor time for much work on the Old Testament, for in 1528–29 Luther was serving as town preacher in the stead of Johann Bugenhagen at Wittenberg, engaging in a "church visitation" to thirty-eight parishes throughout Saxony (with all the attendant practical problems which any district superintendent knows, finances, leaky roofs, and squabbles over liturgies), and at the same time he was undertaking a revision of his German New Testament. On the other hand, the weeks at Coburg Castle in the summer of 1530, during the Diet of Augsburg (which Luther could not attend because of the ban against him), were quite productive, and the basic translation of the remaining Major and Minor Prophets was completed then.

Unfortunately we have no firsthand picture of how Luther went about his work on the New Testament in the solitude of Wartburg Castle. For the Old Testament, certain contemporary documents survive which describe details, as do some working manuscripts in Luther's own hand (a few of which were destroyed in World War II). It has already been indicated that Luther employed the latest texts, grammars, and lexicons available to him, whether by Jews, humanists, opponents, or scholars who shared his views. Melanchthon was a particular support, and for the Old Testament so was Matthäus Aurogallus, Professor of Hebrew at Wittenberg. Luther probably had more help for the Hebrew than for the Greek. Friends did most of the translating in the Apocrypha, when in 1532–33 Luther's illness and other duties threatened long delay. The Wisdom of Solomon, Ecclesiasticus, and the Prayer of Manasseh (which Luther dearly loved because of its contrite spirit and majestic portrait of God and his mercy) had however been completed long before, all probably from Luther's own hand.

Stories are plentiful as to how Luther went about his work

after the Wartburg exile. He would quiz a German butcher as he slaughtered rams, or would inspect the Elector's collection of jewels and precious stones, or would study a thunderstorm to ascertain the proper German terms and get the sense for a passage. Luther used dark ink for writing a first draft and red ink for revisions and corrections that were made. The *Lutherzimmer* or study where he labored in the home provided in the former Black Cloister at Wittenberg was constantly cluttered. Chairs, window sills, and even the floor, as well as his worktable, were loaded with books and papers which Kathie had the sense not to disturb. It was here, in the house surrounded by its garden, stable, little chapel, and *Brauhaus* (brewery), that Luther met with what he called his "Sanhedrin," a company of scholars who helped him in translation work. A contemporary has recorded something of how these sessions were conducted in the 1530's, even after the Bible was complete, in order to revise the translation. Meetings usually lasted about two hours or so in the late afternoon (like many a modern university seminar). Luther presided, with the Latin, German, and Hebrew before him. "Master Philip" Melachthon was the expert in Greek. Creuziger had a "Chaldean Bible," presumably an Aramaic targum, other professors the rabbinic commentaries. Bugenhagen, Justus, Aurogallus, each might speak in turn, and George Roerer, the "corrector" for the Luther Bible, kept a summary of decisions. Some protocols from these sessions have been found in recent years and reveal a bit of the arguments, the methodology, and humor that entered into these meetings. (Our records of modern Bible translation committees are often less complete as to their "inner workings.") In the group, Luther stands out as the leader who seeks clear, vivid German to express the sense of the original.

Certain books gave special trouble. A letter of 1530 notes that three or four days might be spent on a few lines of Job, the sublime style of which has challenged many a translator. Job, said Luther once, seems "much more impatient with our translation than with the consolation of his friends"; he feared Job might persist "in sitting upon his ash heap" and that perhaps the author of the book never wished it translated. The prophets, Luther complained in a letter of 1528, "do not want to give up their Hebrew and imitate the barbaric German," any more than a nightingale would imitate a cuckoo; "O God, what a great and hard toil it requires to compel the writers against their will to speak German!" Luther characteristically refers to sweat as a part of the translator's chore. The result of all this labor, however, was a translation which captured the hearts and minds of contemporary Germany and helped shape the German language itself. Luther not only translated, but he made the Gospel speak German. This was Luther's goal: a Bible really in the language that men understood; Moses and Christ speaking not in some holy "Bible patois," but the way men talk in the market place.

One other contribution which Luther made, though it is often overlooked, is of such significance that it cannot be omitted from our account: he revised his work. As long as he lived, Luther was interested in improving his translation. The New Testament was radically revised in 1529 and altered in further minor ways even after that. The years 1539–41 saw large-scale revision of the Old Testament. The "Sanhedrin" was in session as late as 1544, in spite of Luther's poor health. At the time of his death in 1546, corrections were still being made by the faithful Roerer from marginal notations in Luther's own personal copy. Traditionally, however, a 1545 edition, which lacks some of these last alterations which Luther did not personally see through the press, has been regarded as the *Textus Receptus* of German-speaking Lutheranism. For a century or more the Luther Bible towered over the field in German, so that few rival translations were even launched.

Language inevitably changes, however, and errors can creep in, even with a printed text. By 1690 the Pietist leader August Hermann Francke noted some three hundred departures from Luther. In the eighteenth century the Bible Society founded by

Francke's friend, C. H. F. von Canstein, took the lead in establishing a proper text for the cheap editions in which it pioneered. The German territorial churches in the nineteenth century worked out a plan for bringing the Luther Bible periodically up-to-date. The method was followed of providing first a "test edition" (*Probe-Bibel*), where changes might be tried out over a period of years before finally being incorporated. Such revisions were carried through, after long testing, in 1892, and more recently for the New Testament from 1938 to 1956 and for the Old from 1956 to 1964. In this way, the Luther Bible has been kept broadly contemporary, while still maintaining the old traditional lines. This seems to have been done without all the hue and cry which has attended efforts to revise the King James Bible in English, and over a period of time longer by a century than for the K.J.V. Luther's own example of periodic revision has surely contributed to the continuing reign of his Bible.

"Luther's legions," it may finally be noted, were multilingual. His Bible translation was soon put into a host of other languages besides the High German in which he wrote. Though Luther's own translation enjoyed enormous success—200,000 copies of the New Testament were sold between 1522 and 1534, it has been estimated; there were twenty-two editions of the New Testament and 250 of the entire Bible in Germany before Luther's death, somewhere between 750,000 and a million copies of the Scriptures, in whole or in part, before 1546; even Roman Catholic adversaries like Emser and Eck drew on Luther's renderings—the versions made under his influence in other languages were also of signal importance in spreading the Reformation. Luther's High German enjoys the distinction of being the first complete Bible translation from the original languages into some modern vernacular of Europe. Many of the "daughter translations" likewise were "firsts" of one sort or another. Whether the language was Swedish, Dutch, or English, the pattern was roughly the same. In almost every case there had been earlier, but often only partial, translations. Now under the influence of the Reformation's emphasis on Scripture in the language of the people, a new translation was made. Often it depended on the Luther Bible, though there were regularly other sources too, frequently the original languages themselves. In many cases Luther's students at Wittenberg were involved. At the least, the foreign translators had read Luther, and some of them came to Wittenberg to meet the man. For through Dr. Luther the university had acquired a greater name for itself. It experienced a growing popularity, attracting students from other parts of Germany and beyond, particularly from 1515 to 1519 and then from 1526 until Luther's death. The average number in the student body in the 1520's was two hundred, but Luther's appeal to the German authorities to push local education, especially in Greek and Latin, so that university-trained leaders for church and state might abound, raised the number to over five hundred in the early 1540's.[3] Students who came, churchmen, translators, all were influenced to make the Bible as living as it was when Professor Luther expounded it.

The list of translations sparked by Luther's work is impressive. Low German translations, by unknown hands, appeared almost as soon as any part of the Luther Bible was on the market. In Holland, where a translation from the Latin New Testament had been printed in 1522, a Dutch rendering of Luther's New Testament was published by 1523. The first complete Bible printed in Dutch in 1526 drew on Luther's work in all portions which were available by then. In Danish, though there had been significant endeavors in pre-Reformation times, the first complete New Testament translation appeared in 1524, and it was based heavily on Luther. The entire Bible in Danish was completed in 1550 under the auspices of the state (Lutheran) church, the work especially of Christiern Pedersen and the "Danish Luther," Hans Tausen. This "Christian III" edition served for Norway as well. As for Swedish, a New Testament translation became available in 1526, prepared in all likelihood by Olaus Petri, a blacksmith's son who had attended Luther's lectures at Wittenberg. He and his brother, Laurentius Petri, Archbishop of Uppsala, were later responsible for putting the entire Bible into Swedish, the so-called Gustaf Vasa Bible of 1541, which is the "Authorized Version" for that language; again the dependence on Luther was considerable. The Icelandic New Testament, published in Denmark, 1540, borrowed much from Luther, and the complete Bible in Icelandic, printed in 1584 at a press set up on the island after men had been sent to Copenhagen and Hamburg to learn printing and bookbinding, was also the product of the work of Lutheran bishops in Iceland. Michael Agricola, a Finn acquainted with Luther at Wittenberg, began translation into Finnish, 1548–52. The Pentateuch was put into modern Greek in 1547, and the Four Gospels into Polish in 1551–52. By the end of the century there was a translation of the New Testament into Hebrew for use in a polyglot Bible and also for possible missionary work among Jews. János Erdösi, who made the first Hungarian translation of the New Testament (1541), had been a student at Wittenberg. There was also work in Lithuanian, Lettish, and Wendish, under Reformation auspices, before the turn of the century. A Bible in Slovenian, the language of that part of modern Yugoslavia from which the Lutheran theologian Matthias "Illyricus" Flacius came, was published at Wittenberg in 1584, obviously in the Lutheran tradition, as was also a Croatian New Testament printed in both the Glagolitic and Cyrillic alphabets (1562–63) for use among Slavs, even in the Turkish Empire.

English is a special case. Down to 1555 English translations and translators like Tyndale and Coverdale were under Lutheran influences, and the work must be reckoned a phase of the continental Reformation. At the same time Luther's views were often diluted or obscured. "Lutheran" was applied to a range of views which Luther never espoused. L. J. Trinterud's opinion is probably correct that even Tyndale "used Luther rather than agreed with Luther,"[4] for on crucial points Tyndale was closer to

Zwingli and Basel than to Luther and Wittenberg. Luther was not without influence on English translations, but often at third or fourth hand, and decreasingly so after 1555.

THE TRANSLATOR'S PRINCIPLES

The Luther Bible and the Reformer's views on translation wielded great influence in northern Europe and to a lesser extent in the British Isles. But what really was the approach to Scripture embodied in the work of Luther? The external facts tell only a part of the tale. " 'Luther's view of the Bible,' " Professor Ragnar Bring of Uppsala warns, "does not refer to just a single aspect of the Bible that he could expound as a learned man. Rather it must have reference to his whole understanding of God's revelation and its continuing activity. His view of the Bible includes his preaching of and obedience to the gospel, which is actually the Word and voice of the living God."[5]

Luther himself, while he could write of the Bible in terms analogous to the incarnation of Christ and could call Scripture "Christ's spiritual body," insisted that the Word of God is actually "not that which is in books and composed in letters, but rather an oral preaching, a living word, a voice which resounds throughout the earth."[6] He regarded writing as a necessary evil, an "emergency measure." Accordingly, translations are to be regarded as needful, but primarily as aids for the spoken proclamation of the Word. This is to put Bible translation immediately in the context of proclamation. It removes it from the scholar's worktable and sets it in the framework of the individual's obedient faith and the community's life. In terms of the traditional reasons for translating which have held ever since *The Letter of Aristeas*, Luther, for all his interest in literary aspects, had an eye on usage of the Bible in worship, education, and evangelism. It is significant that at the very time he was engaged in translating Scripture, he was also constructing liturgies, addressing his countrymen about the need for education (and that as a teacher himself), and was ever concerned about winning men to the pure Gospel. He who translated also taught in the academic arena, mounted the pulpit (Luther sometimes preached as many as 170 sermons a year), and prayed fervently that the Word would have its course in all the world.

But if any "philosophy of translation" on Luther's part is to be discerned, it is ultimately on theological grounds, and in terms of personal religious experience, that his approach must be grasped. Luther's personal conversion, an encounter with God which is deeply bound up with his study of the Bible, provides the key. Without taking this event into consideration, one can never understand how Luther went about his translation of the Scriptures.

This "conversion experience" is usually termed the *Turmerlebnis,* the name deriving from the tower (*Turm*) at the Black Cloister at Wittenberg where Luther had his study chamber. The "Tower Experience" took place probably in 1513 or 1514 (the later accounts by Luther do not allow us to date it precisely, any more than do the accounts of Paul's similar conversion experience). Descriptions of the incident are given by Luther in a preface written in 1545 for his Latin works and in accounts preserved by friends in the *Table Talk.* As with other incidents written up only in after years (such as the story of Johanan ben Zakkai's escape from Jerusalem), not all details agree in the several versions, but the substance is clear. And while the incident has often been analyzed along psychological lines, it is better understood as an exegetical discovery out of the biblical text than as an "experience" that is somewhat mystical.

In 1513–15 Luther was lecturing on the Psalms. His mind was also on Paul and his Epistle to the Romans. The study where he worked in the monastery tower was a small, heated room, later destroyed in remodeling. The luxury of a private room had been assigned to him when he was made subprior of the cloister. Here Luther wrestled with an exegetical, seemingly academic problem. Behind it was a personal quest for a God who would be gracious to Martin Luther in his sin. Luther had, as he said, "a passionate desire to understand Paul" and in particular Romans 1:17, "the justice [or righteousness] of God is revealed in the Gospel." He was perplexed over the term "righteousness" here and also when it occurred in a similar sense in the Psalms, where it was written, "Deliver me in thy righteousness." Luther had learned from the medieval dogmaticians that God's righteousness or justice means that quality in God whereby he punishes unrighteous sinners. That sort of God, of wrath and law, was discomforting, and His righteousness repulsive. How can "righteousness" deliver? But, Luther says, "I kept hammering away at those words of Paul . . . , I . . . pondered the problem for days and nights." Then, his account runs, "God took pity on me and I saw the inner connection" (which Luther had not seen before) between "the justice of God revealed in the Gospel" and the Old Testament verse which Paul quotes, "The just shall live by faith" (Romans 1:17*b* = Habakkuk 2:4*b*). Luther had made his now famous discovery that God's righteousness is not a demand, but his saving power "by which He takes pity on us and justifies us by our faith." God's justice or "righteousness" is not a threat against us, but precisely man's hope. Luther describes his reaction in this way: "I felt as if I had been born again and had entered Paradise through wide-open gates. . . . This verse of Paul's became in truth the gate to Paradise for me."[7] We may be somewhat surprised to read these words, which sound more like John Wesley or Bunyan's "Pilgrim," but this is Luther laying bare the deepest experience of his soul. However, his actions immediately after making his "tower discovery" are also typical: "I then went through the Holy Scriptures, as far as I could recall them from memory," to check the phrases used analogously with "the righteousness of God" to see whether the sense discovered was really so. Here was the Bible scholar at work, checking a theological insight. And when he ascertained that the phrase was parallel, as he notes, to such terms as "the work of God," which means the work that He works in us, and "the strength of God" through which He makes us strong, or "the power of God" which He imparts to us, Luther knew that he had stumbled on a clue to the meaning of all Scripture. In the cloister tower he "had stormed the pope" and all theologies of self-righteousness.

In a moment of insight, in what he termed "a wonderful experience," through what was really an exegetical discovery, of how a righteous God rescues sinful men, Luther found personal rebirth. But more, he discovered the center of the Bible and the center for all theology. For, he reasoned, if Scripture is a unity, and this insight holds for Romans 1:17 and for the Psalms and for Isaiah, then the experience of God's saving righteousness must hereafter control the way we look at all the Scriptures. In this manner Luther's approach to the Bible grew out of his encounter with God's righteousness. It was henceforth to be controlled by his theology of "righteousness by grace." One by one, in succeeding years, he cast aside the medieval standards for treating the Bible: the church's authority, the patristic opinions, the allegorical sense. Luther went about his treatment of the Bible, as with all other things, firm in his conviction of the central place of the "evangelical experience," of reconciliation with God by grace, such as he had received in that moment of illumination from the Word of God.

The primary place which Luther assigned to his conviction about justification does not mean, however, that he jettisoned all else in biblical study. He was not some sort of charismatic, only subjectively in touch with God; he was also a man of the Renaissance world, and a member of the Christian community with its heritage of the entire Bible. Properly Luther's approach to the Bible can be spelled out along three lines, and even though the theological side is dominant over all else for him and is the part which in the final analysis really matters, there are other elements which have a necessary place.

First of all, Luther welcomed the *historical-grammatical approach* to Scripture. Generally he came to champion this literal sense in place of the medieval theory which looked for a fourfold meaning in each verse. The Schoolmen had prized, beyond the literal, an allegorical sense, a moral meaning, and the mystical or eschatological "heavenly" sense, and had let the allegorical dominate all else. Luther at this point was endorsing the exegetes of the School of Antioch against the allegorists of the School of Alexandria in their struggle in the fifth century A.D. He was joining hands with the humanists of his day who desired to study the Scriptures historically, just as any other ancient book. For such an approach it was "the fulness of the times." The Renaissance was releasing a veritable flood of new information about the biblical documents, and to a considerable extent Luther was alert for, and ready to use, this material. Examples can be quoted to show how time and again Luther's treatment of the Bible reflects the probing, critical, historical type of analysis then in its infancy. He is concerned, for example, about historical background in commenting on Isaiah. He says of Hebrews, "It is not St. Paul's. . . . who wrote it is not known." He questions the tradition that Paul was in Spain, and faces up frankly to several of the Synoptic discrepancies. Even his disparaging view of James—expressed in the damning statement that the Epistle is not by Jesus' brother or by an apostle, but that "some good, pious man . . . took some sayings of the apostles' disciples [thrice removed!] and threw them thus on paper"—even this opinion (which seems so motivated by Luther's theological bias against the "works-righteousness" he found in James) can be shown to have been a contemporary critical view on the authorship of that epistle. Erasmus the humanist and Luther's opponent Thomas de Vio, Cardinal Cajetan, both seem to have shared this view on the authorship of James. "Be diligent in appraising historical matters," Luther urged. He thus left a place for reason and for critical inquiry, though, as we shall see, it must be informed by the Holy Spirit.

Secondly, Luther the translator and exegete worked *biblically*. He sought to find the meaning of a given text not by piling up and counting opinions from the commentators (a method we

moderns are still sometimes prone to use—"tally up the authorities!"), but rather by searching out the sense from the biblical
context. Here Luther was rejecting the myth of a "patristic
norm," the notion that in the Church Fathers we can find a consensus which serves as authority. With all due respect to the
venerable authorities of past centuries (and Luther cites the
Church Fathers fairly frequently), he was not content to balance
Athanasius and Clement against Chrysostom and call it truth.
Luther desired to know what the text itself said, the text tested
by the whole counsel of the Scriptures. "Scripture is itself its
own best interpreter," he insisted. That is why he sensed that the
meaning of "righteousness" at Romans 1:17 had to come out of
Paul and the Old Testament and not from Aristotle or elsewhere.
Though in the eyes of some Luther treated certain biblical books
with a shocking freedom, he had a profound and abiding respect
for the Bible. He ranged over both testaments. His published
commentaries deal with five Old Testament books (Genesis,
Psalms, Isaiah, Habakkuk, and Jonah) and three from the New
Testament (Romans, Galatians, and Hebrews). Such evidence
suggests that Luther's outlook was quite Bible-oriented. He
assumed that Scripture is "simple and open" (hence he took the
tremendous risk of putting vernacular copies into the hands of
the laity and the clergy and even those outside the church). He
felt that "Scripture alone should reign"—*sola Scriptura*. He
could even speak of the Bible as "the Holy Spirit's own peculiar
book," with God "in every syllable." But such statements must
be kept in context by the third, overarching principle which
dominated even Luther's biblical emphasis. That is the theological.

Luther's approach to Scripture emphasized, thirdly, the de-
terminative role of a *personal comprehension of the Word of
God*—personal, though *within a confessing community*, comprehension by a *Christ-centered conscience held captive by the
Word*. This standard of authority, so real for Luther yet so hard
to define, replaced for him the dogmatic ecclesiastical norms by

which the Bible had been surrounded for centuries. At this point Luther was transforming the "evangelical experience" into a criterion for Bible usage and translation. His own dramatic words at Worms, where he allowed an appeal to reason and to the Bible but above all rested on "a conscience captive to the Word of God," were a striking profession of this principle. From this outlook stems the boldness with which he handles certain texts. Here, at work in his exegesis of the Bible, is the confidence of a man who has been "born again," who has experienced justification, and "entered Paradise." One might refer to this third area as the "theological" aspect of Luther's view of the Bible, since it has to do with the relationship with God. Or it might just as well be termed the "existential" side, since, beyond merely historical study or Bible context, it is concerned with and speaks to the human situation here and now before God. Customarily it has been summed up by saying that beyond the historical and biblical, the element which was decisive for Luther was the Word of God.

This crucial, dominant third aspect is what distinguishes Luther, ultimately, from the humanists. He used the same historical tools as they. Some of them surely treasured the Scriptures as much as he did and worked over them just as devotedly. But there was a vital difference on the theological, existential side, in the appreciation of the Word of God. Luther's position here has even distinguished—and estranged—him from other Protestants. Because, however, this whole, important area has often been left rather vague and even mystical, it is worth calling attention to four factors implicit in Luther's outlook here. (1) The *experiential emphasis* has already been noted. Luther's contention was that just as in any other area personal experience is vital before a thing can really be grasped, so religious experience, specifically the joyous confrontation with God in Christ, is necessary to comprehend the Christian Scriptures. (2) Coupled with this is a *community context*. The Christian experience never leaves a man in lonely isolation but puts him in a fellowship or church with those who have shared the same experience and who join with him in the new life. He translates in the company of his "Sanhedrin." Nothing from Luther reflects these first two factors better than his last written words on February 16, 1546, two days before his death:

> No one can understand Virgil in his *Bucolics* and *Georgics* [poems about rural life] if he has not himself been a shepherd or a farmer for five years. No one understands Cicero's *Letters* [which frequently refer to political affairs], I contend, unless he has held some important state office for twenty years. No one should think that he has tasted Holy Scripture adequately unless he with the prophets has led the congregations for a century. So tremendous is the miracle . . . of Christ. . . . We are beggars. That is true.

Here is Luther's emphasis on personal involvement, and with it a churchly setting. The would-be translator must "see it from the inside," within the witnessing community, from the office of preacher, teacher, and shepherd of souls. Luther thus had a churchly context for his work, though not the same ecclesiastical institution that dominated for many of his predecessors.

(3) An absolutely *Christocentric emphasis* marks Luther's work. "To place the Bible in a central place had been done by theologians of earlier centuries. To place Christ in the center of the Bible, so totally as he did, was previously unheard of," the Dutch scholar Kooiman says.[8] Christocentricity—"Christ in my head, Christ in my heart, Christ in all, Christ over all"—characterized Luther's view of the Bible, and of the canon, and of theology. What mattered in the Bible was what brought Christ to the reader. A translator should hold Christ before his eyes. It was Luther's loyalty to the living Christ which allowed him to be so little alarmed about some of the historical problems and contradictions in Scripture.

(4) The power of the *Holy Spirit* is what made the biblical words become Word of God, proving, judging, illuminating everything, in Luther's view. The Spirit, he said, is the inseparable companion of Scripture (though he insisted on no particular

theories as to how "inspiration" works), and prayer is the proper corollary. Because of the Spirit, the Bible is more than an object for antiquarian research. It is to lead to proclamation. And because in proclamation the Spirit accompanies the scriptural text, Luther looked to the Bible for the Spirit's action, rather than to new revelations as some of the Anabaptists did. The Scriptures proclaimed were a trysting place for God's Spirit and his people. Hence the claim that "Nobody can understand God or God's Word aright unless he has it directly from the Holy Ghost." But when men have that illumination, then, like the apostles of old, they, "filled with the Holy Spirit, speak the Word of God with boldness" (Acts 4:31).

How Luther's approach to the Bible operated, combining historical, biblical, and theological factors, can be seen from one of his most controversial renderings, that at Romans 3:28. The Greek says simply, "man is justified by faith, without deeds of the law." Everyone knows that Luther added the word "alone" after "faith" and castigated his critics as "asses-heads" when they stared at the word, "like cows at a new door." In defense of his translation, Luther claimed that clear, strong German demanded the addition, even if it wasn't in the Greek. But one suspects that his own doctrinal preference for "faith alone," to the exclusion of everything else, was a factor in determining the translation. Thus, the theological seems to have overcome the literal. But Luther was doubtless convinced that "faith alone" is what *Paul* meant, and that "faith alone" is the theme propounded in the total Pauline *corpus*. It is interesting to note that modern exegesis tends to support Luther's decision with a variety of observations. The Epistle of James, where the author is trying to defend Paul's gospel against a perversion of it, is evidence, in the eyes of some interpreters, that already in the first century Paul was understood to have meant "faith alone" (James 2:24). Origen, the greatest exegete of the third century, is now known to have inserted "only" at the same place Luther did. The R.S.V. translation in our own day has done exactly the same

thing at Romans 11:20, adding the word "only" to the Greek
phrase "through faith." Finally a recent Roman Catholic commentary in Germany suggests that Luther's phrase brings out
Paul's thought here well. Thus in this verse, Luther's oft-re-
proached boldness may be exactly what good translation demands. How Luther—or any other translator—went about his
task can scarcely be understood, however, without noting all the
factors apparent in his work, the historical emphasis, the biblical
concern, and the theological convictions.

It is a curious irony, nonetheless, that each one of these factors
has been at times taken by itself, away from the total synthesis,
and developed independently. The historical-critical approach
has of course blossomed enormously in modern times, but often
in isolation from other concerns. Taken alone, by itself, this
historical approach has sometimes been anything but a blessing
for sound exegesis of the Scriptures. But this historical approach
can look back on Luther as one of its pioneer supporters in the
Reformation Church. The biblical emphasis, taken by itself, has
often led to biblicism. When some of Luther's statements are
taken out of context, he can be made to sound like the father of
modern Fundamentalism. And if the theological is stressed by
itself, the result can be a Protestant scholasticism or Lutheran
orthodoxism; or, in the case of emphasis exclusively or excessively
on the Holy Ghost, there results some variety of pietism. Thus
Luther can be claimed as champion of the historical approach, or
as a Fundamentalist, or as a rigid dogmatist, or as a "Spirit-ist," if
the totality of his view of Scripture is breached and one aspect
is taken by itself exclusively.

"INSPIRED" TRANSLATION?

Luther's unified approach to the Bible, though making an
appeal to historical-critical and biblical aspects, definitely emphasized the theological. One of the most arresting analyses in
recent years of how Luther treated the Bible has been presented

in a book-length essay on biblical translation by W. Schwarz of University College, London.[9] The presentation, which, for all its vast learning, has received all too little attention, serves to tie Luther and our study of *The Letter of Aristeas* together in a striking theory.

Schwarz suggests that in the period of Reformation controversy there were three views on biblical translation. The one he calls the "traditional." It was espoused by the scholastic theologians and emphasized church dogma. It regarded the Latin Vulgate text as indissolubly linked with the teachings of the church. Ecclesiastical doctrines and the views of the Church Fathers provided the agreed context for reading Scripture. Accordingly Bibles of this "traditional" approach looked rather like rabbinic editions. To take a typical example, in a Bible printed at Basel in 1498, the Latin text stood in the middle of the page in large letters. Between its lines was an "interlinear gloss" and around it an "ordinary gloss." These glosses were a sort of paraphrase with commentary, incorporating a chain of quotations, mostly of a theological nature, from Church Fathers through the centuries. In addition, this particular Basel Bible contained the *Postillae* of Nicholas of Lyra, a Franciscan at Paris (d. 1340), whom Luther especially admired, plus further moral and other comments. These "aids" suggested the fourfold senses of each significant term and helped direct exegesis along the paths chosen by the Schoolmen. The biblical text was surrounded, and imprisoned, by churchly theology and tradition.

The second view is called by Schwarz the "philological." It was developed by the humanists who embraced the new scholarship of the Renaissance, men such as Reuchlin (1455–1522) and Erasmus. The former pioneered in the study of Hebrew among Christians and engaged in an historic controversy with Roman Catholic officials when he opposed the desire of some to destroy Jewish books. Though Melanchthon was his grandnephew and Reformation adherents tried hard to win him over, Reuchlin remained a loyal, if critical, son of the Church of Rome. Erasmus (*c.* 1466–1536) enjoyed a reputation as the greatest classicist of the day. His Greek New Testament editions promoted biblical study, as did his elegant "modern" Latin translation. He too was often satirically critical of the church and its hierarchy, but he felt no sympathy either with Luther's cause and engaged in a bitter exchange of letters and pamphlets with him. Perhaps Erasmus' work on the New Testament text enjoyed overmuch prestige. He had assembled it at a breakneck pace, and at places actually inserted Greek words found in no Greek manuscripts, translating them himself on the basis of the Latin, for example at Acts 9:5f. and Revelation 22:16–21.[10] But everyone, Luther included, employed the tools forged by these men. The humanists, in translating Scripture, encouraged a style that was scientific, scholarly, literal, word-for-word. If the ruling passion of the "traditionalists" was dogma, that of the humanists was "philology," the love of learning and of linguistics.

Luther's view of translating is the third approach, and to describe it Schwarz uses the word "inspirational." Luther, he is well aware, did not "fight grammar" and in fact eagerly accepted the grammatical explanations of Erasmus and Reuchlin. But Luther did not stop there. He assimilated all this into his own theology, so that it was consonant with the "evangelical experience." Grammar dare not rule over meaning. And since the true meaning comes ultimately and only under the Holy Spirit, Luther's approach may rightly be called "inspirational" or "inspired." Schwarz does not mean by this that Luther regarded his German as divinely dictated, but he does mean that Luther was conscious of the Spirit's presence and power in his handling of the Bible. The approach might also be termed "prophetic," since the expositor is in many ways akin to a prophet in Bible times. Perhaps "grace" is an even better term to describe what Luther emphasized—"the grace given to me," "this grace in which we stand," the graciousness of God which has set me "in Christ" and enabled me to behold a new world, to see the map of the Scriptures from a fresh vantage point, to know God as gracious. Schwarz is clear in indicating how Luther preferred a free, idiomatic rendering, not the word-for-word type of the "philologists" (though Luther knew times when he must be quite literal, as with the phrase, "This *is* my body"). He pays tribute too to Luther's desire to catch the spirit of the author and to have collaborators in translation, like Melanchthon and the "Sanhedrin," not just to work as an individualist.

It is, however, the feature of "inspiration," the accompanying role of the Holy Ghost, in Luther as translator which stands out most sharply in Schwarz's analysis. This is what distinguishes Luther from the "philologists" and, of course, from the "traditionalists" too. This makes him both exciting and subjective, brilliant and controversial. In framing his picture of Reformation times, Schwarz suggests that the controversy then was really a reenactment of one which had occurred several times in previous centuries. The same contrast appeared, for example, in connection with the Septuagint, he feels. *The Letter of Aristeas* wanted to give a picture of Septuagint origins that stressed the philological. The learning, the erudition, the philological abilities of the Seventy are therefore impressed on us by *Aristeas*. But Philo and later writers, especially the Church Fathers, Schwarz says, play up the role of divine guidance, of the Holy Spirit at work; their picture of the Septuagint is "inspirational." Finally Schwarz would see the same debate occurring between Jerome and Augustine in the fifth century. Jerome, the grammarian, became convinced that it was only from the original Hebrew that the true sense of the Old Testament could come; therefore he bypassed the Septuagint and repudiated many of its renderings in making his Latin translation on the basis of the Hebrew. Augustine, the theologian, on the other hand, was convinced that the Septuagint was inspired. He saw no need for "shaking people up" with a new translation which was contrary to what they were accustomed to, just on the chance of getting closer to the "original Hebrew." Letters are still extant in which Augustine reproached Jerome for his Vulgate. Again there is the conflict between the

philologian and the "inspirationalist." In chart form, these are
the parallels and contrasts suggested by Schwarz:

	The "Philological" Approach	The "Inspirational" Approach
16th century	Erasmus	Luther
5th century	Jerome	Augustine
Antiquity	*The Letter of Aristeas*	Philo, Church Fathers

Is this fascinating analysis altogether accurate? Most reviewers
have hesitated to agree fully with it.[11] The classifications are too
exclusive. As for the Septuagint, Schwarz must strain over that
obvious hint of the miraculous in *Aristeas*, the statement that the
seventy-two translators completed their task in exactly seventy-
two days. Other elements in *The Letter* also point not to a
"philological" outlook, but to the genre of religious propaganda,
to a notion that "this is the way men are who study the Law of
God." Their brilliance is related to the revelation in the Torah. In
its own way, *Aristeas* is also oriented to the wonder of God and
his gifts of grace to men. As for the element of "inspiration"
plainly found in Philo, it is worth asking to what extent Philo
reflects a *Hellenistic* view of inspiration, compared with a more
characteristically *Jewish* concept that *Aristeas* might have had
two centuries before. The Greek world knew theories about men
and also about books "breathed into" by God; the sacred meaning, in the case of such books, is there, waiting for the hearer or
reader to find it. Judaism, especially in its apocalyptic circles,
knew a different idea of inspiration, the idea of inspired interpreters who, under the Spirit's prompting, could get the real
meaning from a text that God intended. The whole notion of
"inspiration," whether of author or of interpreter or of both,
needs further analysis. Perhaps it is not so much a matter of
contrast as that Philo heightens what was implied in *Aristeas*.

The contrast between Jerome and Augustine does have interesting links to Luther's day. Luther regarded Jerome as a

good grammarian but a poor theologian, whereas Augustine was his favorite theological expositor. However, even though he felt that Augustine (who also had had something of an "evangelical conversion experience") knew God's grace better than did Jerome, Luther was not willing to cast Jerome's work completely aside or agree with Augustine on everything. Schwarz himself cites evidence to show that Luther regarded Jerome's Vulgate as a very good translation, perhaps the best of the versions. He scarcely shared Augustine's view of the Septuagint as inspired, for Luther regarded the Seventy as men ignorant of Hebrew who falsified the text to avoid attributing divinity to Christ. Is it too simple to claim that Luther had his own opinions as to the scholarly capabilities of each man, but regarded Augustine as the better theologian—a view which many would share?

As for the analysis of Luther, to call his view "inspirational" is wrong if one understands by that a sort of biblical alchemy where all is geared to an unpredictable will-o'-the-wisp Spirit not correlated to the fundamental revelation in Jesus Christ. Luther never abandoned the discipline of historical and biblical study. Nor did his emphasis on the Spirit lead him into paths not Christocentric. On the other hand, the view is correct (though the term may readily be misunderstood) if by "inspirational" one means that the theological, existential aspect dominates, that the "evangelical experience" is what matters most, that the speaking of the Word of God to us is far more important, in Luther's view, than philological details or biblical cross-references. Luther remained committed to the historical, literal sense. He wanted exegesis from the original languages, and continually urged study of Hebrew and Greek. He saw no conflict between such study and the theological sense he prized. But ultimately his decision as to what a passage means rests on a theological criterion: how does the interpretation fit with the doctrine of the Gospel? Or, more properly, with the correct understanding of Law and Gospel? Of this ultimate theological criterion and his emphasis on linguistic, philological study, Luther is quoted as saying:

In translating the Holy Scriptures I follow two rules:

First, if some passage is obscure I consider whether it treats of grace or of law, whether wrath or the forgiveness of sin [is contained in it], with which of these it agrees better. By this procedure I have often understood the most obscure passages. Either the Law or the Gospel has made them meaningful, for God divides his teaching into Law and Gospel. . . . So every prophet either threatens and teaches, terrifies and judges things, or makes a promise. Everything ends with this, and it means that God is your gracious Lord. This is my first rule in translation.

The second rule is that if the meaning is ambiguous I ask those who have a better knowledge of the language than I have, whether the Hebrew words can bear this or that sense which seems to me especially fitting. And that is most fitting that is closest to the argument of the book. The Jews go astray so often in the Scriptures because they do not know the [true] contents of the books. But if one knows the contents, that sense ought to be chosen which is nearest to them.[12]

Thus Luther prizes the philological, linguistic side of exegesis and translation. But he ranks even higher the theological criterion of Law and Gospel. To plumb this deepest meaning, the gift of grace, of the Holy Ghost, is a necessity.

We must be careful here, however, to distinguish Luther from those who stressed the Spirit to the exclusion of all else—as in the mystic who becomes absorbed in God apart from any dependence on the revelation witnessed in the biblical text, or in the pietist who despises learning and gets his "illumination" direct from God without any exegetical striving. Luther had harsh words for those who claimed new revelations from the Spirit superseding the biblical Gospel. At this point, of course, Luther stands in a "hermeneutical circle": the Spirit-given Book is one focus of the ellipse, the Spirit-filled interpreter is the other. What the interpreter gets from the Book depends greatly on the vision of the Gospel which he has received. But just what this Gospel is depends in turn on careful study of the Book. All this is to say that Luther's emphasis on the Spirit does not mean for him new

revelations but precisely the old but inspired biblical Gospel
coming through to him.

Luther's synthesis of the historical, biblical, and theological,
coupled with his overwhelming concern for proclamation, where
God's Word speaks here and now, had in it all those elements with
which certain Christians today are struggling as they search for
a "new hermeneutic" to make the Bible come alive for our world.
To those for whom the "philological" alone suffices, Luther's
talk about the theological, "inspirational" aspects will always
sound like an unnecessary intrusion, a foreign factor which tres-
passes on scholarly ratiocinations about the text. This is so. Involved for Luther was the supposition that the God of whom
the text speaks is not locked out of his world or from the scriptural witness to his revelation. He is a "factor," or better "actor,"
who is not at the exegete's beck and call or under the translator's
control. But this awareness of God's presence is precisely what
gives Luther's translation and proclamation its living quality.
Men of Luther's ilk see themselves in the glorious succession of
patriarchs, prophets, and disciples in the Scriptures. They see
their own experiences mirrored in the stories of Abraham or of
Paul, and find Adam and Jesus Christ in their daily lives. They
move in the apostolic train, "ruling the churches with the
prophets for a hundred years," proclaiming "boldly the Word
of God" because they too are "filled with the Spirit." They even
find themselves alternately walking the Via Dolorosa and ex-
periencing resurrection life. Their existence is "a perpetual
passion play,"[13] sustained by the continuing gift of grace, the
presence of Jesus Christ. They are aware of something in Bible
translation therefore that lies beyond the bounds of philology or
"traditionalism."

It is Melanchthon, the quiet Reformer, a man who lacked
Luther's drama and who appreciated the scholarly even more
than Luther did, who has perhaps best put into words this outlook. "We are," he said, "first grammarians, next dialecticians,
then witnesses." First, he says, comes exegesis—historical, critical,

literal, employing the languages; then we are systematicians too, theologians, logicians, aware of the dialectic of theology, grasped by God's Law and Gospel, which shape our exegesis; finally there is the goal in all this, to proclaim the Word. On another occasion Melanchthon wrote:

> I have not the mistaken view that the holy can be penetrated through the industry of human talent. There is something in the holy that nobody can see unless it is shown to him by God: and Christ cannot be known to us without the Holy Ghost teaching us.[14]

Holy Scripture requires God's light and Spirit, if we are to comprehend its message.

Many will not agree with the way Luther formulated the Gospel. Many will reject his contention of a theological or "inspirational" aspect to translation. "Why not translate the Bible *exactly* like any other book?" they ask. They will not agree that there is anything at all about the Bible that differentiates it from other books. But there are undeniable differences among the men who take the Bible up. Luther's case makes plain how much a man's religious outlook and theological convictions can color the way he handles the text. So does Marcion's, or Aquila's, and that of many other translators. It may be added that even the attempt to exclude such convictions in handling the Bible is a presupposition too, for the absence or denial of such notions is likewise an assumption about God and about what Scripture is, and about man and history. While judgments will probably always vary as to how one is to approach Scripture, with what theological assumptions he is to translate, many a person in the parade of Bible scholars since Luther's day has unquestionably experienced something there of the power of the Spirit about which Luther spoke so fervently.

E. V. Rieu, a British classicist and the editor of a series of translations for Penguin Books, in 1952 published a rendering of the Four Gospels in "Penguin Classics."[15] When his son, C. H. Rieu, also a classics scholar, who has translated the Acts of the Apostles for the same series, heard that his father had begun the task, he commented, "It will be very interesting to see what Father makes of the Gospels." Then he added, "It'll be still more interesting to see what the Gospels make of Father."

In 1953, over a Third Programme broadcast of the B.B.C., the translator himself, E. V. Rieu, reported the results. He had, he said, come to the conclusion that over the centuries "translators of the Bible have been influenced . . . by religious rather than literary considerations." As for himself, he confessed, "It— changed me. My work changed me. . . . these works bear the seal of the Son of Man and God. And they are the Magna Charta of the human spirit."[16] In even stronger terms, Martin Luther would have agreed.

Four

Scholars and Saints—
and Some Not So Saintly:
The Parade of Bible Translators

W HO SHALL TRANSLATE SCRIPTURE? DOWN THROUGH THE
centuries the strangest assortment of men and women that
can be imagined have put their hand to this task—scholars,
bishops, sages, priests, housewives, learned professors, audacious
amateurs, reformers, pillars of orthodoxy, heretics, monks, and
businessmen. In short, just about every type of which we can
think, for there are no real limitations other than a text to
translate, some linguistic ability, and the time and will to per-
severe. We may want as translators only those "authorized" by
church or state or academic competence. But history proves that
contributions have been made by the most unlikely candidates
and that the man ecclesiastically or academically suspect by some
of his contemporaries has sometimes left a significant impression
on Bible transmission and translation. "The wind blows where
it wills." The parade of translators moves on, enrolling in its
ranks participants we could scarcely predict.

There is the story that Ambrose of Milan had the habit of
making his own little addition to the petitions of the litany. Ambrose liked to insert a word of thanksgiving for translators and
grammarians. The three men whom I choose to mention here may
scarcely seem to rate a line in a litany. All of them were scholars,

but they appeared anything but saintly to many of their contemporaries. They faced opposition and were at times harassed, even called heretics. Yet Origen, Jerome, and John James Wettstein, each of whom had to leave his native land because of ecclesiastical dissension, made lasting contributions to the story of Bible transmission and translation. They rate an occasional word of praise, perhaps a prayer of thanks, from us.

ORIGEN, SCHOLAR AND MARTYR

Origen we have already mentioned as the Christian of Alexandria, who about A.D. 230 attempted to rescue the Old Testament text from the confusion into which the varying Greek versions had fallen during the crucial second century. His heroic efforts at reconstituting the text by sorting out the various forms and comparing the Hebrew were his chief contributions to biblical studies, but his massive scholarship and literary production and the details of his colorful personal career are likewise highlights in his life's story.

Origen has been hailed as the greatest theologian of the ancient church, barring only Augustine. Surely he was the most daring and controversial one. He has been called the creator of "scientific theology" and the founder of more precise biblical and especially textual criticism. He was without doubt the source for "Origenism," a series of theological tenets hotly debated for three centuries after his death, and he produced an Old Testament edition, even the fragments of which we are grateful for today. Origen is also the first Christian literary figure we can be sure was born and raised in a Christian home. When a venerable professor in his middle sixties, he suffered prolonged torture in an imperial concentration camp during the Decian persecution, and died ultimately of that maltreatment; in this sense, he can be reckoned a martyr. He was famed for the rigor of his ascetical discipline. Yet in spite of all these excellencies, Origen has never been canonized as a saint but rather came to be called "a hydra of heresies."

G. L. Prestige, a student of the Church Fathers, has none-theless termed him "one of the greatest teachers ever known in Christendom, an Abelard without his arrogance, a Newman who never misled his disciples . . . the greatest of that happily small company of saints who, having lived and died in grace, suffered sentence of expulsion from the Church on earth after they had already entered into the joy of their Lord."[1] A German expert in patristic history writes in a similar vein: "Although his theology may be contested and open to attack, there can be no doubt of the fact that Origen was a disciple of the Lord, who seeks men of such sort in the history of the church."[2]

The future scholar was born about A.D. 185 in Egypt, most likely in Alexandria which was to be his home until his mid-forties. His name was Egyptian, for "Origenes" meant "child of Horus," the ancient falcon-god. His father bore a Greek name, Leonides, and the boy's second name was thoroughly Greek, Adamantius, i.e., man of steel (cf. "adamant"), a name which in many ways was to fit his resolute character. The family, how-ever, was Christian, and Leonides made sure that, in addition to secular studies, young Origen was thoroughly instructed in the faith, especially in the divine Scriptures, from childhood on. The father saw to it that the boy applied himself diligently, and the son amazed and pleased his father, and even worried him a bit, by the way he pressed on beyond the literal sense to seek an "inner, inspired" meaning to the Bible. Origen was a precocious child, and his father gave him the encouragement and advantages to go along with his ability. Eusebius, who records much of what we know about Origen's life, regards him as most noteworthy, "from the time of his swaddling clothes," as he puts it, and seems to have known even more details than he narrates.[3] Leonides seems to have been aware of how unusual his oldest son was and is said to have looked often on the sleeping child and then to have kissed the lad over the heart, reverently and tenderly, "as if a divine spirit were within," Eusebius says.

In A.D. 202, when Origen was seventeen, a persecution against

Christianity broke out under Severus. First an imperial decree forbidding Jews to proselytize was promulgated, then a similar one against Christians. Perhaps the decree was only local in its scope, but pressure mounted against the Christian community in Alexandria. There were martyrs. Leonides was arrested, and Origen himself, always a passionate person, was swept along by the excitement of the events and by his own faith, so that he too sought martyrdom. He wrote to his father in prison, "Keep up your intent not to alter your convictions in any way on our account." The family would be distinguished by a martyr—such was the young man's hope. But not only did he thus encourage his father to die; Origen himself burned with desire to rush out of the house, turn himself in to the authorities, confess his faith, and die a martyr too. His mother, fortunately, was of a more practical stripe. One martyr in a family was enough. When her words failed to divert the son, she solved the matter in the simplest way possible: she hid all of Origen's clothing. Since you can't very well be a decent martyr without any clothing, the young man had to stay at home, and so his life was spared, as the persecution came to an end.

Leonides had been beheaded, though, and his property confiscated. Origen was left as the chief breadwinner for his mother and six younger brothers. The persecution had also driven out of Alexandria the teachers who had been providing catechetical instruction for those who would attach themselves to the Christian faith. Through such teachers a sort of school—more a school of thought which arose out of the questions and discussions in the catechetical situation than a formal academy—had arisen in Alexandria late in the second century, first under Pantaenus, a convert to Christianity from Sicily who taught in Alexandria before moving on, perhaps to India, and then under Clement, a pagan convert of Pantaenus, who left Egypt for good during the persecution of 203. Origen had heard lectures from both these men. Now because of his family's pecuniary needs and because of the fact that no other Christian teachers were available, the course of his life for the next thirty years was shaped.

First Origen was befriended by a wealthy lady who became his benefactress and apparently took him into her home so that he could continue his studies. Next Origen became a teacher himself. He soon had such a reputation that even pagans came crowding to study under him, and Bishop Demetrius made him head of the catechetical school before he was twenty. In this position Origen remained for many years teaching, studying, traveling, writing. Eusebius records an illustrious stream of pupils whom Origen taught over the years, men and women both, some of them doubtless the keenest minds of the day, whom he led into the Christian faith. They in turn became church leaders, one a bishop in Alexandria later on, teachers, and in some cases martyrs like Origen's own father. Pupils were said to fill the lecture rooms in shifts from morn to night. When the "teaching load" got too heavy—for Origen's school embraced not only catechetical instruction but the whole span of "secular" learning, an assistant was called, one of Origen's former pupils, Heraclas.

The master teacher himself continued studying too. He is reported to have attended the lectures of Ammonius Saccas, the founder of Neoplatonism, perhaps the most brilliant thinker of the day in philosophy, exceeded in the next generation only by his pupil Plotinus, author of the *Enneads*. Like Plotinus, Origen listened too, taking what he found helpful for expounding the Christian faith.

It needs to be emphasized that Origen was no pagan convert clutching on to ties from his past. He was not even a man of two worlds seeking to build bridges between Athens and Jerusalem. Origen was Christian born and bred, and he sought, from the central bastion of his faith, to let the Christian message have its course into all areas of life. Basic to that faith was the scriptural witness, and so Origen devoted his efforts especially to exposition of the Bible; for all his interest in philosophy, this was to remain primary. Even in these busy years he began the study of Hebrew, one of the first Christians so to do. Perhaps already in this period his great textual project was beginning to take shape in his mind.

Origen traveled often during these years at Alexandria. He went to Arabia to lecture. He traveled to Rome. He was invited to Antioch by Julia Mamaea; the mother of future emperor Severus Alexander, she ruled not only her son's life and wife but virtually the empire too, attaining the title "mother of Augustus . . . and of the fatherland." It was on one of these trips that an incident occurred which led to bad blood between Origen and his bishop, Demetrius. While at Jerusalem and Caesarea, Origen was invited by the local bishops to give public lectures. While it may have been the practice in some areas to allow a layman thus to speak (the busy teacher had never been ordained), Demetrius expressed his disapproval and recalled Origen home. That incident was to have later repercussions.

It was literary work that busied Origen most during his Alexandrian years—hundreds of letters, text studies, commentaries, a long apologetic against an attack on Christianity by Celsus, and a systematic theology *On First Principles*, plus other treatises. The ancients assigned over six thousand writings to him and described his works as "more than any man could read" in number. That is an exaggeration, but not too much of one, for we know that a wealthy patron (Origen seems to have had the ability to attract them), a man named Ambrose, a convert of Origen's, provided for him seven shorthand secretaries to take down his dictation, seven transcribers, plus other copyists.

We must picture Origen in this period as a brilliant teacher, working himself as hard as he could, for the sake of the faith and its study. He was inclined toward asceticism and seems not to have had any interest in the comforts which his toil could have accumulated for him. Instead he subsisted on a few pennies a day. He disciplined himself to study long hours, to fast, to restrict his hours of sleep, and to forego a bed in order to sleep on the floor. He proved a warm, courageous friend to those led off to martyrdom and braved mob action to comfort them on their way to death. He took the counsel of the gospels in a literal way where Jesus is quoted as saying, "Take no gold, nor silver, . . . nor sandals" (Matt. 10:9f.); Origen regularly for many years went barefoot.

It is against this general background that a tragic youthful action is to be understood. While still a young teacher, Origen decided that the words of Matthew 19:12 were directed to him: "There are eunuchs . . . who have made themselves eunuchs for the sake of the kingdom of heaven. He who is able to receive this, let him receive this." Origen determined to emasculate himself in literal fulfillment of this precept, and he did. The matter soon became public knowledge. Bishop Demetrius was amazed at the daring deed but seems to have accepted the sincerity of the action and to have urged Origen to devote himself the more to his work of teaching. But the step was to have the effect of serving as a barrier to ordination, for canon law came to exclude eunuchs from the priesthood (as a legal parallel to Old Testament rules). While we today are likely to find Origen's act incomprehensible, it should be remembered that some of his work brought him into contact with women. The breath of scandal can always blow. Charges were common in antiquity as to how religious leaders acted when they got into women's houses. II Timothy 3:6–7 hints at such activities.[4] Marcionites must have been charged with just such irregularities, and in his version of the Gospel of Luke, Marcion seems to have made an attempt to defend his movement against such charges.[5] Doubtless orthodox teachers must have been aware of such dangers too, and Origen's self-mutilation seems to have been an effort on his part to remove himself from any such possible charges in his work as a teacher among women.

All of these incidents culminated in the events of 231. A year or so before, Origen had been sent on a mission to Greece and took the opportunity to visit his friends in Palestine on the way. Before he left Alexandria, he, for one reason or another, took the step of designating a successor in the school there. While he was on his journey, the bishops in Palestine ordained Origen a presbyter. Apparently they felt no qualms about doing this, in spite of his physical impediment. That physical impediment might have been Demetrius' reason for never ordaining him in Alexandria, but more likely personal malice and jealousy is what had prevented Origen's bishop from giving him ecclesiastical status. Eusebius hints as much, though it must be remembered that he writes from a Palestinian point of view and was a spiritual descendant of Origen. Demetrius, at any rate, was enraged and in two synod meetings had Origen banished from Alexandria and deposed from his presbyterial status. Some sources tell us that heretical teachings were not a factor in these actions, but only the physical impediment and the infringement of the rights of Demetrius.

Origen then settled in Palestine and from 232 until his death in 254 carried out a second phase in his illustrious career. Ambrose followed him with the secretaries, and soon "publishing house" and school were flourishing again at Caesarea. Pupils flocked to hear him. Typical was a law student named Gregory, a pagan from Pontus on the Black Sea. He happened to hear Origen lecture, became a Christian, and studied under Origen for five years before returning to his native land to become a bishop and win the epithet "Wonderworker" for the miracles he wrought. A panegyric on Origen, composed as Gregory Thaumaturgos left Caesarea, is preserved and gives us a firsthand picture of the teacher and his methods.

All was not easy for Origen in his transplanted life, however. His patron Ambrose was arrested during a persecution, though he eventually escaped with his life. Origen himself had to spend two years in Cappadocia while another persecution raged. He still traveled considerably and wrote and debated with men of all sorts. He corresponded with a pope and with an emperor, Philip the Arabian. All this, and he was still not satisfied that all he wanted to say and do was getting done. Therefore late in life he changed his custom and allowed Ambrose's stenographers to

take down even his sermons and preserve them. Origen's imprisonment during the Decian persecution has been mentioned—
he seems to have been a special target of the persecutors—and
while it is known that he lived for a time after his release, his death
at about 254 at Tyre was attributable to the hardships suffered
during his imprisonment. His tomb, behind the high altar of the
cathedral there, was still pointed out in the thirteenth century as
an attraction more important than that of Frederick Barbarossa,
the Crusader, who was buried in the same church. At least in his
adopted home, the Holy Land, Origen's reputation outlasted the
calumnies of later detractors.

Origen's bold speculations in theology are beyond our interests
here. Infamous as certain of his views became to some, they need
no defense, however. The fact is simply that some of his notions
did not prove to lie in the mainstream of later theological development—his idea of the pre-existence of the soul, for example,
and of a series of reincarnations, wherein souls improve or worsen
their lot; or his theory of an "Apocatastasis," or final restoration
of all things into a harmony with God, when God will save all
men and even the devil. But in Origen's day "orthodox" answers
did not exist to many of the questions which people were raising
or which Origen's own fertile brain might pose. Like many
another pioneer, this trailblazer took some wrong turns—according to hindsight.

Of his work as a biblical scholar, something of the same sort
can be said: Origen was a bold pioneer, some of whose work
followed the wrong path. As an exegete and preacher, for instance, he was given to allegory. He raised allegory to a system
whereby he sought triple meanings in a verse, in New Testament
as well as Old. At times his treatment of the Bible was thus a sort
of "biblical alchemy," transmuting the base material into something else. Today we know the abuses which this process brings,
but in Origen's day the approach was widespread. He merely
intensified it. Technically he was never a translator; his contributions lay elsewhere, though even his greatest achievement

in textual work was to have little lasting influence or, worse yet, helped make matters more confused in the Greek Old Testament.

But on the positive side, we may observe that Origen, who sought to relate his faith to all science and knowledge, was the first of whom we know by name among the Christians to concern himself really with problems of text. He set a standard not to be matched for centuries. He trained others in his school who would be concerned to lift high the torch of learning with regard to Bible and theology. He gathered or had gathered a great library at Caesarea, the nucleus of which was his own collection of books; this library was in existence until the Arab Conquest in the seventh century.

Origen seems to have made some contribution to the New Testament text as well as to the Old. There are scholars who think they can identify a "Caesarean text type" used in Origen's voluminous writings after he settled in Palestine. If true, this would give us a geographical text type from Palestine along with those of Egypt, Antioch, and the western part of the Roman Empire. Other investigators have claimed that this "Caesarean type" also appears in Origen during his Alexandrian period. Exact details are still being debated. It should not surprise us, though, that Origen and Eusebius and others at Caesarea could have worked over the New Testament text in such a way that the effects still show up in our manuscripts. The fact that Eusebius sometimes quotes Matthew 28:19 in a short form as "Go, make disciples of all nations in my name . . . ," instead of with the familiar phrase, "in the name of the Father and the Son and the Holy Ghost," has led a few scholars to conjecture that the Trinitarian reference is an addition from a time later than Origen and Eusebius. For this, however, there is no evidence in New Testament manuscripts, and the wording in a single Church Father has not been enough to persuade translators or many text critics on the point.

In treating the Old Testament, Origen conceived a plan as bold as any in the history of Bible transmission. The confused state of the Greek manuscripts in his day has already been described. Septuagint, Symmachus, Aquila, Theodotion were all jumbled together at times, and none of these Greek versions necessarily agreed with the Masoretic Hebrew text by then in existence. Few Christians knew enough Hebrew even to make a comparison. Origen did, and was aware of how bad the situation was. Therefore he planned a grand enterprise as a solution: to copy out, in parallel columns, the various Old Testament versions; with this evidence before him, one could finally sort out the various readings.

Origen's Hexapla or Six-Column Old Testament put the Hebrew in the first column. Next, since few Christians could read the Hebrew letters (though he wanted to encourage them to master the language), the Hebrew transliterated into Greek; then Aquila, as being most literally like it; then, Symmachus, the Septuagint, and in column six, Theodotion. In most cases, only a word or two could be written in each column, and so it is no wonder that the finished work was some thirty volumes in length. To mark off words in the Septuagint which did not belong there on the basis of the Hebrew and to denote phrases which had to be added to get agreement with the Hebrew, Origen used a system of markings already in vogue in the Library of Alexandria. He also engaged in a certain amount of "field research," turning up three other partial translations of the Greek Old Testament which he cited where possible. One of them came from the area near Jericho where the manuscripts were said to have been found buried in jars—a detail which has led to the conjecture that Origen's material here was akin to our recently found Dead Sea Scrolls.

It is an intricate matter, even for experts, to assess the influence and values of Origen's work. The unanticipated result was that his parallel columns simply helped some scribes to confuse readings all the more. The great tragedy is that Origen's Hexapla has come down to us only in a fragmentary state, a few pages of various copies, occasional quotations, and a Syriac translation which luckily preserves his critical markings. Scholars would be delighted to have any substantial part of the Greek turn up. Let it suffice to say that no one before Origen even conceived of such a project. Few men or groups since then have executed anything so large or potentially significant. There has not passed another figure like Origen—in scholarship or personal color—in the procession of Bible scholars. Lietzmann, the historian, paid him this tribute: "Origen lived in the Bible to an extent which perhaps no one else has rivalled, except Luther."[6] Let Prestige have the last word about his overall stature: "If there had been no Origen, it may be seriously doubted whether the rising forces of obscurantism might not have blocked the entrance of Christianity against the genius of Augustine; and in that case the occasion might never have arisen for an Anselm or a Thomas Aquinas. A degenerate Christianity might well have found its leadership committed exclusively to illiberal imitators of Jerome and illiterate echoes of Bernard."[7] That sort of judgment should make us want to look at Jerome in the procession of translators.

St. Jerome, Translator

It is true that Jerome, who was a man of often parochial partisanship himself, was followed by a series of imitators marked by illiberality and conformity, not daring, in theology. He is unlikely to have stirred up the intellectual excitement that Origen did for centuries. Jerome could rouse great loyalty to himself, especially among well-to-do Roman matrons, but an air of controversy and polemic seems to have hovered round his head, not stimulation of the mind.

Of course, times had changed by the late fourth century when Jerome lived. The world was different from Origen's day. Now the church was established in the empire. There were no more persecutions like those of Decius. Even the "apostate" emperor, Julian, did not launch the sort of attack in which Origen's father had died. One may also note among the changes that the empire, which had split into eastern and western halves, was in a state of decline. By the time Jerome died in 420, Britain had been abandoned, Gaul and Spain overrun by barbarian tribes, and Rome taken by the Visigoths. Christianity had conquered the empire, but Augustine was already drafting his *City of God* to refute charges that Rome's fall to Alaric had happened because worship of the old gods had been abandoned. Along with all these other differences there was one of language too between Origen and Jerome. By now, Greek had died out in the west. Jerome spoke Latin, he wrote Latin, and perfected his Greek only when he was in his late thirties, after he had lived in the east for several years.

Yet there are some basic similarities between the two men. Like Origen, Jerome was deeply ascetic. By now the institution of monasticism had developed in the east as an avenue of ascetic expression. Jerome was constantly attracted to it, and he did much to introduce and encourage the movement in the west. Linguistically both men shared the rare distinction among Christians of knowing Hebrew. Jerome learned his from a converted Jew in Syria and from rabbis in Palestine when he was almost forty. Likewise both men were well educated in the classical tradition as well as in the Scriptures. Jerome came from an apparently wealthy Christian home, and his parents, like Origen's, evidently saw to it that he received sound training. In contrast to Origen's experiences, however, Jerome was permitted to travel and find his niche more slowly; he was not thrust into the role of teacher as Origen had been.

A direct link between the two men is the fact that Jerome, at the outset of his career, admired Origen. He read his works, was influenced by them, and translated some of them into Latin. At one point in his career he even began to translate Origen's Hexaplaric text of the Bible. Among Jerome's earliest works was a commentary on Obediah in the allegorical style of Origen. But later, by 390, he repudiated this approach in favor of a more literal one. He also attacked several of the Origenistic doctrines, and savagely castigated his former friends who had loved Origen, as he had in his own youth. It seems to have been a characteristic of Jerome that when he changed his mind on a doctrine, he assumed that his friends would go along with him. If they did not, he was apt to lash out against them with his acid pen.

"Dearest Rufinus" is a case in point. Tyrannius Rufinus was a presbyter in northeast Italy, with whom Jerome formed a friendship during student days in Rome and later in Aquileia. A series of letters describing Jerome's travels in the east about 375 are addressed to Rufinus, in most affectionate terms—"your mind must not lose sight of me, even though your eyes have"; "friendship that can cease was never real." Yet some twenty years later Jerome had broken with him completely. The issue was Origen. Rufinus had translated some of Origen's works into Latin (just as Jerome had once done). In particular, Rufinus had put into Latin Origen's *First Principles,* hoping to convince people of the orthodoxy of the man. (The book by Origen survives today chiefly in this translation.) But Jerome launched a biting attack on his former friend, withering in its effects. Jerome thus helped fix the labels of "unorthodox" and "heretic" on both Rufinus and Origen. Though he was to make an enormous contribution to translation history, Jerome was a contentious man, lacking the creative, speculative grandeur of an Origen.

Jerome's biography likewise lacks some of the drama of Origen's, though it is not without its interest. Eusebius Sophronius Hieronymus—to give Jerome his full Latin name—was born about 340 or shortly thereafter at a place called Stridon, in the Roman province of Dalmatia, near the frontier of Pannonia. The town, which was destroyed by Goths in 377, is probably to be identified with Grahovo Polje, in what is now central Yugoslavia. The boy was sent to study at Rome under the best of teachers, including Donatus, a grammarian famed for his commentary on Virgil, and Victorinus, a rhetorician, won from the ranks of the Neoplatonists to the church. Jerome listened to the philosophers, visited the law courts, and on Sundays explored the catacombs seeking martyrs' graves and inscriptions. Jerome's parents were

Christians, and orthodox at that in an area where Arians were strong. Somewhat surprisingly, he was baptized only in the year 360 at Rome by Pope Liberius. An explanation for the delay may lie in the fact that infant baptism was not yet fully normative in all orthodox circles in the fourth century—unless the sacrament was postponed in order to receive it at the hands of a bishop who had defended Athanasian orthodoxy.

Jerome was by every inclination a scholar as well as a Christian, and his education was now rounded off by years of travel and further study—a bit like the English nobleman's "grand tour" after Oxford or Cambridge a century ago, or the American graduate student's trip to Europe nowadays. Jerome's letters and other sources picture him now in Stridon, now in Aquileia, studying in Gaul (366–70), or on a trip to the east.

It was on this trip to the east, in Antioch, that a crisis occurred. Illness struck the party. A companion, Innocentius, died of a fever. Jerome himself was stricken, and funeral preparations were made for him. He recovered, but the brush with death caused a change in him. He now determined to give up whatever held him back from God. As Jerome analyzed himself, this was his love for pagan literature. A dream confirmed the matter when Christ appeared and denounced Jerome: "You are a Ciceronian, not a Christian. 'Where your treasure is, there is your heart also.' " Jerome had learned his rhetoric too well. The Scriptures had always seemed to him uncouth in style. Even on his way to Jerusalem, he had brought along the plays of Plautus. He fasted —but then read Cicero. And after that, the prophets or apostles seemed wanting. But Jerome saw his damnation precisely here. He had lied in claiming to be Christ's. He was Cicero's—unless he cast away pagan literature. So he prayed, "O Lord, Thou knowest that if I ever have secular manuscripts in my possession or read them, I deny Thee." Henceforth study of Scripture would be his task, David instead of Pindar or Catullus. In a different way from Origen, Jerome learned that what threatens to offend must be torn away.

The resolve was carried out. From 373 to 379 Jerome lived in the desert near Antioch as a hermit. Solitude, study, privation marked his life. From 382 to 385 he was back in Rome, serving as papal secretary. It was then that the pope thrust the task upon him of revising the Latin Bible. In 385 he returned to the east and settled in Bethlehem, where a monastery was to be his home the rest of his life. While Jerome wrote tracts, biographies, commentaries, and all sorts of occasional literature, it is his work as Bible translator, the Latin Vulgate, that is his chief claim to fame.

Origen's influence was a factor in turning Jerome to the problems of translation, but the real impetus came from his friend, the Bishop of Rome, Pope Damasus. Damasus thus played a role in Bible translation probably paralleled by no other pope. Clement VIII was responsible for printing a famed edition of the Vulgate in 1592, Sixtus V had issued a less happy one two years before; other popes have doubtless encouraged this translation or that. But Damasus was the one who commissioned a translation which has lasted over fifteen hundred years, which down to the present day has been the Bible of the Roman Catholic Church.

Damasus himself provides a story. Of Spanish extraction and said to be a priest's son (in a time when clerical celibacy was not mandatory), he served as a deacon under Pope Liberius. On the latter's death, while some supported Damasus as the next pope, others actually elected a man named Ursinus to the office. A struggle went on between the two claimants from 366 till 381. One contemporary historian, Ammianus Marcellinus, records that 137 persons were killed in the contest, and finally Emperor Valentinian intervened in favor of Damasus. Precarious as his position was during his early years in office, Damasus was nonetheless vigorous in the struggle against the Arians and other heretics. He is credited with a tome or confession of faith, the *Fides Damasi,* and he joined with orthodox leaders in the east, like Basil of Caesarea, to oppose the Arian party. One of the battlefronts on which Damasus fought was in Antioch. Here a confused situation developed at the time of Bishop Melitius (360–81), involving Arian and orthodox factions and, in fact, two rival orthodox parties, one of which distrusted Melitius and consecrated Paulinus as bishop. This Paulinus was the man who had ordained Jerome as presbyter in 379 and was the man whom Damasus backed in the Antioch situation. Therefore it is not surprising that Damasus in 382 called Jerome back to Rome to serve as his adviser on the matter and as his secretary. Damasus also perceived Jerome's scholarly abilities and so put him to work on a revision of the Old Latin gospels then in use.

Such a revision was sorely needed, for the Latin Bible was in perhaps an even more confused state in A.D. 380 than the Greek Old Testament had been when Origen took it in hand. Translations of sections of the Old and New Testaments into Latin had popped up all over North Africa and Italy in the second and third centuries. Everyone had tried his hand, Augustine complained. There was no uniform text, not even broad agreement from city to city. At points the Old Latin (as we now call these pre-Jerome translations) even flatly contradicted the Greek New Testament, and of course the Hebrew Old Testament, though virtually no one knew that—for the Old Latin was generally translated from the Septuagint in the Old Testament, and therefore had all its errors, plus some of its own. Christians in the west, knowing no Hebrew, were often blissfully unaware of this, but some of the glaring discrepancies in the New Testament were more apparent. At Romans 5:14, for example, where the Greek says, "Death reigned from Adam to Moses, even over those whose sins were not like the transgression of Adam," the Latin got exactly the opposite sense in the last phrase because it omitted "not." A commentator of the time, Ambrosiaster, insisted this must be the original reading, "Death reigned . . . over those who sinned in the likeness of Adam's sin," even though it scarcely fits Paul's argument. Ambrosiaster was convinced the heretics had tampered with the Greek.

There was thus good reason for revising the Old Latin, and

Jerome set to work immediately in Rome. When Damasus died in 384, his successor, Siricius, was less cordial, and so in 385 Jerome headed back to the east, but carrying with him plans for Bible revision. He was joined by several Roman ladies who had been members of his Bible study circles and were attracted by the monastic discipline he preached. It was one of these, the widow Paula, who endowed the three nunneries and the monastery in Bethlehem which Jerome and his followers established after several years of travel. This physical migration, from Rome to Palestine, was not without its influence on the translation project.

Jerome's work with the Latin Bible is a classic example of how much more precise the workmanship can get as the translator becomes aware of the problems of text and the resources available. At first Jerome intended merely to touch up the Old Latin. His revised gospels were published at Rome, dedicated to Damasus, and the rest of the New Testament soon followed. Here Jerome relied heavily on the unknown Latin translators before his day. The gospels represent a moderately thorough revision of the Old Latin; other New Testament books felt Jerome's hand only superficially. When he turned to the Old Testament, he evidently expected to proceed the same way. In 384 he completed a revision of the Psalms in the Old Latin form, a rather mild revision on the basis of the Septuagint.[8] Wanting to be more thorough, he made a second revision in 387 based more specifically on the Hexapla's Greek text. This second attempt was especially adopted in Gaul and became known as the Gallican Psalter. It is the one which the Vulgate Bible incorporates. After his return to Palestine, however, Jerome, probably out of his study of Origen's Hexapla, became more and more convinced that a definitive Latin translation must be based on the Hebrew ultimately, not the Greek. Therefore he produced in 392 a third Latin Psalter, this time from the Masoretic Text. It goes under the name of *Psalterium juxta Hebraeos*, "in the manner of the Hebrew," though there was doubtless influence from the columns of Aquila and Symmachus in the Hexapla. Curiously, this presumably most accurate version never came into general use, but it did show Jerome the method he must follow in translating the Old Testament: he must work from the Hebrew.

To supplement the Hebrew he had learned in the hermit days some twenty years before, Jerome now made use of help from rabbis, one from Lydda, another from Tiberias, one named Ben Anina who, like Nicodemus, "came by night" for fear of the Jews—and fear of the Christians too. Jerome was criticized by many of his contemporaries for his use of the Hebrew text and, of course, for aid from non-Christians. His retort was to refer critics to the Masoretic Text (which almost none of them could read), or, worse yet in their eyes, he told them to "ask the Jews" if they wanted to know what a passage meant!

Work went on from about 390 till 405 or so. Samuel and Kings were the first books ventured. Some of the Apocrypha got short shrift; the book of Judith was said by Jerome to have been done in a single night. It is important to realize that what we call the Vulgate, by Jerome, is really a translation produced in varying ways. The New Testament, as noted, is a revision of the Old Latin, not a fresh translation of the original Greek. Most of the Old Testament is Jerome's own, based on the Hebrew; but not the Psalms (in Jerome's "Gallican version" they are based on the Greek), nor all of the Apocrypha (or deutero-canonical books). Jerome did Judith, Tobit, and the additions to Daniel, though with great haste, as if he did not care about them. The rest of the Apocrypha he ignored, because from the rabbis he knew the limits of the Hebrew canon. The Latin of these books in the Vulgate is not Jerome's but that of some earlier translator. Jerome was one of the few Christians of the day to be aware that the Hebrew canon did not include the Apocrypha.

Two other facts round out our picture of Jerome's Bible translation. The Vulgate eventually became the official Bible of the Roman Catholic Church, and a pope had been responsible for its beginnings. Technically, though, all that Pope Damasus seems to have authorized was a revision of the four gospels (and he did not give Jerome a cardinal's red hat, as medieval tradition would have it, for the work). The rest of the Bible was an independent venture, not "authorized" by anyone. The Gallican Psalter was soon widely used, but Jerome's final Psalter never found much acceptance. True, many friends including some bishops welcomed Jerome's Old Testament. But other bishops opposed it. Augustine, who liked the revision of the gospels, couldn't see why Jerome had made all these changes in the Old Testament on the presumed basis of what the Jews said!

The final fact to note is that the translation of Jerome made its way only slowly. Two hundred years later, for example, the best the new translation could claim at Rome itself was that Pope Gregory was using it sometimes.

We have several times referred to its eventual title, the Vulgate, or "common," popular Bible. Jerome used that word not for his translation, but to describe the Septuagint. In the thirteenth century Roger Bacon was still calling both the Septuagint and Jerome's work by the term "vulgata editio." As with so many other things, it was the Council of Trent which fixed the title, just as it fixed the authority of Jerome's text for Roman Catholics. Slowly but surely, however, the Vulgate had become the Bible of the western, Latin-speaking world. Few other single translators, save Luther, have erected such a dominant monument in any language. It is not surprising that Monsignor Knox, who has translated Jerome's Latin into English in our day, dates the preface of each volume on St. Jerome's day, September 30, the anniversary of the day on which Jerome died in 420.

J. J. WETTSTEIN AND THE DANGERS OF A TEXT CRITIC

It is a long jump from Jerome to the eighteenth century and the story of J. J. Wettstein. He was not a translator like Jerome. His contributions were in the area of text study, like Origen's. But he was a scholar and something of a maverick in his day, and he made a contribution for which modern exegetes of the New Testament are still in his debt. He too had bitter enemies and heard the cry "heresy." In such ways he is akin to Origen and Jerome.

By Wettstein's time, in the eighteenth century, the situation was quite changed, of course, even from Luther's day. The battle for vernacular translations was pretty well won. New theological orthodoxies dominated, the decrees of Trent among Roman Catholics, the systems of Protestant scholasticism among Calvinists, Lutherans, and others. The crisis in Wettstein's day was the rise of new knowledge about the Bible and the application of critical scholarship to its pages. J. J. Wettstein provides an example of how slowly and with what dangers the rising number of discoveries was applied in Bible translation and in the study of transmission of the text.

The harbinger of the new day was a Greek manuscript from Alexandria which arrived in England in 1628. Codex Alexandrinus, containing the Old and New Testaments, had been copied in the fifth century, five hundred to a thousand years before the manuscripts on which Erasmus' New Testament and the Received Text had been based. Cyril Lucar, patriarch of Constantinople, had given the codex to the king of England. The manuscript included in its pages I and II Clement, documents not previously extant in western Christendom. Codex Alexandrinus thus restored long-lost literature of the early Christian period to scholarly eyes. But more than that, the biblical text of Alexandrinus frequently differed from that to which people were accustomed and on which the King James Version had been based. Alexandrinus thus had the effect of alerting scholars and translators to the textual problem.

One result of all this was to spur explorers and archeologists to seek out ancient manuscripts in Greece, Egypt, Palestine, and the lands beyond. The nineteenth century proved the climax of such endeavors, and the German scholar Tischendorf provided the most exotic examples of this sort of adventure. Another result, however, was to encourage scholars to examine more carefully the older manuscripts already known to exist in European libraries. There were a number of such codices deserving

careful study. In 1636, for example, just after Alexandrinus had
arrived in England, Archbishop Laud presented to the Bodleian
Library at Oxford a manuscript from the sixth or seventh century of the book of Acts in Greek and Latin. At Cambridge were
two other bilinguals which Beza, the reformer, had secured from
the libraries of French monasteries and brought to England. He
had noted their spectacularly different readings at points but did
not incline to follow these very far in the Greek testaments he
edited. Actually these variants were from the Western Text, the
importance of which has been seen only in the present century.
Dramatic discoveries were being made in the archives of libraries.
At Paris, for example, in 1700 a fifth-century Greek Bible was
perceived beneath a twelfth-century hand which had copied a
commentary by a Syrian saint over the biblical text; unfortunately one could make out very little of the older writing. And so
the story went, at Paris, Oxford, Basel, fresh examination of the
ancient manuscripts.

It fell the lot of other scholars to attempt to survey the rising
quantities of evidence and to report the textual variants in an
orderly way—perhaps even to try to make sense of them. While
work went on slowly in the Hebrew Old Testament (since there
were not many manuscript discoveries to provide further evidence), New Testament studies developed steadily and with
increasing speed. In 1657 Brian Walton, later a bishop at Chester,
completed his six-volume Polyglot Bible, giving evidence from
manuscripts like Alexandrinus and the two of Beza at Cambridge. By 1675 the Dean of Christ Church, Oxford, John Fell,*

* This is the same Dr. Fell (1625–86), a distinguished patron of the
Oxford University Press, who has achieved a popular renown of a different sort in Tom Brown's poem,
> I do not love thee, Doctor Fell,
> The reason why I cannot tell;
> But this alone I know full well,
> I do not love thee, Doctor Fell.

Actually the student poem is a translation of one of Martial's epigrams,
with the victim made to be Dr. Fell because his name rhymes so well.

published a New Testament with readings from some one hundred Greek manuscripts. Another Oxford don, John Mills, was able in 1707 to list thirty thousand variants from the Greek manuscripts for the New Testament. Mills also took the daring step of venturing to correct the Received Text in a few places on the basis of such evidence. He was roundly condemned by those who felt that faith stood or fell on the basis of the traditional text, and a long and angry controversy ensued. Traditionalists deemed such work inimical to Christianity. Among the verses involved in the controversy was, as we might expect, I John 5:7. Jonathan Swift tells the story of one rake who, when he heard that this proof text for the Trinity did not belong in the Bible, thanks to Dr. Mills, promptly concluded that he could "defy the parson" on other biblical teachings too and indulge in wine and women as he wished! Others, however, praised Mills' work as "a good Providence and a great Blessing."

The fracas caused by such work on the biblical text indicates the temper of the times. Some years later, in 1734, when J. A. Bengel, of Tübingen, the Lutheran pietist, published his Greek New Testament, he was sure that the increasing accumulation of manuscript evidence had to be classified into families, and some attempt made at deciding which groups were earlier and preferable. But it is also indicative of the times that Bengel printed the traditional text and indicated his alternate preferences only in the notes and apparatus below. It was not until 1831 that a reconstructed critical text based solely on early manuscript evidence, not later traditions, was printed by Karl Lachmann of Berlin. It was in such a heresy-hunting atmosphere, when the hue and cry was instantly raised about any departures from the Received Text, that John James [Johann Jakob] Wettstein lived and did his work on the New Testament.

Wettstein was born at Basel in 1693, the son of the pastor at St. Leonhard's, a fifteenth-century church approached by quaint steps rising above Barfüsser Platz. The Wettstein family moved in Basel's patrician circles and had a long tradition of education and service in church and state. A great-grandfather had been burgomaster in the time of the Thirty Years' War and achieved such fame as a statesman that the "Wettstein Bridge" over the Rhine was named after him. The boy John James grew up in a parsonage in the shadow of Basel's red sandstone Münster or cathedral. Behind the Münster was the Pfalz, a terrace where the bishop's palace once stood on the hill, affording a splendid view over the Rhine and toward the Black Forest beyond, a fine place for children to play. Not far away was the house of Johann Froben, who had printed the first Greek New Testament, the same house in which Erasmus had died. Also nearby was a wall-painting from the Middle Ages, the *Totentanz,* or dance of death, suggesting some of the grimmer aspects of medieval theology and, perhaps, of the strict Calvinistic orthodoxy which held sway over pulpit and town council alike in Basel.

The boy studied at the university in his home city, matriculating at the age of thirteen, taking up first philosophy and then theology. His grandfather, director of the city mint, had established a chair in theology at the University of Basel, and a brother of his grandfather, John Rudolf Wettstein (1614–84), had been rector of the university. This John Rudolf had contributed to the famous patristic lexicon compiled in 1682 by Johannes Suicer (or Hans Schweitzer, to give him his name in it unlatinized form), and had also been one of those who opposed the Formula Consensus Helvetica, a Calvinistic confessional statement which insisted that even the Hebrew vowel points and the very Greek letters of the traditional text were divinely inspired. John Rudolf never accepted this document and only his personal prestige prevented the authorities from taking steps against him. A similar viewpoint, though with different results, was to appear in John James. It may finally be mentioned, as part of the family background, that another branch of the family had set up in the printing business at Amsterdam. Suicer's *Thesaurus* had appeared from the press of Henry Wettstein there. This Amsterdam connection was to shape the second part of J. J. Wettstein's career.

Professor J. L. Frey advised the young student to devote himself to the text of the New Testament. He collated Codex Basiliensis, an eighth-century manuscript of the gospels in the university library, more accurately than Mills had done, and then, after completing his basic studies, set out on a literary journey to examine other manuscripts in other Swiss cities, in Lyons, Paris, and then in England. At Cambridge he met that odd genius Richard Bentley, Master of Trinity College. Bentley was without question the most brilliant text critic of the day and had achieved lasting fame by an "immortal dissertation" exposing as spurious the "Epistles of Phalaris." Bentley was also an eccentric who built a marvelous library by borrowing books which he forgot to return and who engaged with the fellows of his college in a bitter feud which lasted till his death.

Two things happened in England which helped set the course for the rest of Wettstein's life. The one incident had to do with the reading of Codex Alexandrinus at I Timonthy 3:16. In the traditional text the little hymn there begins,

"God was manifest in the flesh,"

and the line had traditionally been taken as a proof for the deity of Jesus Christ. The Greek word for "God" is *theos,* and the usual custom among scribes was to abbreviate it with the first and last letters, *th-s,* or in uncial letters (such as Alexandrinus uses) $\overline{\Theta S}$, the line above the two letters indicating an abbreviation. Wettstein by close examination was able to show that the line above was written in the hand of a later corrector, and further that the dash through the middle of the letter was not part of it but came from a letter on the other side of the page, a stroke of which had come through in the middle of the circle. If line and dash are later additions, then the original reading was simply OS, and that is a different Greek word, *hos* (as it would be pointed), meaning "who," the relative pronoun. The original meaning therefore was,

"who was manifest in the flesh,"

a reading confirmed by later manuscript discoveries and subsequent research. R.S.V. and most modern translations take it this way, rendering the line, "He was manifest," and explaining in a note that the Greek literally means "who" and that other (later) manuscripts have "God." The hyperorthodox of the day were not pleased, however, for they felt that Wettstein had removed a "proof" of Christ's divinity just at a time when radicals were attacking his deity.

The second happening involved Wettstein's work as chaplain for a troop of Swiss soldiers then in the service of the Dutch, a position Bentley helped him secure. Wettstein preached and ministered to these mercenaries in 1716–17. A fellow chaplain soon came to question his orthodoxy, however. He reproved Wettstein for speaking more like a Socinian than the pastor of a "pure congregation of the Lord." Thus a reputation for inclining toward the Socinian movement—the Unitarian heresy (in Calvinist eyes), named for sixteenth-century Italian teacher, Sozini, who was anti-Trinitarian—attached itself to Wettstein's name. Nothing happened for the time being, but in the course of Wettstein's later troubles this chaplain gave testimony against him.

In 1717 Wettstein was able to return to Basel where he became a popular preacher in his father's church, but the two incidents from the literary tour were combined in rumors about Wettstein: he was going to prepare an edition of the Greek testament, it was said, which would assail the divinity of Christ, along Unitarian lines. It would "reek of Socinianism," some claimed. It was true that Wettstein was planning an edition of the Greek text. His contacts with Bentley encouraged him to do so. His continued study since student days provided the materials for the work. His former teacher J. L. Frey had led him into the task in the early 1720's. But Frey's attitude now changed, as did that of other Basel theologians. Jealousy of the young scholar was no doubt a factor. So was pressure from other Swiss cantons, which resented Basel's looser attitude toward the Formula Consensus and saw a chance to take vengeance on one of Basel's sons. But Wettstein's own pride and stubbornness never helped to ease strained situations. He seems to have had an ability to antagonize need-lessly at the wrong time. Without going into all the details of the controversy, we may simply note the result, that J. J. Wettstein was deposed from his ministerial office by the Basel town council in 1730 for unorthodox teachings.[9]

On leaving Basel, Wettstein went to the obvious haven, Amsterdam, where his cousins ran a publishing business. Here too classical learning was esteemed, and the attitude a bit more tolerant. Wettstein was able to have his Prolegomena, setting forth a plan for his Greek testament, printed there in 1730. In 1751–52 he was finally able to publish in two volumes the New Testament to which his life had been devoted. In Amsterdam he was also invited to teach in the seminary of the Remonstrant Brotherhood or anti-Calvinist Arminians. The Basel government in 1732, after a long, involved debate, in which Wettstein felt he was contending for the freedom of New Testament textual criticism, reversed its former sentence, and he was permitted to take up his post in Amsterdam. Local opponents, though, insisted that he teach only Hebrew and philosophy, avoiding the New Testament or any expression of Socinian views. Wettstein thus lived out the last twenty-four years of his life in comparative quiet, a teacher in a seminary, a bachelor who seldom traveled save for research, a savant at work on his beloved New Testament edition.

His Greek text, ironically, proved something of a dud. It was handsomely printed, though not without mistakes. For all of Wettstein's presumed radicalness, however, the Greek he finally put down as the text was the traditional form, the Received Text, much as it had been printed in Holland by the Elzevirs since 1633. In the apparatus, it is true, something different was to be found. Here Wettstein cited the readings from more than 225 manuscripts, a hundred of which he had personally examined. Between the text and the notes he gave the readings which he personally preferred, the readings which his opponents disliked. Even here, however, he did not follow out the elaborate rules which he had proposed, but tended to accept "majority opinion" in the manuscripts, so that the mass of late witnesses outvoted a few ancient ones. It remained for Semler and Griesbach in Germany twenty-five years later to formulate the rules which future critics followed and to print a text other than the received one. Wettstein's work thus had less influence than he hoped it would.

But another feature which he had tossed into his New Testament of 1751–52 as an "added attraction" proved the element on which Wettstein's lasting fame is based. All his life he had collected quotations from Greek, Latin, and rabbinic literature which might illustrate New Testament verses. These he added in the notes of his New Testament edition. His commentary was thus not theological but philological, illustrating the meaning of the words from contemporary sources. This illustrative material, gathered so tirelessly by Wettstein, continues to be the basis to this day for many discussions of New Testament terms. More than a few commentators, wishing to show ancient contemporary applications of a word, got their material from Wettstein, often without acknowledging the fact. More than one preacher, quoting some commentary when he illustrates a Bible word with a citation from Philo or Cicero, really is employing data which Wettstein first related to the New Testament.

Of course, our knowledge of the ancient world has grown enormously since Wettstein's day. However, no single work has ever replaced or updated his volumes of 1751–52. Only in our own time have scholars begun to produce a "new Wettstein." For the rabbinic sources a large commentary of quotations out of the Talmud and Midrash illustrating New Testament verses was produced in the 1920's by an industrious parish pastor in Germany, Paul Billerbeck.[10] In 1910 another German, Georg Heinrici, set in motion a plan for redoing the Greek and Latin material in Wettstein. It was apparent that it would now have to be done in two parts, one presenting Jewish-Hellenistic material, the other providing strictly Gentile sources. Work went on enthusiastically during World War I and the 1920's. As editor, von Dobschütz and then Hans Windisch succeeded Heinrici. They promised publication "soon," but the size of the undertaking, the depression, and then the Hitler period and another war interfered. Kurt Aland, a church historian and New Testament text critic, managed to get the Jewish-Hellenistic part under way again; it is today under the leadership of Professor Gerhard Delling at Halle, in East Germany. The Gentile-Hellenistic part has had a more romantic trek. The Corpus Hellenisticum, as it has come to be known, became a sort of "war orphan" and was evacuated to Sweden by Anton Fridrichsen, of Uppsala, in the 1940's. In 1956, to facilitate work, Professor W. C. van Unnik had it brought to the University of Utrecht, in Holland—which is perhaps only appropriate, that this part of a "new Wettstein" should return to the land in which the original Wettstein's volumes saw the light of day.[11]

J. J. Wettstein, Origenes Adamantius, and Eusebius Sophronius Hieronymous are not names we normally recall when we read Scripture. But without these men and others like them the text we read and the meaning of the words would be less accurate. Something less than orthodox they may have seemed, and perhaps none of them are men we would choose for personal friends. But "heretic," contentious, contumacious or not, they are men to whom we owe a word of thanks in the parade of translators. Perhaps, even, a prayer of gratitude for them, a tribute such as Browning voiced in "A Grammarian's Funeral":

> This man decided not to Live but Know—
> . . . Here—here's his place, where meteors shoot, clouds form,
>   Lightnings are loosened,
> Stars come and go! . . .
> Leave him—still loftier than the world suspects,
>   Living and dying.

Five

Philadelphia's Patriot-Scholar:
Charles Thomson (1729—1824)
and Bible Translation

THERE WAS SCARCELY EVER A LESS LIKELY CANDIDATE FOR A place of honor in the procession of Bible translators than Charles Thomson. He lived in Philadelphia at the time of the American Revolution, far from Europe's citadels of scholarship. He was woefully short in formal training and had no strong ecclesiastical allegiance, thus lacking both the customary academic and religious spurs to translate. He also suffered from the handicap that he was a businessman most of his life and got seriously into Bible translation only at the age of sixty when he retired. And Charles Thomson is probably the only translator ever to have served as secretary to a political insurrection.

Yet his Bible, published in 1808, is a landmark which has been reprinted in our own day. Charles Thomson is one of the few men ever to have put both Old and New Testaments into English. Moreover, he did it by himself. Luther had had helpers; only men like Moffatt and Ronald Knox are comparable with this colonial pioneer on that score. Further, Thomson also published a harmony of the gospels. His translation has a number of miscellaneous distinctions: the first English New Testament to be translated and published in America; the first Bible to be printed by a woman. More significantly, he made the first English translation of the

Septuagint (for he rendered the Greek Old Testament, not the Hebrew), and it was the first such translation anywhere into any modern European language. In fact, there has been only one other English translation of the Septuagint in the century and a half since Thomson's day.

This singular scholar-patriot was born in 1729 in County Derry, northern Ireland. His mother died when he was a boy, and the father, John Thomson, decided to emigrate to America with his six children. But John Thomson died at sea, and so Charles and his brothers and sisters landed at New Castle, Delaware, completely on their own in 1739. By his own wit the orphan boy managed to earn an education for himself, after he ran away from a blacksmith's shop where he had been apprenticed. He picked up Latin and Greek at a private academy run by Dr. Francis Alison, a clergyman, who later founded what is now the Presbyterian Ministers' Fund, the world's oldest life insurance company.

Charles Thomson's first career was as a teacher of the classics in a Latin school run by Benjamin Franklin. In 1760 he entered business and grew wealthy as an importer of dry goods and hats, as well as from investments in the iron furnaces near Egg Harbor and in the Pennsylvania Bank. His business interests drew him into civic affairs. Because of his reputation for fairness, the Indians welcomed him in their negotiations with the settlers; Thomson was even adopted into the Delaware tribe and given the name, "The Man Who Tells the Truth."

Civic and business ties also drove him on a collision course with the British government. Repressive economic and political measures roused the ire of Thomson and other colonials. Hence he helped force the local agent for the hated Stamp Act to "resign" and himself served as secretary for the Stamp Act Congress in 1765. He organized a public meeting where Paul Revere, the Boston patriot, could speak; Thomson's own oratory that night was so impassioned that he fell to the floor in a faint. The Tory Joseph Galloway called him "one of the most violent of the Sons of Liberty," and John Adams wrote in his diary, "This Charles Thomson is the Sam Adams of Philadelphia."

It is not surprising therefore that the Continental Congress elected Charles Thomson its secretary in 1774. Then "for fifteen years he sat at the secretarial table, listening to the debates, minuting the birth-records of a nation."[1] As its "perpetual secretary," he kept the journals in an accurate shorthand. He maintained contact with ambassadors abroad and with spies behind British lines. He dug into his own pocket to help the patriot cause and suffered the loss of his mansion along the Schuylkill River when the redcoats burned it to the ground looking for secret documents—Thomson himself escaped with his papers, probably because friendly Indians warned him of the raid. He is said to have been one of the two men who signed the Declaration of Independence on precisely the fourth of July. He it was who carried word to Washington of his election as the Republic's first President, and with William Barton he designed the Great Seal of the United States.

His government service completed, however, Charles Thomson retired in 1789 to the estate of his wife's family, Harriton, near where Bryn Mawr College now stands. Here he lived and did his translating, until he died in 1824, in his ninety-fifth year. Declining offers to run for the Senate or to serve as Commissioner for Indian affairs, he devoted his time to the translation project, publishing *The Holy Bible, containing the Old and New Covenant* when he was almost eighty, and completing the *Synopsis* seven years later.

Why did Charles Thomson translate the Bible? A variety of answers, some worthy of consideration, others naïve, have been given over the years or are suggested by details in Thomson's life. To begin with, Thomson had a certain interest in Scripture and religion from his youth. His teacher, Dr. Francis Alison, was a Presbyterian clergyman, and the school was subsidized by the Synod of Philadelphia; it is not unlikely that there was some emphasis on instruction in religion and biblical content.

After he finished his training there, Thomson was urged by friends to begin the study of theology. "For this purpose they recommended to him the reading of certain theological works. It is related that he at once inquired from whence these writers drew their religious knowledge. His relatives answered: 'From the Holy Scriptures, most assuredly,' and seemed to be surprised at his asking such a question. 'Well then,' replied young Charles, 'if they whom you so highly recommend as models drew their religious instruction from the Scriptures, I shall apply directly to the same source, instead of taking knowledge at second hand.' Although he had no intention of preparing for the ministry, he at once began a careful study of the Bible, and laid the foundations of that intimate knowledge of the Scriptures which he displayed in later years," a biographer reports.[2] Thomson never did take up theological studies, but throughout his years in business and politics he was known for his interest in things biblical, as his correspondence sometimes shows—a long letter to Thomson in 1771, for example, seeks to explain to him the physical causes for the flood in Noah's day.[3]

John F. Watson, an early biographer, gives a most romantic account of how Thomson's specific interest in the Septuagint was awakened. "His first passion for Greek literature was induced, as he told me, by a seeming accident. Passing an auction store, he heard the crier proclaiming the sale of an 'unknown, outlandish book;' he bid a trifle for it and got it. It proved to be a part of the Greek Septuagint. When he had mastered it enough to understand it, his anxiety was extreme to see the whole; but he could find no copy, until, strange to tell, in the interval of two years, passing the same store and looking in, he actually saw the remainder selling off, when he joyfully bought it at a few pence. I used to tell him the 'Translation,' which he made from that copy . . . should have been furnished with the story as a proper subject for its *preface*. For this great work . . . is strangely enough without any introduction or advertisement to the reader. It wanted something of the kind. . . . His modesty kept him from

giving any preface; and being offered for sale without any published commendations from others, it did not receive its meed of
praise. . . ."[4]

Watson's version undoubtedly has elements of truth in it:
Thomson probably did secure part of the Septuagint at a Philadelphia secondhand store and may well have gotten the rest of it
at the same store later on. But the implication that he translated
the Bible merely because he happened to pick up the Septuagint
at various sales seems an example of nineteenth-century roman-
ticism—like Parson Weems's stories about George Washington.
Actually the Greek Old Testament was not an "unknown book"
in America in Thomson's day. "The Septuagint was studied in
the colleges, and Ezra Stiles examined it for entrance to Yale,
besides teaching it there."[5] Moreover it is inconceivable that the
practical merchant and political leader would devote years to a
translation just because he happened to own certain books.
Thomson had far better reasons for his undertaking, and although this legend has been widely repeated, he himself was wise
enough to omit it as a preface to his edition of the Holy Bible.

A similarly unsatisfactory story is given in a newspaper account in Poulson's *American Daily Advertiser* for Friday, July
29, 1825. It reports how Thomson's nephew gave to Allegheny
College, Meadville, Pennsylvania, part of the library of "the late
Secretary of the old Congress." It goes on, "The late venerable
Charles Thomson, a scholar, patriot and Christian, was an intimate friend of Dr. Franklin and agreed with him in everything,
except religion. To counteract the infidel sentiments of the great
American philosopher, he devoted more attention to the subject
of divine revelation, than he would otherwise have done, vainly
hoping to be enabled to convince him of his errors. It was on
this ground he undertook the translation of the Septuagint."[6]

This appealing tale of Thomson's motive for translating the
Bible appears to have little real basis. Benjamin Franklin's attitude toward Scripture was, of course, scarcely as sober as Thomson's. Franklin, for example, loved to hoax people by quoting a

"parable against persecution" which he told them was in Genesis. Solemnly Franklin would open the Bible and pretend to read how Abraham once turned a man out of his tent because he did not join in giving thanks to God with him. But God, according to the story, then reproached Abraham and got him to invite the man back, telling Abraham, "Why do you lose patience with him in one night when I have borne with him for eighty years?" Franklin, we now know, might have gotten this story through a Latin form of an incident in the Babylonian Talmud, so he was not without knowledge of things biblical. But any concern for the Greek Old Testament is another matter. Thomson was acquainted with Franklin, but there is no evidence the two ever discussed the Septuagint together. Franklin was scarcely a Christian, it is true, but Thomson himself was far from the orthodox faith in many ways; he never seemed to have had a passion for converting the atheists of his day. Once he mentioned the "awful impression on my mind that I was attempting the translation of a book containing the immediate revelation of God's will";[7] but on the whole his character was modest and reserved, and the translation can hardly be called an evangelistic tract. The most convincing argument against this whole theory is that Franklin was in Europe much of the time when Thomson was dabbling in Bible translation and died in 1790 when Thomson was just beginning his period of retirement, the time when most of the work was done.

Still another motive is suggested by Lewis R. Harley, Thomson's most voluminous biographer. "After our Revolutionary War was terminated, and before the adoption of the present Constitution of the United States, our country was in a very deplorable state, and many of our surviving patriotic fathers, and Mr. Thomson among the rest, could not easily rid themselves of gloomy apprehensions. Mr. Thomson's resource (and who will say it was not a noble one, and worthy of a vigorous, cultivated and pious mind) was to soothe his painful feelings and await the developments of divine providence in the study of the sacred

Scriptures. There was then no translation of the Septuagint into the English language, and he determined to make one; and to this, when accomplished, he added a version of the New Testament, varying very considerably from that in common use—in language, but not in sense. Delighted with his employment, he was reluctant to quit it, and his last work was a Harmony of the Four Gospels in the language of his own version."[8] On this theory, Thomson buried himself in biblical studies as a soothing relief from political distresses of the day. There may be some truth in this view. The Continental Congress gradually deteriorated in quality after the Revolution. Thomson was no longer so busy with his secretarial duties and found more time, especially after his retirement, to devote to Greek. So his undertaking may have been therapeutic. A letter to Thomas Jefferson in 1808 states: The translation "has kept my mind employed, so that I can say I have not during the last nine years found one hour hang heavy on me."

The most convincing reason, however, is the one Thomson himself indicated in a note in his handwriting on the fragment of a detached leaf in his notebook. This Commonplace Book, now in the Historical Society of Pennsylvania, is filled with jottings for his translation. The inscription seems to be a sort of preface— Watson had advised Thomson to write one—and it is found in the book Thomson used for gathering his material. The fragment gives a plausible motive for translation, for it reads: "As the quotations which the writers of the New Testament make from the Old, either to shew that the predictions of the prophets are fulfilled in J[esus] C[hrist] or to confirm and enforce the doctrines they delivered, or convey their own thoughts on different subjects, are chiefly taken from the Sept[uagint]; and as, upon inquiry, I could not find that there was any translation of this in English. . . ." Albert J. Edmunds, who first called attention to this fragment, comments, "It is pretty plain that the writer is saying that he was led to translate the Septuagint (1) because he found it quoted so often in the New Testament, and (2) because it was untranslated in our tongue. . . . That the New Testament was his inspiring motive is moreover stated by Watson himself in these words . . . : 'Dr. Adam Clarke declares that no man can adequately understand the New Testament Scriptures who has not diligently read the Septuagint. It was a similar conception which made Mr. Thomson decline the proffered offices of President Washington, that he might give his days and nights to this his favourite study.' "[9] New Testament scholarship, then, seems to have led him to the Septuagint.

To sum up, Thomson, interested in Greek and Scripture all his life, happened across a copy of the Septuagint. Its relation to the New Testament interested him, and, as events allowed, he devoted time to it. Partly it was a relaxing hobby, partly a contribution to scholarship, and all the while there was a growing interest in polishing and publishing the completed work.

Coupled with this whole question of motive is the problem of Thomson's own religious background. Nominally he was Presbyterian. His Scotch-Irish background indicates this. In Delaware, where he settled, "in the mid-eighteenth century the most rapidly growing denomination . . . was the Presbyterian."[10] Thomson was educated in a school sponsored by that denomination and in Philadelphia was "a pew-holder in the Market Street [Presbyterian] Church, and was a ruling elder of First Presbyterian Church of Philadelphia," where he was a trustee for one year beginning May, 1774.[11] It is possible that this connection with First Church came about because his old teacher and friend, Dr. Alison, was assistant pastor there from 1755 on. There seems no evidence that Thomson ever formally severed his connection with the Presbyterian Church.

There was, however, considerable Quaker influence in his life. Philadelphia was, of course, the Quaker capital. Thomson's second wife, Hannah Harrison, and most of her family were Friends, and so it is likely that Thomson became increasingly attracted by tenets of the Society of Friends the latter part of his life. Watson believed "his affections . . . were most accorded with the Quakers," and it has been suggested Thomson's translation might be regarded as "the Quaker testament." In 1764 Anthony Purver tried to make a Quaker Bible but failed because he was no scholar. Thomson may have been inspired by his friends among the Friends to make another attempt.

During the years at Harriton there was also a strong connection with the local Baptist Church. Charles Thomson worshipped there. He became quite friendly with the minister, the Reverend Horatio Gates Jones, and supported the church financially. In 1817 Thomson presented the Baptist Education Society with one hundred copies of his *Synopsis of the Four Evangelists,* for which he was duly made a life member of the Society. Reverend Mr. Jones was frequently a dinner guest at Harriton on Sundays, and it was he who preached Charles Thomson's funeral sermon. The Baptist Church today in Lower Merion has a window portrait of Thomson.

Thomson the translator himself spoke of his religious affiliation thus: "Attached to no system nor peculiar tenets of any sect or party, I have sought for truth with the utmost ingenuity, and endeavored to give a just and true representation of the sense and meaning of the Sacred Scriptures."[12] That Thomson regarded himself as a seeker after truth, emancipated from denominationalism, is quite in harmony with the rationalistic spirit of the times. Thomas Jefferson, who shared a similar outlook, commented on his *Synopsis* in a letter to Thomson, January 9, 1816: "This work bears the stamp of that accuracy which marks every thing from you, and will be useful to those who, not taking things on trust, recur for themselves to the fountain of pure morals. I too have made a wee little book from the same materials, which I call the Philosophy of Jesus. . . . It is a document in proof that I am a *real Christian*—that is to say, a disciple of the doctrines of Jesus; very different from the Platonists who call *me* Infidel and *themselves* Christians and preachers of the Gospel. While they draw all their characteristic dogmas from what its author never said nor saw, they have compounded from the heathen mysteries a system beyond the comprehension of man. . . ."

Charles Thomson felt he was a real Christian. The pious legends about his motive for translating the Bible show others thought this too; so does a letter preserved from a man in York County: Your Bible "will give a savour to your memory infinitely more superior to what could be derived to Tho. Pain[e] from all the boasted productions of his pen, either on religion or politics." By early nineteenth-century standards, Thomson was quite orthodox, especially compared to Tom Paine (1737–1809), whose pamphlet, *Common Sense*, helped spark the American Revolution but whose book *The Age of Reason*—actually written to help refute the atheism of the French Revolution—struck many contemporaries as "the atheist's Bible" and caused them to regard Paine himself as the antichrist.

A translator cannot work without tools. What equipment did Thomson use for his translations? As a Septuagint text he used Field's edition, printed at Cambridge in 1665, which in turn was based on the great Sixtine edition of 1587, a compilation following chiefly the Vatican Codex (B). Field's text was a so-called Puritan Septuagint including the books approved by the Westminster Confession of 1643–48 but omitting the noncanonical Alexandrian books, the Apocrypha and the hymns in the third chapter of Daniel. The books were arranged according to the order of the King James Bible, however, There were two additions: a 151st Psalm, beginning, "I was little among my brethren," and an added ending of Job. The copy of the Greek text from which Thomson himself worked has disappeared, although his manuscript from which the translation was printed is preserved at Allegheny College. On the first page of the manuscript is written, ". . . translated from the Vatican copy of the Septuagint by Charles Thomson." A copy of Thomson's Bible in the Ridgway Library, Philadelphia, has a note opposite Genesis in Thomson's hand verifying this information.

For the New Testament the textual problem is not so clear.

The late Kendrick Grobel, who made the most thorough study of the subject, believed Thomson employed "some uncritical copy of the textus receptus [and] consulted Woide's edition of Codex Alexandrinus (London, 1786)."[13] He departed from the Received Text in Acts 9:20, 11:20, I Cor. 9:22, and I John 5:6–8, the latter a place where the Received Text had been in error ever since Erasmus' Third Edition.

In working out his translation Thomson made use, where possible, of other versions and translations, as well as suggestions from friends and commentaries. He had learned Latin in school, and Grobel thought it "likely he consulted the Vulgate"—at least there are examples of its influence in some of his renderings. Grobel also credits Thomson with a secondhand knowledge of Syriac and Arabic, and there is the possibility he acquired a smattering of Hebrew late in life.

Since there are many verses in Thomson's translation exactly like the Authorized Version, he doubtless consulted the King James Bible. His notebook mentions that he did not like Harwood's translation[14] and names three others he intends to get. A letter to John Vaughan, January 21, 1796, states: "I should be very glad to see Doct Geddes' translation of the Old Testament.[15] Mine which I have now finished is from the Septuagint Version. I have heard that a like work has been undertaken by some person in England and that a part of it has been published, but I have been disappointed in all my attempts to get a sight of it." We do not know what English publication he referred to, but it is certain that Thomson was on the lookout for other translations; a later letter tells us he examined Geddes' work that same year.

Other New Testament translations which appeared during the period in which Thomson worked include those of Worsley, a "dissenter," in 1770; Wakefield, 1791; Archbishop William Newcome, in 1796; and the Universalist Nathaniel Scarlett, in 1798. The most important (and worst) of these influences was probably Gilbert Wakefield (1756–1801), a man who had been ordained by the Church of England and later became a Unitarian. This erratic scholar published a translation in 1791. Thomson commented caustically on it in a manuscript now at the Massachusetts Historical Society, but often followed Wakefield's blunders, as Grobel illustrated in his article.

Many times in his extant letters to friends Thomson made reference to his translation and its progress. Once, at least, he sent samples of his translation of John Vaughan. In a series of letters of 1809–10 he secured advice on Greek terms from the Reverend William Sinclair, who was then at Baltimore College. No doubt there were similar consultations with other friends. Charles McClenachan, one of the grandchildren of Hannah Harrison Thomson's brother Thomas, is even reported to have "aided his uncle in making the translation of the Bible from the Septuagint version."[16]

Father Vincent Pottle has made the most important suggestions on the Greek grammars and lexicons Thomson used. The first lexicon to appear in America with definitions in English was not published until 1826. Therefore one in Latin—probably that of Schrevelius or J. G. Schneider—was used. The first Greek grammar printed in this country, Wettenhal's, was printed in Philadelphia in Latin, 1803, and Thomson most likely knew of it; however, his translation was well worked out by that time. Among the commentaries, those of Matthew Poole and Adam Clarke are possibilities; Clarke is mentioned in Thomson's notebook but was not published until 1816. Thomson's manuscript of the Old Testament, preserved today at Allegheny College, contains several pages of excerpts from articles on Greek and oriental studies which Thomson evidently copied out for himself.

Charles Thomson's own rules for a translator are given at the beginning of his notebook. He wrote, "To translate well is: 1, to give a just representation of the purpose of an author; 2, to convey into the translation the author's spirit and manner; 3, to give it the quality of an original, by making it appear natural, a natural copy without applying words improperly, or in a meaning not warranted by use, or combining them in a way which renders the sense obscure, and the construction ungrammatical or harsh." To achieve these ends, Thomson copied and reworked his translation of each biblical book, four or five times in some cases. And behind this was often much preliminary investigation. His notebook contains discussions with such sentences as, "I have chosen to translate . . . ," or "I acknowledge the Greek word signifies . . . but I have adopted. . . ." These studies served as raw materials for his final renderings.

A window into Thomson's habits of translation is provided by a newspaper story of 1839: "We are informed by his nephew . . . that he never left his dwelling without a copy of the Greek New Testament in his pocket, and that he would wander in the woods and sit for hours in study, making notes, and preparing for his evening task of translation." This description apparently refers to the translator's period of retirement at Harriton. During his years in political life, Thomson undoubtedly had a far different schedule, perhaps relaxing over his Greek at night or writing translations in spare hours.

One chance passage in a letter from Thomson to his wife during the years he was Secretary to Congress shows he maintained an interest in things literary even amid the heaviest duties of office. On April 6, 1785, he wrote from New York: "You see by the tenor of this letter I write just for the pleasure of writing to you. The ancients had the advantage on us in point of conciseness. When Cicero who wrote almost as often to his Terentia as I do to my dear Hannah had nothing particular to say, he used to make his whole letter consists [sic!] of these few words. Si vales bene est et ego valeo. Vale. That is, I say you are well, that is well, I am well, farewell. You remember our good friend S. Emlin's sermon when he quoted a scrap of latin and desired the women to apply to their husbands for an explanation of it. As you have not had the opportunity just now of making an immediate application to yours, though I hope you soon will, I have sent the translation of mine and conclude in the true Ciceronean stile [sic] with most earnest entreaties to take care of your

health." Not only does this letter indicate Thomson's attachment
to the classics; it also gives us an example of his fondness for
word-play. His translation of Cicero is not strictly literal, to be
sure, but it does "convey . . . the author's spirit and manner."
And this was one of the things he sought in his biblical translation.

There is some debate as to when Thomson made his translations
of the Old and New Covenants. Harley states that it was after
he retired from political office: Thomson "saw his country safely
through the perils of war, and then retired to give his days and
nights to his favorite study. . . . It appears that Thomson began
work on the translation early in the year 1789, and that he was
almost constantly employed in it until 1808." [17] This conclusion
is based solely on the sentence in Thomson's letter of January 6,
1801, to the Reverend Samuel Miller, that the translation "has
occupied my closest attention . . . for more than twelve years,"
which gives us the year 1789 for the start of the project.

However, the truth of the matter is that Thomson had begun
the undertaking some years before, *during his term as Secretary
of Congress*. A letter from Timothy Pickering to his wife,
December 16, 1789, says: "He is now revising his translation
of the Bible, which one day perhaps may be published to the
world."[18] Obviously, if Thomson had only begun his work
that year he would not have completed his translation of the
Bible and be revising it by December—assuming that Pickering's comment is accurate. Presumably, Thomson had been
working over his translation prior to 1789, and the conclusion
which should be drawn from his letter to the Reverend Mr.
Miller in 1801 is that the project occupied his *full* time after
retirement in 1789. Also to be noted is Pickering's reference to
the possibility of publishing this Thomson translation. That
urge was to grow stronger during the years, and it is quite
possible that even in 1789 the sage of Harriton had some hopes of
seeing his Bible through the press.

Other letters during the period 1789–1808 give us inklings

of how the work was proceeding. A letter to his brother, Alexander Thomson, in 1792, mentions "a translation of the Bible or old testament which I have just completed and which I may possibly give to the public." In January of 1796 Thomson was worried about "the precious state" of his health (he was then sixty-six years old) but reported he had finished his Old Testament translation of the Septuagint; to this he added: "I am now engaged in a translation of the new testament and am not without hopes of accomplishing it, if it please God to spare my health and life a little longer." Three months later, however, things had progressed well enough for him to write to John Vaughan: "I send you a specimen of my translation from the Septuagint. Having finished the old testament, I ventured to undertake the New, and have now nearly got through both for the last time. Though the labor has been great, the pleasure attending it has made ample compensation." And by 1800 Thomson was able to send another friend, J. P. Norris, a copy of his New Testament translation for examination. A year later he had completed his fourth revision and was going over some books for a sixth time and planning further revising! Moreover by this time he had added a few notes, but since the Bible appeared in 1808 without notes of any sort, these may have become the basis for his *Synopsis* of 1815.

All this suggests that the work begun so many years before and seriously prosecuted from 1789 on unfolded as follows. The Old Testament was ready in a rough but complete way by 1792, with revision continuing until perhaps 1795. About that time the New Testament was written out in full and was ready for critical eyes by 1800. Then followed more study until publication in 1808. The length of time consumed in the process is to be explained by Thomson's age and ill-health and his careful habits of polishing his work for publication—his self-criticism was so keen he destroyed a history of the Revolution he once began, though here other motives too might have prompted the action.

By the time Thomson's translation was finally published in four volumes, public interest in it, one might expect, should have been high. After all, Charles Thomson had been a leading businessman in America's largest city and was an important figure in the struggle for freedom. It had been almost twenty years since Pickering had first intimated the patriot-scholar might one day publish his Bible. It was therefore with some justification that J. P. Norris said in a letter to Thomson on July 2, 1808 (just thirty-two years after the momentous events in Independence Hall): "I suppose you must have nearly got thru . . . the great work you have so long had in hand . . . a great many people are impatient for a sight of it." Some were quite interested. Thomas Jefferson was one of the subscribers. William Dickson ordered nine copies and believed that many men at the coming session of the Pennsylvania Legislature would order the volumes. The most enthusiastic endorsement came in 1816, from Peter S. Du Ponceau, a secretary of the American Philosophical Society. He wrote: ". . . the time will come, it is to be hoped, . . . when your excellent translation of the Sacred Writings will be preferred to a version made under the authority of a foreign government. The adoption of a national translation would stamp upon this country a character not only of independence, but of proper self-respect." Du Ponceau also suggested a preface should be appended on the superiority of the Septuagint over the "corrupted Hebrew copies"!

Luckily for the future sanity of American scholarship and religion, this proposal was never taken up. However, it is apparent that some sort of preface to the work (not necessarily following Du Ponceau's outline or embodying the romantic version Watson urged) would have aided the dismal sale of the books, for Thomson's *Holy Bible* "did not receive . . . its proper pecuniary reimbursement."[19] In fact, Ebenezer Hazard, Thomson's partner in the publishing venture, soon bought out the edition; it was stored in his garret and finally sold for waste paper after Hazard's death. Thus most of the copies were destroyed. Hazard, who had been Postmaster General, 1782–89, was probably disappointed at the whole affair, and was not associated with Thomson's *Synopsis* of 1815.

Throughout the years Charles Thomson's *Holy Bible* has fared little better than it did in its initial sale. It has been mentioned from time to time by scholars, but only occasionally has it aroused much interest, and then under unusual circumstances. For example, only brief mention was made of Thomson as a biblical scholar in 1844, when there appeared another rendering of the Septuagint.[20] This second translation was by Sir Lancelot Charles Lee Brenton, whose Rhode Island-born father, Jahleel Brenton, had been an admiral in the British navy. Brenton had heard of Thomson's efforts, finished four decades earlier, but failed to make any real use of them in his work.

Brenton's preface sees real values in the Septuagint and makes the interesting suggestion that it might be used as a textbook for children in place of classical authors. His reference to Thomson is found in the preface's next to the last paragraph: "In the notes also, though very rarely, there appears the name of Thomson, the American translator. The writer has himself never seen that work, but some alterations and improvements were made from it by a friend (Mr. Charles Pridham) who had the opportunity of comparing the two. . . . While thus acknowledging our obligations to Thomson, we are of course not likely to speak slightingly of his work. If there are faults, they are probably those of a vigorous and independent mind, better fitted to engage in original attempts than to submit to the drudgery of translation."[21]

About sixty years later Thomson again came into the limelight when an Englishman, S. F. Pells, stumbled across his Bible. "Stumbled" is the proper word, for he happened quite by accident upon the Thomson Bible in a secondhand bookshop. Pells himself had long been interested in biblical matters and had worked out an elaborate study on Hades.[22] He was also a man convinced that the traditional Hebrew (Masoretic) text had been utterly corrupted by Jews who opposed Christianity. In his opinion, the Septuagint and the Peshitta—respectively, the Greek and Syriac translations of the Old Testament made, he assumed, before this Jewish corruption set in—and the Vulgate, the Latin translation of the Septuagint, preserved the original meanings. The Greek Old Testament, therefore, and not the Hebrew, is the church's real Bible. Pells stated that Christ himself had been instructed as a child in the Septuagint and that He and the early church constantly used this Greek version as their Bible. Hence, he held, English translations should be made from the Septuagint, not the Hebrew.[23]

Pells had studied Brenton's translation but apparently was little attracted to it. Just as he was completing his study on Hades, he discovered the Thomson Bible. He was, of course, delighted to see that there were so many references to Hades in the American's version. He was also delighted to discover that Thomson had had such an illustrious, romantic career. He conceived the idea of republishing the Thomson Old Testament, incorporating a few references to Thomson into his own book on Hades, and publishing both at the same time. By the summer of 1903 he had these projects ready for the printer.

There is one other bit of unusual background. Six years earlier Pells's wife had died. Her death gave him the means and the time for such literary work. He himself was greatly impressed at the way he had discovered Thomson. Pells wrote: "Is it to be wondered at, then, having just finished my work on "Hades," and believing that it contained . . . a great discovery, that I should ask myself the question—How came this unknown and very scarce copy of the First English Translation of the Septuagint into my hands in which the word 'Hades' occurs so frequently?" He was also amazed at the fact that a letter from a friend encouraging him to go ahead with his publications arrived "on the 5th of January, 1903, the sixth anniversary of [his] widowhood, being the very last day of the *seventy-second* month, the same as that sacred number that the original *seventy-two* translators had remarked on when they had finished their translation [of the Septuagint from Hebrew] in exactly the same number of days." In this sacred arithmetic, S. F. Pells saw the hand of God.

And so in 1904 there appeared from the presses first *Hades,* the treatise on the place of the dead, to which an appendix on the Septuagint and Christ's use of it was added, and secondly, a reprint of the Thomson Old Testament. This was the first time Thomson's Bible had been printed since 1808, and a lengthy preface was added, setting forth many of Pells's views on the Septuagint. In the years which followed, Pells became more opinionated, and when he republished the Thomson translation of the Septuagint in 1907 an even longer preface was added. The prospectus for this edition, a sixteen-page pamphlet, describes the Thomson Old Testament as "The Septuagint in English, the Bible used by our Saviour and the Apostles, Used in the Churches of England for a thousand years—First English translation." By these and other means Pells tried mightily to organize a society to spread his views on the Septuagint. The Archbishop of Canterbury, who had commented favorably on the 1904 edition, was approached to aid in the scheme but, diplomatically perhaps, found himself too busy with an Education Bill to be concerned with a matter relating to business affairs. The Septuagint, nonetheless, was described in glowing terms by Pells's prospectus:

> It was the Bible used by Christ and the writers of the New Testament . . . it would be altogether improbable to suggest that each writer of the New Testament translated direct from the Hebrew.
>
> Our ordinary Bible . . . is taken from the Hebrew, but not from the same text as the Septuagint was translated from. The original is considered by scholars to be irretrievably lost or destroyed, and the only Hebrew now extant is none other than the Bible of the spurious Messiah, Bar Cochiba—a new text made in the second century by the Jews out of opposition to Christianity. . . . [This Hebrew text] was never the Bible of the Christian Church, and

never can be by right, but must remain a corrupted text made by the enemies of Christ.

Pells then goes on to make the most boastful claims ever advanced for Thomson's translation of the Septuagint.

The reviews on the Thomson Bible and even on the editor's preface were generally favorable. The *Expository Times* and *The Jewish Quarterly Review* duly noted the volumes. The Church of England *Pulpit and Ecclesiastical Review* (May 4, 1907) objected only to the "prohibitory cost." The Glasgow *Herald* explained of the second edition on January 24, 1907: "within the last two or three years the editor has acquired a vastly increased sense of the importance of the Septuagint, and consequently of this translation which he has taken under his wing. . . . Now . . . he maintains that . . . the Hebrew text is 'one that Christ would certainly have repudiated, and against which the blood of the martyrs crieth out,' and that the great Bible Societies of Britain and America are sapping the foundations of Divine truth . . . [with] the adulterated text of Rabbi Akiba."

In spite of such vigorous statements, Pells was never able to form the society he dreamed of; nonetheless he kept on championing the Septuagint. *The Church's Ancient Bible,* a book published privately by Pells sometime after 1911, is the strongest and most detailed presentation of his cause. Believing "the day is gone by for any . . . attempt to defend the Masoretic Text" against "the altogether superior claims of the Septuagint," he was especially angered at "that Great Octopus," The British and Foreign Bible Society, which ignored the Septuagint. To those who desired "a more authentic Bible than our Authorized Version or the New Revision [English Revised Version, 1881–85]," he wholeheartedly recommended "the excellent English translation of the Septuagint made by Charles Thomson." He even suggested ecumenically that if Protestants adopted such a Bible or one based on the Syriac Peshitta, then there would be "a better prospect of a reunion of the Churches," since there is but little difference between the three Bibles of Christendom, the Septuagint of the Greek Church, the Old Latin used by Rome, and the Syriac Peshitta, to be adopted by the Protestants.[24] For the time being, Thomson's English translation of the Septuagint should be used.

The final plea of the book is pathetic in its sincerity: "I am an old man, and am the sole proprietor of this admittedly beautiful reprint edition of Thomson's . . . which I should be only too pleased to hand over to a Committee, or Syndicate, if such could be formed. . . . This opportunity therefore may not occur again. . . . Consequently, unless a patron . . . comes forward . . . there is every probability that it will again return to that oblivion which unfortunately befell Thomson's first edition!"[25] Yet in spite of the valiant efforts of S. F. Pells, Thomson's *Holy Bible*, 1808, did sink back into oblivion. And perhaps, in this case, it was just as well, for while the patriot-scholar of Philadelphia had a strong and vigorous mind of great independence, there is something incongruous in linking his translation with the extremely partisan views of Mr. Pells. The Thomson Bible deserved a better fate than becoming a foil in the quarrel over the merits of Greek versus Masoretic texts, or theories about Hades.

That history can repeat itself in some ways is suggested by the fact that another reprint of Thomson's Septuagint appeared in 1954.[26] The editor, C. A. Muses, has subtitled his reprint, "The Oldest Version of the Old Testament," a claim which is certainly true if one recalls the technical sense of the word "version," i.e., that the Septuagint is the oldest translation of an original Hebrew text. Some of the advertising for the reprint has been extreme in its claims as when it states that here is the Bible which Jesus used, for example, in his discussion of Scripture in the Temple as a boy of twelve. It is a fact that many of the gospel citations of the Old Testament follow the Septuagint form rather than that of the Hebrew Masoretic text, but this evidence scarcely proves that Jesus quoted the Greek form rather than the Hebrew. Use of the Septuagint by the evangelists might simply have been an accommodation for their Greek readers. What is more, practice varies among the evangelists. While Luke regularly quotes the Septuagint, Matthew gives his numerous Old Testament citations sometimes in the Hebraic form, sometimes in the Septuagintal, and sometimes in a sort of free composite. In the interest of enhancing this reprint of Thomson, a complicated matter has been misleadingly simplified. The 1954 editor also shows a preference in his introduction for accepting the Aristeas legend and has ventured to change Thomson's original punctuation, paragraphings, and spellings of certain proper names. He has also undertaken to insert some corrections made in Thomson's hand in his personal desk copy now preserved by the Library Company of Philadelphia, though Muses has rejected the change from "Lord" to "Jehovah" which Thomson seems to have adopted in his own notations. Finally Muses has added the Septuagint's additions to the Book of Esther which Thomson chose to omit from his translation. Readers should thus be warned that the 1954 reprint is not "pure Thomson" at many points. Reviewers have criticized certain features of the volume and even the fact that it was done at all.[27]

In the face of all this, what can be said of the values of *The Holy Bible, 1808?* Perhaps it is fairest simply to quote what some men have written who came in contact with the Thomson Bible. In 1824 Orme's *Bibliotheca Biblica* said of the translation: "This transatlantic work is creditable to America and to the learned author. It is the only English version of the Septuagint, and is therefore worthy of attention, as well as for the fidelity with which it is executed. The New Testament contains many improved renderings and improvements."[28] An interesting summary of Thomson's work was given in 1839 by Thomas Hartwell Horne, a British commentator: ". . . upon the whole, faithfully executed. . . . The translation of the New Testament is much improved . . . in the arrangement of the objections and replies that occasion such frequent transitions in St. Paul's Epistles."[29]

Dr. Francis Bowen, of Harvard University, has offered a striking comment contrasting the work of the scholars on the Revised Version of 1881–85 with that of Thomson: "This solitary and unaided scholar . . . living in what might have been viewed from the English standpoint as a small provincial city, having at his disposal none of the rich means and appliances of scholarship which were collected in the Jerusalem chamber of Westminster Abbey, and in fact probably possessing hardly any books available for his purpose except an English Bible and a copy of the Textus Receptus of the Greek New Testament and Septuagint, has yet produced a work which may well challenge comparison with the best results of the united labors, during the last ten years, of two companies containing thirty or forty of the best scholars in England and America."[30]

One thing is surely clear; the "perpetual secretary" of the Continental Congress who had patiently "minuted the birth-records of a nation" also wielded an industrious pen in the service of his God, and Charles Thomson of Harriton, the Irish lad who became a business success and political hero, found an uncommon hobby for a layman, that of biblical scholar. He stands without equal in the parade of Bible translators.

Six

The "Manuscript Detective":
Constantin Tischendorf (1815—1874)
and Bible Translation

BIBLICAL SCHOLARSHIP AND DETECTIVE FICTION WOULD SEEM to have nothing in common. True, some theologians do like to read detective stories. H. Wheeler Robinson, the famed Old Testament expert at Oxford, was, for example, once reproached by a clerk in a country bookstore, where the professor (who was on holiday) couldn't find a single "who done it" which he hadn't read; the girl made the retort that it would do him good to read something a little more serious![1] Perhaps theological professors simply enjoy relaxing with a good story like the rest of us, or perhaps, as some people darkly allege, they like detective stories because there virtue always triumphs (or at least with more regularity than in daily life) and the "goodies" overcome the "baddies." At that point, though, they may merely share a prejudice with many a nontheologian who likes detective stories or is a "Westerns" fan.

It is a curious fact, however, that several ranking theologians and biblical scholars have tried their hand at writing detective fiction. Dorothy Sayres comes immediately to mind. No mean lay theologian, she initially achieved fame with her stories about that peerless amateur detective, Lord Peter Wimsey. It can even be argued that there is a continuity to her work, from the Lord

Peter novels to her Christian apologetics, and that *Gaudy Night* is but a step toward *The Mind of the Maker*.[2] M. R. James, editor of the New Testament apocrypha in English, once compiled an anthology of ghost stories, and H. H. Farmer, the Cambridge philosopher-theologian, has reflected in one of his lectures his interest in tales of the uncanny. From among the ranks of biblical translators, it is well known that Ronald Knox published several detective thrillers. Less known is the fact that E. J. Goodspeed once published a novel with the intriguing title, *The Curse in the Colophon*.[3] It may not be the greatest suspense novel in terms of plot, but it does provide a pleasant way of learning a great deal about text criticism.

On a deeper level, though, there is a certain affinity between biblical scholarship and detective work. Each depends on evidence, deduction, and logic. Each starts from certain clues— some words, an artifact, a report—there is a problem or a question. Further clues must then be patiently unearthed through searching, intuition, or careful reconstruction. Then a theory must be developed to explain all the facts, and that theory, in turn, must be investigated to the hilt, for it must stand up in the court of inquiry. In terms of biblical scholarship, in examples we have seen: the Septuagint rendering of a Hebrew word, Luther's view on "repentance" or "the righteousness of God," Akiba's hermeneutics as practiced by Aquila, or the reconstructions of Origen's text—all these exist for other investigators to consider and to accept or reject. In a sense, with Bible translations, the reader is ultimately the judge, and by his reactions a verdict is constantly being rendered.

Besides these comparisons in matters of methodology, there exists in some cases an even closer parallel to detective work in the almost romantic adventures of certain scholars. Their investigations and discoveries have an aura of excitement about them and are often quite as intriguing as mystery fiction. This is especially so with regard to the unending accounts of how biblical manuscripts have been discovered (and still are being found, for significant discoveries are being made in our own day in caves near the Dead Sea and in burial grounds along the Nile). Some incidents here even sound a bit like a Perry Mason case.

No one fits better into this category and is more deserving of the title "manuscript detective" for the Bible than an amazing German scholar, Constantin Tischendorf, whose career was at its height exactly a century ago. As we so easily read the pages of the New English Bible, the Revised Standard Version, or any other recent translation, we should occasionally pause in thanks for the labor of Tischendorf and men like him who have pushed back the centuries, to bring the text of our Scriptures ever more close to what was originally written. For no translation is ever better than the Greek (or Hebrew) text on which it is based. Hence the genuine contribution of these "manuscript detectives" who ferret out ancient copies of Scripture.

Outwardly, Tischendorf's career seems serene. An encyclopedia might list, "Lobegott [Aenotheus or "Praise-God"] Friedrich Constantin von Tischendorf, 1815–74, Evangelical-Lutheran, New Testament textual critic," and then trace out his course of honors, from early schooling in the classics to appointment as a lecturer on the faculty of theology at Leipzig, then as associate and finally regular professor there.

But actually most of Tischendorf's life was spent in rigorous travels seeking manuscripts and then in painstaking work publishing them. No ivory-tower recluse, he spent much of twenty years, from 1840 to 1860, roughing it in remote parts of the world. His work might be said to center about three particular cases, "The Hidden Writing," "The Guarded Codex," and "The Missing Manuscript." In helping solve them he strengthened Christian faith for many people.

Tischendorf was a physician's son from Lengenfeld, south of Leipzig, and as a youth received a sound training in Latin and Greek in the gymnasium at Plauen. While studying theology at the University of Leipzig from 1834 to 1838, young Tischendorf worked particularly under Johann G. B. Winer, a famous New

Testament grammarian whose treatise on biblical idioms was standard reading for students in Germany, England, and America for three-quarters of a century. Winer interested his student in work on reconstructing a better, more ancient text of the New Testament, on the basis of the increasing manuscript material then coming to light. Luther and the King James translators had made their renderings from a small group of late manuscripts. By 1840, however, manuscripts far better (because they were older) than these medieval ones were available. There was in London *Codex Alexandrinus,* written in fifth-century Egypt, given to the king of England in 1627 (sixteen years too late to help the King James translators). Another codex in the Vatican at Rome, called *Vaticanus* or "Manuscript B," was believed to be even more ancient, but it was little known because papal authorities jealously guarded it. Two were in Paris which called for closer study, though the faded, hidden writing of the one defied all efforts to read it. Wettstein and his successors had done yeoman service, but much remained to be accomplished. Tischendorf, when he was given permission to lecture at the university in 1840, determined to apply himself to examining just such manuscripts in an effort to arrive at the oldest possible text. He was in part influenced too by Karl Lachmann, Professor of Classical Philology at Berlin, who in 1831 began to publish his reconstruction of the Greek New Testament as it stood in the fourth century A.D., based solely on the evidence of ancient manuscripts, quite apart from the traditional Received Text of later centuries.

Such an attempt as Tischendorf now undertook was not just purely academic, "scholarship for the scholars' sake," but intensely practical for everyday Christians. In 1835–36 David Friedrich Strauss had published his *Life of Jesus* in which he dismissed much of the gospel narratives as made-up myths, "fish stories" that never happened. Bruno Bauer, in the very year 1840, began to bring out his opinions that "the original gospel" did not appear until the early second century and that Paul's epistles were forged about A.D. 170. The views of F. C. Baur, of

Tübingen, were immensely influential; he held that only Galatians, Corinthians, and Romans were genuine, the rest of "Paul's" letters second-century forgeries. In the face of this situation, more orthodox Christian scholarship had to devote itself to demonstrating the authenticity and basically first-century date for the New Testament documents. This could be done only by laborious examination of ancient manuscripts and the establishing of a more sure text. To the chore Tischendorf gave himself. He wrote to his fiancée, "I am confronted with a sacred task, the struggle to regain the original form of the New Testament."

At the age of twenty-five, armed with a meager grant from the Saxony government and additional money from his brother, Tischendorf set out on October 30, 1840, for Paris where he was to spend three years from 1840 to 1843 and solve brilliantly "the case of the hidden writing." At the National Library the young German examined in detail the pages of a number of manuscripts and prepared the contents for publication, including an important copy of the letters of Paul written in both Greek and Latin during the sixth century. This bilingual manuscript had been in a monastery at Clermont, France. The religious wars of the sixteenth century had brought it into the hands of the scholar-reformer Beza. Now Tischendorf's work made its contents available for all. But when he turned his attention to the other important manuscript known to be there, his efforts met with a smile of derision.

For "Codex C" was a palimpsest, a manuscript in book (codex) form which had been "scraped again" for use a second time. Originally in fifth-century Egypt the Old and New Testaments had been copied onto its pages. Corrections were made in the sixth century and the ninth, but by the twelfth its letters must have been rather faded. The librarian of some monastery, short on writing materials and having evidently many "better" (for him, more recent) copies of Scripture, erased the biblical text and wrote over the pages some sermons by a Syrian saint named Ephraem. Thus the manuscript, scraped and reused, became a palimpsest. How precious would the fifth-century Bible text be, if it could be recovered! But great scholars like Wettstein and Griesbach had tried and given up. The director of the library, Capperonier, believed no one would ever read Codex C. Six years before, an attempt to bring out the faded, hidden letters by use of Gioberti tincture (made with magnesite) had done nothing but spoil the manuscript.

Tischendorf was armed only with extraordinarily sharp eyes and patience. He diligently worked over the pages until he recovered the fifth-century "hidden writing" with such accuracy that modern ultraviolet lighting serves only to confirm his work. He was even able to distinguish the original hand from the two later correctors. Tischendorf published his finds in 1843–45, to the admiration of the world. Now the doors of libraries all over Europe were open to him. In London, Oxford, Cambridge, Utrecht, Basel, and half a dozen Italian towns Tischendorf pored over manuscript treasures and set up a program of publishing results, not just from individual Greek manuscripts and Latin ones, but also for comparison of them as the basis for a New Testament text. He went to work also on critical editions of the Greek Old Testament, the New Testament apocrypha and pseudepigrapha (Christian gospels, acts, and epistles not in the New Testament), Philo, and even of Luther's German Bible.

In Rome, 1842, however, he had his first contact with what must be called the least successful of his endeavors, "the case of the guarded codex." Scholars knew that in the Vatican archives rested an extremely important copy of the Old and New Testaments, "Codex B." They knew of it because one professor, J. L. Hug, got a look at it in 1809 when Napoleon carted it off to France as war booty. But now the manuscript was locked away at Rome, and permission to examine it was very difficult to obtain, in spite of the pope's personal good will toward Tischendorf. The explanation lay not merely in a Roman Catholic hostility then toward Protestant emphasis on Scripture or in rivalry among scholars of different nations, but even more in the fact that Angelo Cardinal Mai had prepared an edition of Codex B which was sloppily done and unworthy. Mai had done much important work on unpublished manuscripts, but his examination of Codex B left much to be desired. Mai therefore jealously kept scholars away from the original, lest his poor workmanship be known. In spite of letters of introduction and a kindly reception by Pope Gregory XVI, Tischendorf found he was allowed to see Codex B for only six hours spread over two days, and that under close supervision. Another scholar spent five months in Rome and did not even get permission to examine it at all. The codex remained guarded.

Later in his life, full of subsequent successes, Tischendorf returned to Rome to try again. In 1866 he was allowed to spend three hours daily for fourteen days (seven times as long as before), but still it was an impossibly brief time to go over 390 pages. The best he could do was copy quick notes and memorize the beginning of lines on some twenty pages and in that way reconstruct a portion of "the guarded manuscript." Tischendorf's work, however, was probably more accurate than any editions put out by Vatican scholars until a photographic reproduction was issued in 1889–90. Is it too much to say that Tischendorf's persistent interest and exacting standards helped bring about this solution, so that Codex B is today available for anyone to study?

Tischendorf's most adventuresome work, however, concerns "the missing manuscript." Between 1844 and 1860 he made three trips to the Near East, searching out old manuscripts. This was a period when travel in Egypt, Palestine, or Greece was just as dangerous as a trip to America's "Wild West." The East was infested with bandits and disease, and had little of "European civilization." At this time Robert Curzon was just beginning his similar searches for ancient manuscripts and art described so vividly in a book called *Visits to Monasteries in the Levant*

(1849).⁴ Schliemann, the Lutheran minister's son from Mecklen-
burg, who was later to rediscover Troy, was in 1858 making
hazardous explorations in Arabia. Tattam and Cureton were in
this very period securing and cataloging important manuscripts
from the Coptic monasteries in the Nitrian desert, west of the
mouths of the Nile, toward Libya. Later in the century, two
amazing sisters from Cambridge, Mrs. Lewis and Mrs. Gibson,
were to make their way to Cairo and the Arabian desert where
they discovered Syriac manuscripts of enduring significance.
Such was the world when Tischendorf thrice made expeditions
to Mt. Sinai in search of an elusive manuscript treasure.

He set out first in 1844 following his Paris success and his
initial experience in Rome, to seek "blessing for the church, for
science, and for fatherland"—for those were days of rivalry
among scholars of different nationalities. The Orthodox monastery of St. Catharine on Mt. Sinai in the Arabian peninsula was
his particular goal. Here, on the spot where, tradition said, Moses
saw the Burning Bush and received the Law, the Christian
emperor Justinian had built a monastery about 530. It bore the
name of St. Catharine of Alexandria, greatly revered in medieval
piety because she spurned a pagan Roman emperor and over-
came the heathen philosophers in debate before being martyred.
Legend has it that her body was borne by angels to this site on
Sinai. Here in this mountain retreat, at one of Christendom's
oldest monasteries, might well be important finds for the "Bible
detective."

Hoping for great discoveries at Sinai, Tischendorf ventured
the twelve-day trek on camel-back from Cairo. The small cara-
van moved daily from dawn till ten A.M., and five P.M. till eleven
o'clock, resting during the heat of the day. There was no Suez
Canal as yet, and the party crossed the Red Sea near where the
children of Israel had centuries before. At last the fortress-like
monastery loomed ahead. It had a minaret atop one tower, built
hundreds of years earlier to make the Moslems think St. Catharine's was a mosque and leave it unmolested. High walls pro-

tected the monks, and there was no gate. Messages could be sent
inside via a basket dropped from an opening thirty-five feet
above the ground, Tischendorf discovered, and when his papers
were found to be in order, a stronger rope with a crossbar was
lowered for him. Clutching this, Tischendorf was hauled by a
windlass into the strange world of St. Catharine's. The scholar's
life is not always an easy one! Since disaster as well as achievement might come at any time, he needed the sort of faith of
which he wrote in a letter home: "Should I succumb . . . I
should quickly find, instead of the empty grave, the Hero of the
Easter Morn."

About life in the monastery little need be said. Tischendorf
found it "a burned-out crater," devoid of scholarly attainment
or religious zeal. The Rule of St. Basil commanded "No wine,"
but the brothers, typically, reasoned this did not cover liquors, so
they specialized in a type of palm brandy called *araki*. The
traveler complained of the monks, in spite of their endless
liturgies: "I should be doing a good deed if I threw this rabble
over the walls. It is sad to see how man carries his baseness and
wretchedness into the lofty grandeur of this mountain world."

And manuscripts? There were some of interest in the ill-kept
library room, but none of the New Testament, much to Tischendorf's dismay. As he was about to leave, however, he saw a huge
wastepaper basket filled with scraps of books of all sorts. Cyril
the librarian explained, "Lately that basket has twice been filled
with such rubbish, but we have thrown it all into the fire so as to
get it out of our way." The scholar's sharp eye, however, caught
sight of a number of larger pages with Greek writing amid the
"rubbish," and quick examination showed they were from an
ancient manuscript of the Old Testament.

There was no trouble in getting permission to take along
forty-three pages once destined for the fire, loose parchment
leaves which lay together, but eighty-six other pages which
belonged with these the abbot refused to give. Tischendorf noted
their contents and urged the monks to take good care of them,

and set out with the forty-three pages he did have. Back in
Leipzig he ascertained they had been written in the fourth
century, a hundred years before even the Alexandrinus manuscript, and he published them as *Codex Friderico-Augustanus*
in honor of the king of Saxony. He did not indicate, however,
where he had come across the find, lest a rival, from the British
Museum, for example, might go to Mt. Sinai and secure the pages
still there. A good detective conceals his source for information,
and Tischendorf himself hoped to get more of the manuscript
from St. Catharine's for study by the Christian world.

Cherishing this hope, he made a second oriental journey in
1853, again to the monastery at Sinai. This time, however, he
not only failed to secure those elusive eighty-six pages but discovered that they could not be located anywhere. Even Cyril
did not know what had become of them. The frustrated scholar
was convinced that the librarian and the others were telling the
truth. No one knew where the eighty-six sheets were. Now
there was a mystery of a missing manuscript, and Tischendorf,
after a thorough search of the library, could only conjecture that
some traveler to St. Catharine's in the past nine years had
acquired the pages and would publish them in time. The sole
reward of this journey was a tiny scrap of Genesis 23, just eleven
lines long, being used as a bookmarker for a volume on the lives
of the saints. He now published the fact that he had discovered
the forty-three pages at Sinai and saved eighty-six others from
the fire in 1844, thus making his claim to be original discoverer
—and then he held his breath, waiting for "Mr. X" to publish
those missing pages. But no one did.

Finally, in 1859, Tischendorf set out on a third and final journey to Mt. Sinai. He was unable to rest at the thought of those
missing pages, perhaps somewhere in possession of monks who
might kindle fires with such treasures. This time he went under
the auspices of the Russian government, a great advantage since
the Czar was looked upon as secular head and protector by all
Eastern Orthodox Christians. The monks at St. Catharine's

welcomed the aging scholar all the more therefore. But they knew nothing of the missing pages, nor did thorough search reveal a thing. Accordingly the order was given to have camels ready to depart on February seventh.

Two days before this date, Tischendorf climbed to the summit of the Mount of Moses for a final look over the beloved country-side, yet with heavy heart, for his quest had failed and he knew that health would never permit him to visit Sinai again. On the last day he visited the plain where the Israelites were supposed to have stood when the Law was given. His companion was a monk from Athens who served as *oikonomos* or steward at the monastery and who grasped something of what Tischendorf had spent his life doing. At dusk, on return to the monastery, the dejected German wanted to retire to his room, but the monk persuaded him to come to his cell for food and more talk. Perhaps inspired by all their conversation of the day, he volunteered, "I also have a Greek Old Testament here in my cell. I will show it to you," and brought forth a large manuscript tied in a red cloth.

When Tischendorf untied the knots he found parchment sheets, four columns to the page, from the same hand he learned to know fifteen years before. Here were not only the missing 86 pages, but 112 more of the Old Testament, plus the New Testament, and to his utter amazement two other early Christian writings: the Epistle of Barnabas, known previously only through a very poor Latin translation, and "The Shepherd" of Hermas, a second-century composition, only the title of which had been known before. The persistent detective efforts had met success at the last, unexpected moment.

What now to do? To protest too much about "value for scholarship" might make the monks cling all the more tightly to the manuscript. First Tischendorf, trying to hide his excite-ment, asked to take the codex to his cell—and then sat up all night, by candlelight, in icy cold, copying Barnabas! Who could sleep under such circumstances? Next he asked to buy the book as a gift to the Russian Czar, but his offer of money was refused. Then he sought permission to take it to Cairo for copying at a monastery of the same order, but one monk, the keeper of the altar plate, objected. (It turned out that, after Tischendorf's visit in 1844, the bulk of the manuscript was located in this man's storeroom under some church furniture, and the eighty-six pages were put there too, so that in 1853, truthfully, they were not in the library, and no one could remember what had become of those "missing pages"!) His objection could be overruled only by an order from the abbot, who, as luck would have it, was in Cairo. Tischendorf made the twelve-day trip in seven, secured permission, and swift Bedouin messengers had the precious book in Cairo in another twelve days. Here at Hôtel des Pyramides Tischendorf enlisted the services of two Germans who knew Greek, a druggist and a bookseller (or doctor, according to some accounts), and in two months they transcribed 110,000 lines.

The story is involved after that. Tischendorf made a number of hurried trips to get Russian authorities to regularize possession of the manuscript and reward the monks. Finally it was arranged, by 1869, that the codex remain as a gift with the Czar and be placed in the library at St. Petersburg (today, Leningrad); in return, the Czar favored the monastery in an ecclesiastical election and bestowed lavish gifts on it. There has been great debate over the years concerning the precise role which Tischendorf played in these long negotiations and concerning the legal ground on which he stood at times. Enemies have charged him with robbing the poor monks at Sinai of a priceless possession for a pittance. Friends have written that he acted with scrupulous honesty throughout an involved situation. The debate has gone on till the present day. In 1960, for example, a scholar in East Germany located and published for the first time a copy of a receipt from Tischendorf to the monks, preserved in the Leipzig archives at the university where Tischendorf had taught.[5] Written in black ink on yellow copy paper, it reads:

I, the undersigned, Const. Tisch., sent to the Orient on a commission of Alexander, Czar of all the Russias, testify through this document that the Protosyngelos of the monastery at Sinai, Mar Agathangelos, together with his brothers, gave me, for the purpose of reading and study, an old manuscript of both testaments, containing 346—three-hundred forty-six—leaves and a small fragment, a possession of the same monastery, and I give my word that after one and a half months I shall return this manuscript complete and unharmed. In confirmation of this promise, the consul-general of Russia has also signed with me.

    C. Tisch.   Lagovosky

In Cairo_____.

The document was presumably written in February of 1859 and represents but the start of the lengthy discussions over disposition of the manuscript. Pastor Lauch, who published this receipt, concludes, after an examination of the whole episode, that there is "nothing against Tischendorf" and that no fault should be found with him. However, in the same year of 1960, during a visit to St. Catharine's at Mt. Sinai, Professor Ihor Ševčenko, of Columbia University, turned up five hitherto unpublished documents dealing with the affair.[6] They were stored in an envelope, in a chest, in the new library of the monastery, and include letters and a draft memorandum from the years 1859 to 1869 or so. The full story is not yet clear, even with these finds, and vital documents which would settle points one way or another are still missing. Tischendorf was forced increasingly to claim *possession* of what certain monks thought was merely *loaned*. It is certain that the whole affair was caught up in contemporary political matters involving the Czar's maneuvers in the Near East, and also in ecclesiastical politics concerning the election of a new archbishop to head the monastery at Sinai. It is clear too that the monks were not completely naïve but possessed considerable shrewdness in negotiating, and that Tischendorf, while not exactly guilty of falsehoods, was vague on some points in his reports (do monastery libraries have wastebaskets? how well does parchment burn?) and on questionable legal grounds on others. But then, in a desert monastery, one can scarcely expect the exactitude of a Philadelphia lawyer. Tischendorf's chief concern seems to have been to secure the manuscript for scholarly purposes, and he himself got caught in a series of events where men not particularly concerned about his professional or personal honor called the decisions. This was, after all, the century in which Lord Elgin removed the marble friezes from the Parthenon at Athens, and consular agents were shipping home all sorts of treasures of antiquity for the British Museum or the Louvre.

Whatever the exact details on the machinations involving the Czar's bureaucracy, the ecclesiastical rivals, and Tischendorf—how many rubles the monastery was promised, how much it received, and who was awarded which Russian decorations—for Tischendorf it was honor enough to edit the manuscript for publication. At great haste he pushed through the task with four large volumes by 1862 for the thousandth anniversary of the Russian monarchy. It was decided that photography, then in its infancy, could not make satisfactory reproduction of the faded letters. To print an exact duplicate, Tischendorf supervised cutting of three different Greek alphabets to match the varied hands (seven varieties of one letter were made!), so as to incorporate precisely the 1,600 corrections made in smaller handwriting on the manuscript. Even the detail of how far one letter is from the next gets exact duplication; thin metal leaves, usually 2,500 to the page, were inserted between letters in the type!

Tischendorf was also able to ascertain that Codex Sinaiticus, as he now named the manuscript from Mt. Sinai, had originally been written about 330–40 and that before it found its way to the monastery there, perhaps as a gift from Justinian himself, it had been corrected at the great Christian center of Caesarea. One note at the end of Esther reports how it was compared with an ancient Christian Bible which was marked by notes from the

hand of Pamphilus, a martyr in the final wave of Roman persecution, who had in turn made use of the magnificent edition
of Scripture prepared at Caesarea by Origen himself. Here was
a veritable "apostolic succession" of scholars, tracing back and
establishing the text in Sinaiticus. To bring the story of this
manuscript up-to-date, it must be added how in 1933 Codex
Sinaiticus made its way to the British Museum (where Tischendorf in 1853 suspected it might end up). The Communist government in Russia had no especial interest in biblical manuscripts
and therefore was willing to sell it for £100,000, some of which
was contributed through the pennies of Sunday School children.
Today, therefore, at the Museum, one may see it in a place of
honor, with Codex Alexandrinus and the Magna Charta. Scholarly study of it still goes on. In 1960, for instance, the results of
one man's study on certain statistical aspects of the manuscript,
such as how many letters appear in each line, were published.[7]

For his accomplishments Tischendorf received many honors.
A special professorship was created in 1859 at Leipzig to recognize his work in biblical paleography. In 1869 he was given the
right to insert the term "von" in his name, the sign of nobility.
After his success at Sinai, von Tischendorf went right on working, however. His definitive edition of the New Testament, based
especially on Sinaiticus, appeared between 1864 and 1872. In the
midst of several projects and on the eve of a trip to the United
States he suffered a stroke in 1874, and after a period of paralysis
died on December 7 at Leipzig, worn out at fifty-nine by his
strenuous, exacting labors. Fittingly the funeral text for the
"Bible detective" who had done so much to recover a more
accurate text for the Scriptures came from Exodus 33:20–23,
when God said to Moses at Sinai, "Behold there is a place by me
where you shall stand upon the rock . . . you shall see my back,
but my face shall not be seen."

Detective stories always have some loose ends to be picked up,
before the "summing up" in the last paragraph. So here. Tischendorf's manuscript projects were taken over and in some cases

completed by an American from Philadelphia, Casper René Gregory, it is interesting to note. A Lutheran who was graduated from Princeton Seminary, Gregory went to Leipzig in 1873 to study under Tischendorf. He remained, after the latter's death, to be pastor for a brief period of the American chapel there and then for the rest of his life a professor. A volunteer in the German army in World War I in spite of his age, Gregory was killed in France. He had, however, written a lengthy introduction to Professor Tischendorf's Greek New Testament and was his "heir" in scholarship.

The life of Tischendorf has often been retold, notably in a little book called *Search on Sinai*[8] by Ludwig Schneller (1858–1953), who was a son of the founder of the famed Syrian Orphanage begun in Jerusalem just over one hundred years ago. Born in Jerusalem, widely traveled in the Middle East, and a well-known writer and mission leader, Ludwig Schneller married Katharina Tischendorf. She, as anyone might guess, was named for the monastery at Sinai, where her father had made his greatest manuscript discovery just prior to her birth.

But what of Constantin Tischendorf's major concern, the text of the New Testament? His contributions here were immense. Tischendorf collated, edited, and published more Greek uncial manuscripts than any other man in history. He edited over twenty editions of the Greek New Testament. These editions fall into distinct phases and exhibit the editor's increasing erudition and growth in critical judgment. His earliest Greek testaments, undertaken during the days of poverty in Paris in the early 1840's for the French publisher F. Didot, provided a Greek text closely approximating that behind the Latin Vulgate, in the so-called *editio catholica* (1842), though in another *editio non catholica* (Paris, and also Leipzig 1841) Tischendorf indicated a preference for other readings, those which occur in the older Greek manuscripts. The later editions exhibit increasing knowledge and mastery of the actual textual evidence. Tischendorf boldly follows what the earliest manuscripts have and not what later tradition made of the readings. Conservative scholars, like the Englishman F. H. A. Scrivener, a man who vigorously defended the traditional text, criticized Tischendorf for departing from it in his mature work, but the tide of scholarship in all lands was on Tischendorf's side. His greatest achievement was perhaps the *editio octava maior* in two volumes, 1869–72. This eighth edition earned a lasting place in New Testament study because of its extensive and careful citation of the Greek variants. It has been reprinted in 1964, and when scholars throughout the world today plan for a definitive edition of the Greek New Testament, incorporating as much evidence as accurately as possible, they speak of it as a "new Tischendorf," in deference to his important achievements as an editor.

By means of all this textual work, Tischendorf sought to be a defender of the essential authenticity, and a supporter of a first-century dating, of the New Testament. True, his discovery of Sinaiticus and work with other manuscripts established the fact that the earliest copies of Mark ended at 16:8—thus the R.S.V. rightly puts 16:9–20, an added ending, in different, smaller type. His research showed that the words "at Ephesus" do not appear in all copies of Ephesians 1:1, and that the words in the King James Bible at John 5:3–4, about an angel troubling the water of the pool Bethesda, are an insertion. Sinaiticus corrects the King James Bible at all these points. But all this was a gain for truth which made the solid reliability of the rest of the New Testament stand forth all the more. To establish this general point, Tischendorf wrote popular little treatises on "Why were our Gospels written?" and "Have we got the genuine writings of the Apostles?" in defense of the faith.

In England study of the New Testament text such as Tischendorf engaged in, in order to refute the claims of the radical critics, came only twenty years later, especially in the efforts of the "Cambridge School," three scholarly churchmen, Westcott, Hort, and Lightfoot. Constantin Tischendorf, in Germany, at an earlier date had seen the same problems and gave himself to the work which helped rebut opinions like those of Strauss, Bauer, and the Tübingen School. Textual criticism thus became a defense of the faith, and when we read our New Testament today with confidence and ease, we should do it with gratitude for such scholars as the "Bible detective," Tischendorf.

Seven

The Twentieth Century
New Testament (1890–1904):

A Company of Amateurs
and Their Bible Translation

TAKE A TELEGRAPH ENGINEER, A CRUSADING JOURNALIST, AND the wife of a Congregationalist minister who has lost his church. Add some Church of England clergymen who can't decide whether they want to remain in holy orders; a twenty-year-old boy, a socialist-minded school teacher who has disowned the doctrines of classical Christianity; an ex-cowboy, and a housewife, the mother of six children, who knows not a word of Greek. Put them together with some two dozen other people of similarly varied background, often just as unstable religiously and politically, and sickly or hypochondriacal, during late Victorian times in England. Let these people correspond and meet occasionally over a dozen or more years. The result is scarcely likely to be a milestone in Bible translation. Yet such is precisely the story of *The Twentieth Century New Testament,* one of the earliest "modern speech" versions, a trailblazing work recently reprinted in paperback,[1] because some think it is one of the most effective translations ever made!

The last decade or so of the nineteenth century, when this New Testament was in the making, was an exciting time in biblical translation work. Tischendorf's adventures had caught the public eye and had brought to the public's consciousness

163

something of the need for Bible revision and fresh translation. So had the papyrus discoveries in Egypt, from which Pastor Adolf Deissmann was able to demonstrate that the language of the evangelists and apostles was no ornate Greek with elaborate literary pretensions, but the language of everyday speech—Greek in "work clothes," not dressed up lavishly or in the styles of a bygone age. Deissmann's discovery led to the obvious conclusion that if this was the style of the Scriptures originally, then the New Testament today also ought to be in everyday language, not in archaic or fancy terminology.

But at this time the King James Version still reigned supreme, even though it was almost three hundred years old. In German, the Luther Bible flourished similarly, though there had been a recent revision, bringing it up-to-date somewhat. Already in 1817, Claus Harms, in publishing at Kiel a new set of Ninety-Five Theses, seeking to awaken the church of his day, had argued that "a translation in a living language must be revised every century if it is to remain alive." By 1867 the New Testament was issued in a "trial revision," and the Old Testament in 1883. Thus an updated Luther Bible was in use.

In England a similar revision of the King James Bible had been made, the English Revised Version, its New Testament appearing in 1881 and the Old Testament in 1885. But the revision was generally conservative in style. Changes were made where the K.J.V. was inconsistent, obscure, or inaccurate according to the older manuscripts then available. But any corrections were put not into the language of the day, but into the language of the seventeenth or sixteenth century. You don't touch up a Gothic cathedral, it was held, with Victorian gingerbread. In fact, if alterations were made, they were put, if not in King James phrases, then in wordings from even *earlier* English translations —as if "Perpendicular" architecture must be patched up only with Norman features, not with modern Gothic. The result was a Bible excellent for study purposes but scarcely for reading. "Strong in Greek, weak in English," was Spurgeon's famous comment.

A few people were experimenting in Britain on their own. For example, Ferrar Fenton, a London businessman, dabbled in Bible translation as a hobby, publishing the New Testament in 1895 and the Old Testament in 1901–03. Fenton claims to have read the New Testament in Greek for some forty years in preparation for his work, and to have seen, as early as 1852, the need for a direct translation which broke with all past endeavors. His results were often amateurish, but Fenton's work was a harbinger of things to come. Such was the situation when *The Twentieth Century New Testament* came to birth.

The woman who set the project in motion was Mrs. Mary Ann Kingsland Higgs, the wife of a Congregationalist minister at Oldham, a mill town northeast of Manchester on the way to Huddersfield. She had four children of her own and was active in church youth work, and later proved herself a pioneer in religious education. The daughter of a Congregationalist minister, she had been educated at Girton, a college for women newly established in 1869 at Hitchin, and transferred to Cambridge only the year before she took her degree in 1874. She was the first woman to receive a science degree there, and she remained as a lecturer at Cambridge until she married at the age of twenty-five. With her husband she then served in various parishes till they found themselves at Oldham. At thirty-four her health broke down (though she recovered and lived until 1937), and at the very time she was beginning the New Testament translation project her husband lost his parish. So her situation scarcely seemed advantageous for launching such an undertaking as a New Testament translation.

In her work with youth, Mrs. Higgs had observed that children did not understand the Authorized Version of the Bible. The E.R.V. was no improvement. Nor did any of the other efforts on the market in the late 1880's satisfy. So she did two things. The one was to begin her own idiomatic translation of Mark, and the other was to write a letter to a magazine, setting forth her plight. Thus, because a mother interested in church work wanted a Bible for children and young people, the adventure of this strange company of translators got under way.

The magazine to which Mrs. Higgs wrote was the *Review of Reviews*, edited by an unusual and dynamic Englishman named William Thomas Stead, the sort of engaging individualist in which the Victorian age seems to abound. About this same time in 1890 Stead had received another letter from a layman on the east coast of England, some sixty miles from Oldham, Ernest de Mérindol Malan. He too complained that the traditional English Bible was difficult for his children to understand in family devotions, and he added that a modern French version he had consulted was far ahead in clarity. Stead brought the two letter-writers into contact, Mrs. Higgs and Malan, and they decided to undertake a translation of Mark in collaboration, and later set their sights on other parts of the New Testament. In 1891 W. T. Stead ran a notice for them in his magazine seeking additional workers to translate the gospels and Acts "into our every-day speech." The aim was a translation for "working men and women, and children of all classes, a version which they could read without difficulty." At first, twenty persons associated themselves with the project, later some fifteen more.

Since the preface to the New Testament which these amateur translators finally completed in 1904 makes no reference to the story of how the project began and is signed simply by "The Translators," with not one of them being named, facts about the company of translators and even their identity are not widely known. Luckily, Malan in 1892 asked for an autobiographical sketch from each participant, and fifteen of them responded. These sketches and other records were deposited in the John Rylands Library, Manchester, in 1933. The late E. J. Goodspeed, himself a Bible translator, had heard of the group's project as early as 1898, and knew of the records in Manchester. However, it remained for Professor Kenneth W. Clark of Duke University to go through the file of material and to publish something about the makers of *The Twentieth Century New Testament* in 1954, on the fiftieth anniversary of the completion of their work.[2]

The catalyst for the project, who brought Mrs. Higgs into contact with the rest of this glorious company of amateurs, was W. T. Stead (1849–1912). He, like Mrs. Higgs, was the child of a Congregationalist clergyman. He entered business first but soon turned to journalism. At thirty-one Stead went to London and became the editor of the *Pall Mall Gazette*, where he made a name for himself by introducing the "interview,"a technique borrowed from America. Articles in the *Gazette* had wide influence and were probably responsible for sending General Gordon on his ill-fated expedition to Khartum. But a series of articles on "Maiden Tribute of Modern Babylon," exposing outrages legally permitted against women and children, written during debate over a proposed amendment of the Criminal Law Act, forced Stead from the newspaper staff and led even to a three-month prison term for "dealing in pornography" in connection with his crusade.

It was on leaving the *Pall Mall Gazette* that Stead in 1890 founded the *Review of Reviews,* in which Mrs. Higgs's letter appeared. Stead was a man of many passions, including psychic research and pacificism (he opposed the British government over the Boer War in 1899), and he wrote sensational-sounding books with titles like *The Truth about Russia* (1888) or *If Christ Came to Chicago* (1893). It was he who brought the *Twentieth Century* translators together, who advised them on business organization, and who in 1897 helped arrange for publication of the work in book form. Stead was to die on April 15, 1912, in the sinking of the *Titanic,* on his way to a peace congress in New York.

The prime mover in the project seems, however, to have been Ernest de Mérindol Malan, the other person to write to Stead. His middle name is a clue to his background. Mérindol is an area in Provence where his family, of Waldensian origin, had dwelled, until expelled from France when the Edict of Nantes was revoked. His grandfather, César Henri Abraham Malan (1787–1864), grew up at Geneva (where the family had settled), was converted to a staunch, rigorous Calvinism, and earned a reputation as a fervent preacher throughout western Europe. He eventually became a member of the Church of Scotland.

His son brought the family more fully into English life. César Jean Salomon Malan (1812–94), who preferred to anglicize his first names to Solomon Caesar, went to Oxford, taught briefly in Calcutta, and then served Church of England parishes in southwest Britain. Solomon Caesar Malan had an enormous reputation as a scholar. He knew twenty-five or thirty languages and is said to have been unrivaled as a linguist in Oriental tongues. He wrote extensively on the Bible and translated books from Russian, Armenian, Arabic, Syriac, Coptic, Ethiopic, Georgian, Chinese, and Japanese. Thus immense linguistic learning and an interest in Bible translation lay in the Malan family tradition. So far as biblical criticism went, however, S. C. Malan was rigidly conservative. In 1882 he attacked the textual theories of Westcott and Hort on the Greek New Testament, and opposed the E.R.V. New Testament of 1881. In fact, he joined with John William Burgon, Dean of Chichester, that champion of lost causes, in assaulting the new revision.

From such a family background, Ernest de Mérindol Malan quite naturally had linguistic and biblical interests, but that he would spearhead a project so radically different from the Authorized Version as *The Twentieth Century New Testament* was to be, is a bit surprising. In 1890 at the time when Malan had found, as Mrs. Higgs did, that the traditional English renderings did not speak to the situation in family devotions and had written Stead about the matter, he was living at Hull. He is described in the autobiographical sketch of 1892, when the translation project started, as thirty-three, a signal and telegraph engineer, the father of four children. He had been educated in England and Switzerland, baptized and confirmed in the Church of England, but was later active in the Congregationalist Church. In Hull he joined the Wesleyan Church. Professor Clark feels that Malan "carried the heaviest burden in the problems of translating, revising, financing and publishing" the

New Testament.[3] He fell ill in 1892 from influenza, brain-fever, and heavy work, and after 1895 was often out of the country on engineering assignments. For whatever the details are worth as sidelights on the man, Malan was a teetotaler from 1888 on, a man out of sympathy with creeds and dogmas (a reaction to the rigorous family Calvinism?), and he says he was greatly influenced by the book *Natural Law in the Spiritual World*, by the Scotsman Henry Drummond, who sought the principle of continuity in things spiritual that scientists were uncovering in the natural world.

Alongside Mrs. Higgs and Ernest Malan, the other participants can be described more briefly. At least three of them were Church of England clergymen of sorts. The Reverend Edward Deacon Girdlestone, sixty-three years of age when the project started, is one of the more important figures, for he helped see the work through to the end and wrote the preface to the completed New Testament. His father was an Anglican clergyman too, but two years after ordination E. D. Girdlestone wanted to leave the ministry. Indecision over his calling marked his entire life. However, marriage to a well-to-do first wife allowed him to "retire" at a young age to a life of writing and occasional tutoring. Most of his published articles had a socialistic slant.

The Reverend Henry Bazett, an Oxford graduate, of Huguenot antecedents, served the Church of England as a schoolmaster in Wales. After a breakdown he went to America where, he said, he read many socialist books. On his return to England, Bazett submitted a letter of resignation to the Bishop of Rochester, and so he could thereafter describe himself as an "ex-curate." He became active in the trade-union movement and for a while worked as a tutor in classics at Cape Town, South Africa, until health again required him to move. He settled near Brighton on England's Channel coast. Bazett already had an interest in translating New Testament books into the language of the day before he responded to the notice in the *Review of Reviews*. He had prepared a version of the Epistle of James which he published privately as *James's Letter: The people's version* (Bexley Heath, 1891).

An interesting example of a Church of England clergyman concerned with the broader problems of the day was the Reverend Edward Bruce Cornford. He had taken a Cambridge degree in theology and then took up medicine. After travel abroad, Cornford did slum work in London, near the Bermondsey docks. Later he read theology under Charles John Vaughan, Dean of Llandaff, a preacher known for his evangelical warmth, who had done commentaries on several epistles. Vaughan also had a reputation for preparing men for ordination—over 450 by his death, men who were known as "Vaughan's Doves." Cornford was thirty years of age when he joined the translation project.

Three other clergymen were Free Churchmen. The Reverend Ernest Hampden-Cook stands out most strikingly, for he seems responsible for the link between *The Twentieth Century New Testament* and another translator of the period, R. F. Weymouth. Hampden-Cook was only thirty-two in 1892 when he joined in the work, but he had already studied at London University, at a Congregational training college, and at Cambridge, and had served parishes in London, New Zealand, and Australia. More strategically for the work he was going to do on New Testament translation, he was from 1891 to 1896, at the time the project was beginning, resident secretary of the Mill Hill School in London, the revered headmaster of which had been R. F. Weymouth. Weymouth was during these years living in retirement, but at work on his own New Testament translation at Brentwood, a town in Essex some twenty miles northeast of London.

It is almost certain that Hampden-Cook was the man who enlisted Weymouth as a consultant on *The Twentieth Century New Testament*. He was close enough to Weymouth to be entrusted by him with seeing his New Testament through the press and even with revising the manuscript and writing the paragraph headings and certain notes. Hampden-Cook seems to have done the similar chore of drafting paragraph headings for *The Twentieth Century New Testament,* and is the person to whom one ought to look in seeking explanation for similarities in format between the two translations. On the strength of a note in the appendix to the *Schaff-Herzog Encyclopedia,* written while Hampden-Cook was still alive, we may name him as one of the translators of the Pauline epistles in the project. "Theologically," the article says of him, "he is a broad Evangelical and believes in three personal advents of Christ, holding that the second took place in 70 A.D., and that there is a third yet to come."[4] This position was developed in a book of his, *The Christ has Come: The Second Advent an Event of the Past,* published in 1894. One wonders, did he have a hand in the interpretative footnote on Mark 13 in the Weymouth New Testament, that "this discourse makes the Parousia coincide with the destruction of Jerusalem (A.D. 70)"?[5]

Another Congregationalist, the Reverend Peter William Darnton, had a slightly different background from Hampden-Cook's. His father was a manufacturer of musical instruments, and at first the son entered the family business. He went to evening school, however, and at twenty-two took up study for the ministry. He reports begrudging time to sermon preparation and that he was a widower with four daughters. The records show him at a church in Bristol in 1903, as the work of revising *The Twentieth Century New Testament* was drawing to completion.

A retired Baptist minister, the Reverend Henry Charles Leonard, played an important role in the project in several ways. W. T. Stead had been given power by the group to nominate a treasurer to serve along with Malan, who was secretary. This treasurer was to handle funds and records for the group, and since none of the participants knew each other save for their correspondence begun through Stead, it was necessary to make the appointment in such a way. Stead chose Leonard, a man from Isleworth, Middlesex, north of London, presumably with time available in retirement. Leonard is known to have had a hand in doing Mark and in trying to make parallel passages in the Synoptics consistent. He also served as one of the revisers, polishing the translation. Leonard experienced much personal adversity during the years he was involved in the project; his wife died in 1895, he lost an eye and suffered from other infirmities. The fact that the 1898 "Tentative Edition" of *The Twentieth Century New Testament* refers to "The Treasurer of the T.C.N.T." at an address in the Clifton section of Bristol suggests that someone else, possibly Darnton, may have been treasurer in later years.

Of the lay people involved, several shared certain characteristic features with the participants thus far described, such as a connection with a parsonage, a tendency toward ill health, or an interest in socialist ideas. W. M. Crook, for example, exhibits all three characteristics. He was the son of an Irish Wesleyan minister; at twenty-one he had to cease his studies for a time for health reasons, and he espoused liberal causes and Home Rule. He was, however, well educated in classics at Trinity College, Dublin, and that equipped him for translation work.

W. M. Copland, educated at Aberdeen, where he read Divinity for a year, was likewise a man troubled by chronic bouts with illness and a man "Radical in Politics and Religion," as he himself put it. He said he had been dissuaded from orthodox Christianity and led to renounce creeds and dogma by reading Isaac Taylor (1787–1865). A lay theologian, Taylor had written *Ancient Christianity* (1839–46) in answer to the *Tracts for the Times,* then appearing from the High Church "Oxford Movement." Taylor argued that fourth-century Christianity could scarcely be considered as embodying the apostolic teaching and practices without pagan corruptions. Copland was moved therefore to reject the Trinity, the immortality of the soul, and a personal Devil as pagan superstitions contrary to scriptural teaching. At the same time Copland held that the Lord Jesus would come back "to put matters right," and he expected that "the present gigantic preparations for war—Russia's designs on the

East, etc." were all foreshadowings of the Second Coming. Copland's interests thus had much in common with those of certain other translators—Stead's interest in Russia and current events, for example, Hampden-Cook's apocalyptic speculations, and the opposition to traditional dogmas expressed by several of the company. Copland was, however, a man with university training and the headmaster of a school, and could make his contribution to the translation project too.

Mrs. Sarah Butterworth Mee, the other woman who joined the company, was the daughter of a Huddersfield wool manufacturer. She was married to a Wesleyan minister, and had borne him six children. Mrs. Mee was active in church affairs, taught Sunday School, and engaged in temperance work. Seven years after she married, her health failed. She had never learned Greek, and so her work was on the committee which was created to review the English of the translation.

A. Ingram, a widower with three children, was a Presbyterian from Aberdeen. His autobiography describes him as having done the jobs of cowboy, grocer, draper, clerk, and journalist between 1880 and 1892.

The "baby" of the group was Thomas Sibley Boulton of Birmingham, just twenty years old when he entered the undertaking. He was an accountant at sixteen, with socialist leanings. At eighteen he experienced a breakdown in health. Boulton reported he was a consistent abstainer from alcohol and tobacco. He later continued studies in language and music, and noted in his autobiography his concern for "a re-union of Christianity."

It will be observed that these profiles of the translators exhibit a certain pattern, but also great variety. Most of the persons resided in the Midlands area, but some of the translators had ties with the European continent, America, Asia, Australia, or South Africa. Age-wise they ranged from twenty to sixty-three, but a number of the leaders were in their early thirties. Religiously they represented the major bodies in the British Isles (excluding Roman Catholics, Unitarians, and Jews) : the Church

of England (though none of High Church leanings), Congregationalist, Methodist, Baptist, Presbyterian, and, if we count one
of the advisers, Friends. Many had shifted from one denomination to another, or shied away from traditional Christianity and
its creeds. Half were clergy, the rest teachers, writers, businessmen, housewives. There were no university professors or ecclesiastical officials, but a good proportion had had university training in a time when that meant a basically classical education.
Most of them had children of their own or had worked with
youth, and there was a broad sympathy for the working classes.
That such a group should undertake a translation of the New
Testament books, let alone produce and agree on results which
are worthwhile, seems the more surprising the more one gets
acquainted with the translators. The usual caricature of staid,
conventional Victorians disappears; actually few periods in history have produced more genuine individualists—some would
say eccentrics—than late nineteenth-century England. Two
"plus factors," however, aided the translation project. These
were the consultants involved and Malan's careful plan for
proceeding.

One of these consultants, R. F. Weymouth, has already been
mentioned in connection with Hampden-Cook. Richard Francis
Weymouth is doubtless better known than any other person involved in *The Twentieth Century New Testament* by virtue of
his own *New Testament in Modern Speech*.[6] A Baptist layman, he
studied classics at London University and took the first doctor of
literature degree ever awarded at that institution in 1868. Pro-
fessionally a teacher, Weymouth became in 1869 headmaster of
Mill Hill, a public (i.e., private) school run by the Noncon-
formists. In the year in which he retired, 1886, Weymouth published a *Resultant Greek Testament*, based on the readings
preferred by Tischendorf and other editors. This was the Greek
text which he then began to render into English. The translation
was complete, at least in rough form, when failing health compelled Weymouth to let Hampden-Cook finish the task. He died

in December, 1902, before the translation was published in 1903. But in the 1890's Weymouth was in a position to advise the *Twentieth Century* company not only as a scholar (his treatise on the translation of Greek verbs in the aorist and perfect tenses came out in 1894), but also as a fellow New Testament translator, certainly a more experienced one than they. But one wonders how much a man in failing health, busy with his own projects, could do for what was almost a rival endeavor during the period from 1895 to 1897, the years we know he was associated with the company of amateurs. At best there was interchange of ideas and suggestions, but scarcely full participation.

A second consultant enlisted was George Gillanders Findlay, Professor of Biblical Literature at Headingley College, Leeds, in the Midlands. This Methodist New Testament scholar was then writing a number of commentaries and a translation of the Fourth Gospel, which he called "John's Good News." In the summer of 1892, Findlay is known to have agreed to revise the committee's translation of John, but in the fall he resigned, and there is no evidence that he helped on even that one book.

Perhaps the most interesting story among the advisers to *The Twentieth Century New Testament* belongs to James Rendel Harris (1852–1941), like Tischendorf a discoverer of manuscripts, and a "Christian rabbi" famed for his learning and Quaker piety. He is known to have been associated with the translation project at least in 1901, though his exact role is uncertain. However, Harris' great scholarship and personal characteristics doubtless influenced the work quite a bit. Born at Plymouth, England, he was originally a Congregationalist. At Cambridge he studied mathematics, but in 1881 experienced "an estrangement from mathematics, and conversion to criticism" of the New Testament.[7] Harris doubted some of the "clear-cut results" which Westcott and Hort claimed, and came to question their extreme reliance on Codex Vaticanus, looking with more favor on the Western Text. All this was a rather forthright stand —particularly for someone in the university where these two masters taught. At Cambridge Harris also became a "convinced Friend."

After a period in the United States and in Holland, Harris gave up a secure professorship he had taken at the University of Leiden to accept the job of director of studies at Woodbrooke, a Quaker center near Birmingham. Later he was curator of the John Rylands Library, Manchester (where the records of the *Twentieth Century* translators were deposited).

Harris' experiences would fill a book. He often visited the Middle East in search of manuscripts or for relief work among the Armenians. On a trip to St. Catharine's monastery at Mt. Sinai in 1889, he followed in Tischendorf's footsteps by finding a Syriac version of the long-lost *Apology* of Aristides from the second century. Later, in a manuscript until then unread, Harris identified the so-called *Psalms of Solomon* and the *Odes of Solomon,* works of mystical character from early Christian times. He survived torpedoing of the ship on which he was sailing to Egypt in 1915, and on the return trip was on another ship sunk by the Germans. He survived again, but this time only one of six lifeboats made it through an April blizzard. Harris had the experience of watching his traveling-companion, J. H. Moulton, a famed New Testament grammarian,[8] die of exposure and be buried at sea.

During the period of the preparation of *The Twentieth Century New Testament,* Rendel Harris was at Clare College, Cambridge, teaching in the Divinity School, and preaching in the Friends' Meeting House on Jesus Lane. His wide interests and broad sympathies likely encouraged him to give a hearing to the *Twentieth Century* translators. Adolf Deissmann was later to pay him this splendid tribute:

> . . . Cosmopolite,
> Traveller through four Worlds, Odysseus of the Oceans, Guest greatly beloved in the Tents of the Nations;
> In Jesus Lane, in Fifth Avenue, and on the Caravan Routes of the East, ever the same: a Disciple of the Saviour;

. . . Polyglot and Polyhistor, knowing all things, acquainted with
all things, save only Hate:
. . . Virtuoso in Friendship. . . .[9]

What his precise contribution to the translation may have been,
records do not tell. But Harris did dislike the E.R.V. with its
"barbarisms" and "Baboo-English." He also had his own opinions
about the need for "de-clericalization" in English universities
and disliked much about the widely heralded Westcott-Hort-
E.R.V. "establishment."[10] The *Twentieth Century* project must
have had considerable appeal to him.

To whatever extent these consultants may have aided the
translators, the other "plus factor," in the *Twentieth Century*
project, Malan's planning, must have been of equal or greater
importance. As secretary he prepared at regular intervals a series
of circulars and set up a "Word-book" about terms hard to translate, like "gospel," "Christ," and "lord." The Word-book went
the rounds among participants from 1892 on. The second circular, mailed out in December, 1891, outlined a general procedure which is similar to that followed by the 1881 revisers. The
New Testament was parceled out among small groups of three
to five translators. A man did his translation, had it criticized
by his group, then by other groups, and then made his revisions.
For the next step, a Revising Committee was set up, with one
person from each group. This committee could make changes in
a translator's work by a two-thirds vote. Lastly an "English
Committee" examined the results for idiom. A translation might
also circulate outside the company of translators. (Was this the
function of consultants?) The hope for an American committee,
such as advised on the E.R.V., failed to materialize. But Professor
Clark, who has outlined the provisions in some detail, comments,
"Surely no group translation was ever prepared with greater pre-
caution or better safeguards against error or private whims."[11]

Each translator not only worked at his own expense but also
was expected to contribute financially to the undertaking, either
by purchasing shares in the company that was formed or by

giving at least £1 a year. The idea of publishing a "Tentative Edition" before the final one frankly imitates the plan used in revising the Luther Bible in Germany. When the E.R.V. was in process, the Bishop of Worcester had proposed that the 1881 revisers should follow this pattern by allowing their work to circulate experimentally for two or three years. That did not happen with the E.R.V., but the *Twentieth Century* translators felt it would be a helpful step. The device of issuing the translation in parts, as completed (gospels and Acts first, then Paul, then the Pastoral and other epistles and Revelation) paralleled the procedure of Luther with the Old Testament and that of many another translator, including Knox and J. B. Phillips in our day. Part I (1898) sold 40,000 copies in three years. Costs, however, went beyond the money subscribed by the participants. But profits by the end of 1901 allowed for printing of the final, revised edition of 1904. A title for the work was being discussed as early as 1893. Among the suggestions considered were:

> The New Testament in Every-day English
> The New Testament in Modern English
> The New Testament in Current Language
> The New Testament in the English of To-day
> The New Testament: People's Version.

This last title reflects the subtitle which Bazett had used in 1891 for his rendering of James. All the others faithfully express the original purpose of the venture, "every-day speech." Weymouth was to employ the phrase "modern speech." "Modern English" was being used by a translator named Sadler, "current English" as a subtitle by Ferrar Fenton, "modern American" by F. S. Ballentine at Scranton, Pennsylvania. By 1897 Girdlestone's suggestion of "The Twentieth Century New Testament" must have sounded like a natural and was happily adopted.

How well did this disparate company succeed? Certain features will strike anyone who picks up *The Twentieth Century New Testament*. One of them is the unusual order of the canonical books. The gospels run Mark, Matthew, Luke, John, and the epistles are arranged in what is presumed to be their chronological order. Such shuffling may cause trouble for readers, but we must remember that there is nothing sacrosanct about canonical sequence; manuscripts have many different arrangements, and Luther and Moffatt, among others, have not hesitated to make changes with the traditional order.

Leonard, we are told, opposed any footnotes, such as Hampden-Cook wrote for the Weymouth New Testament. His view won out. The only notes in the *Twentieth Century* translation are those to identify quotations. It was a helpful insight to label Old Testament quotations as being from the Hebrew or the Septuagint, where that is significant for Bible study. Citations from classical authors are noted at Acts 17:28, I Corinthians 15:33, and Titus 1:12, though the translators were not yet able to add that at Acts 17:28, in addition to Aratus, a Greek poet named Epimenides is also quoted, from the same poem of his as that at Titus 1:12—a brilliant discovery made by Rendel Harris in 1906.

There are outlines of six points or so for each book, and section summaries printed in bold-face type at the left of certain paragraphs. These same features appear in the Weymouth New Testament, thus suggesting the hand of Ernest Hampden-Cook. The section summaries seem more frequent in Weymouth, and the wording differs in the two. In the "Tentative Edition" of *The Twentieth Century New Testament,* these section summaries appear in only the first of the three parts; even these are revised for the final edition of 1904, where they appear throughout. The major exception to "modern English" is the use of "thou" instead of "you" in prayers to God. At this point the *Twentieth Century* translators combine relevance and reverence.

On textual matters they follow critical views of the day. A verse like Luke 23:34 ("Father, forgive them . . .") is bracketed on textual grounds, as in Westcott and Hort. At Ephesians 1:1, the words "at Ephesus" are rightly put into brackets for the

same reason. In all, fourteen passages are bracketed. Among them
are Luke 22:19*b*–20, 24:12, 36*b*, 40, 51*b*, and 52*a*, all cases
involving Western Text variants, which Rendel Harris was at
that very time helping reassess. Acts 12:25 follows Westcott and
Hort and their "heavenly twins," the manuscripts Sinaiticus and
Vaticanus, in saying Barnabas and Saul returned "*to* Jerusalem"
rather than "*from* Jerusalem," which is read in most other
sources. The problem of the ending for Mark's gospel is handled
as, apparently, in no other English translation. It is recognized
that in the best manuscripts the text ends at 16:8. That verse is
rendered in the *Twentieth Century* translation,

   . . . they were frightened; * * * * * * * *

Then follow "A Late Appendix" (16:9–20) and "Another
Appendix." The asterisks come right out of the Westcott-Hort
Greek edition, but the semicolon is unusual. Seemingly it parallels
the punctuation of Westcott and Hort, suggesting a belief that
the gospel could not have ended so abruptly and that an original
ending must be lost. The whole matter is one to which the translators certainly gave considerable attention; the order of the two
appendices to Mark is reversed in the 1898 and 1904 editions.

The *Twentieth Century* company was aware of other critical
problems besides text. Between Philippians 3:1 and 3:2 they put
not only a space but also a line, since the break is abrupt and some
scholars feel we have fragments of separate letters joined together
at this point. Poetry is arranged in poetic lines. Even the prologue
to John, 1:1–18, is thus set up as poetry. So is the Lord's Prayer.
Certain other prayers are printed in a more narrow column,
indented on both sides.

What, finally, of the translation itself? A detailed study of the
diction in English New Testaments of the period, by Dr. John
Skilton of Westminster Theological Seminary, Philadelphia, has
pointed out a tendency in the *Twentieth Century* version to
paraphrase, inevitable in any translation which seeks to be idiomatic, a certain wordiness (though there is a tendency to avoid
uncommon longish words), a harshness at times, use of some

jaded phrases, and terms which are scarcely from popular language.[12] But there are also many fine passages, vivid renderings, and fresh expressions. Admittedly such phrases as "break my heart," a "deaf ear," "dog their steps," "at death's door," or the description of Luke as "our dear doctor" (Col. 4:13) are cant, but in 1901 and in comparison with the E.R.V. they were like fresh air in a Bible translation. Perhaps it is somewhat erudite to say "the men frapped the ship" (Acts 27:17) or to speak of "vacillating men" (instead of "men of double mind"), "puerile teaching," or of Paul as "this prater" (Acts 17:18), but the translators have often attained striking vividness with phrases like "ringleader" and "public pest" (Acts 24:5). There is something arresting when they refer to judgment at "the Bar of God" (Rom. 14:10), or say that Herod was "trifled with by the Astrologers," or speak of "the priest of Zeus-beyond-the-Walls," (Acts 14:13), as if the temple in front of the gates of Lystra were a counterpart to St. Paul's-outside-the-Walls. One is gripped by the phrase at Hebrews 5:12, "the very alphabet of the Divine Revelation," or by the antithesis of "shadow" and "substance" achieved at Colossians 2:17, a contrast borrowed by the R.S.V. The rendering of "saints" by the phrase "Christ's people" anticipates the New English Bible.

Alliteration occurs: "dulled by debauches or drunkenness" (Luke 21:34), the "Destined Deliverer" (Luke 24:21), "profane prattle" (II Tim. 2:16). A word-play in the Greek of II Thessalonians 3:11 is neatly handled in a phrase about people who, "instead of attending to their own business, are mere busy-bodies." The last word comes out of the Authorized Version; the pun is similar to, but not quite so terse as Moffatt's "not busy, but busy-bodies." There are terms characteristically British—"shilling" and "florin," "gaoler," "barrister," and "corn-measure"—but that is to be expected in a translation into the speech of the people of the British Isles. Certain technical terms are paraphrased; "Pentecost" becomes "the Festival at the close of the Harvest"; "Rulers of the synagogue" are referred to as "presidents." The Greek adjective *aiōnios*, usually rendered "eternal" or "everlasting," caused all sorts of difficulties and comes out as "Immortal Life" and even as "aeonian life."

Theological preferences seem to dictate a few choices, or at least a desire to avoid traditional theological terms. "Grace" is regularly avoided, and there is substituted some word like "loving-kindness," "gift," "blessing," "charge" (I Cor. 3:10), and frequently "love." This latter substitution, whereby *The Twentieth Century New Testament* speaks of "the Throne of Love" (Heb. 4:16) or of the Word as "full of love and truth" (John 1:14), has been paralleled by a modern American translator in his New Testament, William F. Beck.[13] The evangelical outlook of the company of translators comes through in their understanding of "justify" as "to pronounce righteous" (Rom. 3:24). But there is a tendency to tone down "the wrath (of God)" to "God's displeasure" (John 3:36). The rendering of *gnōsis* or "knowledge" at I Timothy 6:20 as "theology" may represent a desire to be contemporary, or perhaps an antitheological bent which some of the translators shared. I think there may also be a bit of Victorian propriety in these verses:

> Luke 1:24   "expecting to become a mother," instead of "Elizabeth conceived" (K.J., R.S.V.).
> John 11:39   "the smell must be offensive," instead of "he stinketh."

The nineteenth century was not the Elizabethan age. Even in America, Noah Webster had begun to revise the 1611 Bible in the interests of more elegant expressions.

For all these less than happy features, however, one is continually struck by the overall level of achievement in *The Twentieth Century New Testament*. In its day it was truly a landmark, and it yet reads well today. It made its mark, far beyond what Ernest Malan, W. T. Stead, or anyone else had a right to expect. There is no finer tribute to it than these words of Professor Clark:

When we read *The Twentieth Century New Testament* in its definitive form, it is difficult to remember that it was produced by so strange a company as we have met. Somewhere along the line, some transforming miracle seems to have occurred. We are forced to conclude that the devotion to their task has made of them better scholars than they were at first. . . . it is amazing to find that the finest scholars of later years paid tribute to their work by adopting many of the same phrases and perceptive insights. . . . under the conditions of half a century ago it was extraordinary.[14]

Philology the *Twentieth Century* company of translators prized; church tradition they cherished somewhat less. But the gift of "some transforming miracle" was theirs.

Eight

Monsignor "Ronnie" Knox (1883–1957):
Roman Catholics and Bible Translation

RONALD KNOX IS PROBABLY THE ONLY BIBLE TRANSLATOR IN history to have his portrait sketched twice by a cover artist for *Time* magazine.

At first glance, a man who achieved fame as a wit and satirist and writer of detective tales does not strike us as a candidate for the exacting role of Bible translator. But this impression begins to change when we learn that Ronald Knox was translating Virgil from Latin at the age of six (and is said to have been making Greek puns at four) and that he was a classicist who took prizes for his work all through Eton and Oxford. When we observe that he earned a reputation as one of the most brilliant English stylists of his day and was hailed as one of the gifted preachers of his time, our opinion is liable to shift even more. And when we discover that Knox carried with him, in his conversion from the Church of England to the Church of Rome, an enduring affection for the Holy Scriptures and that English-speaking Catholicism was ripe for a new translation of the Bible, then it is almost inevitable that Ronald Knox should be expected to turn his hand to rendering the Bible into English.

It is far from certain that future decades of time will concur with the optimistic assessment of *Time* magazine in 1952 that

184

Ronald Knox is "the man who made the great 20th century translation of the Bible,"[1] but it is sure that, for the present, whenever one thinks of Roman Catholic contributions to English Bible translation, the name of Knox comes first to mind. We should be clear, of course, that work by Roman Catholics in Bible scholarship and English translation is by no means limited to the efforts of Ronald Knox, and that perhaps, in view of recent and significant increases in the attention paid to Holy Scripture by English-speaking Roman Catholics, there are factors at work which may well in the long run minimize the import of Knox's work. But for the time being, he provides the popular symbol for his chosen church's contribution to the Bible in English.[2]

In any strict sense, the story of Roman Catholic translation work is virtually synonymous with the tangled fortunes of a single Bible, the Rheims-Douay Version of 1582–1610. There are, of course, reasons for the paucity and delay in Roman Catholic achievements in the world of the English Bible. The use of Latin in public worship worked to exclude the liturgical reason for vernacular translation until recently. The Bible was not in the forefront of Roman Catholic missionary work, education, and piety the way it was with Protestants. On the literary side, English-speaking Roman Catholics labored under certain real disadvantages. Until comparatively recent times in Britain they were, for example, excluded from full rights and privileges in the universities at Oxford and Cambridge and therefore from the literary "establishment." As far as Bibles went, they always had to face the enormous prestige of the King James Version, which was basically a Church of England product, Protestant in its heritage. In America, Roman Catholics suffered from the same disadvantage as Lutherans and certain other groups, the bulk of whose adherents came from non-English-speaking lands on the Continent. It takes a generation and more before such groups can begin even to think of presenting worthwhile translations in English.

The one really significant translation, the Rheims-Douay

Bible, arose in the Post-Reformation period as a Roman Catholic response to the various Protestant Bibles in English. It was prepared by a group of scholars in exile on the Continent because of their religion. Their New Testament was published at Rheims in 1582, and the Old Testament at Douay, Flanders, in 1609–10. The Rheims-Douay Version, as it became known, seems to have carried no episcopal *imprimatur* or papal approval, but it was destined to be the normative translation for English-speaking Roman Catholics. Its English left much to be desired, for the Latin influence was very great. To speak of "our super-substantial bread" in the Lord's Prayer or to employ words like "colinquination," "exprobate," or "scenopegia" is simply not English, and subsequent scholars right down to Ronald Knox have complained of it on this score. Nonetheless, at least the New Testament part did have some influence on the 1611 Bible and strengthened the Latin element there. To a degree, it may be added, Protestant-Catholic controversy gave the Rheims-Douay Version attention which it would not otherwise have had. It is scarcely any wonder, though, that over forty revisions of one sort or another of Rheims-Douay were attempted in succeeding years by Roman Catholics.

One of the most famous was that of Richard Challoner, a priest at Douay, later a bishop, who carried through a revision of the entire Bible between 1749 and 1772. Challoner himself had been born of Presbyterian parents but became a Roman Catholic as a boy. He entered the seminary in Douay at eighteen and remained there in one capacity or another until he was thirty-nine. Though he achieved some fame as a writer of devotional literature later, it may be objected that Challoner lacked the best scholarly training of the day and even the flair for English which would have been cultivated at one of the "Oxbridge" universities or by residence in England itself.[3] Most of Challoner's changes in the Rheims-Douay Version approximate the King James Bible. At points they made Rheims-Douay into a new translation.

A more daring effort was that of a strange, scholarly Scottish priest, Alexander Geddes, who labored in London about the same time that Charles Thomson was working on his Septuagint translation in Philadelphia. Geddes, who was influenced by the rising tide of biblical criticism, had little good to say for the Douay Version and even for Jerome's Latin. He had his doubts about the Masoretic Hebrew text too and regarded it as corrupt. Many were offended by his bold comments and odd translations; he is said once to have translated "Passover" as "Skipover." His "ecumenical" attitude disturbed fellow Catholics. The epitaph he wrote for his tomb in Paddington says, significantly:

Reverend Alexander Geddes, L.L.D.
Translator of the Historical Books
Of the Old Testament,
Died Feb. 26th. 1802
Aged 65.
Christian is my name, and Catholic my surname.
I grant, that you are a Christian, as well as I,
And embrace you as my fellow disciple in Jesus:
And, if you are not a disciple of Jesus,
Still I would embrace you as my fellow Man.

Monsignor Knox, who both deeply opposed the "higher critics" of the Bible and once is said to have remarked in a rather dogmatic *bon mot*, "All the identity discs in heaven are marked R. C.,"[4] would scarcely have appreciated Geddes' denominational broadmindedness or his flirtation with source and form criticism. His contemporaries did not either. Geddes died under censure and without a final Mass. His rudimentary work was not the answer for a Roman Catholic Bible in English.

The most significant revision of Rheims-Douay in the nineteenth century was probably that carried through between 1849 and 1860 by Francis Patrick Kenrick, Bishop of Philadelphia and later Archbishop of Baltimore. He made use of Challoner's several revisions but often reflected an independent judgment of his own. The work was published in sections, as completed, and Kenrick seems to have worked unaided, by himself.

There is for Kenrick's work one interesting connection to England and indirectly to Knox. In 1855 it had been proposed that John Henry Newman, like Knox an Anglican and a brilliant literary figure who had been converted to Rome, should undertake a translation of the Vulgate for Roman Catholics. There was for a time the possibility that Newman would do exactly this, and in 1858 the American bishops urged that Kenrick and Newman should combine forces to produce a single version for English-speaking Roman Catholics. Nothing came of the proposed Newman translation, however, for a variety of reasons, one of which may have been an apprehension that Kenrick's work would be swallowed up by Newman's literary gifts. Accordingly, distinct British and American types of Rheims-Douay Bibles continued to exist. Ronald Knox was, of course, aware of Newman's flirtation with Bible translation, but, ironically, in the period when he was publishing his own translation, the American hierarchy was again involved in a revision of its own of Rheims-Douay-Challoner. Thus in the 1850's and the 1940's both, a common Anglo-American project failed to materialize even in the same Roman Catholic Church.

The American Roman Catholic revision which was beginning in the 1940's is called the "Confraternity Edition," since it was edited under the supervision of the Episcopal Committee of the Confraternity of Christian Doctrine. The New Testament, based on the Vulgate and Rheims-Douay-Challoner, appeared in 1941. But the Old Testament, which began to appear in 1948 and is now nearing completion, reflects the changed outlook endorsed by Pope Pius XII's encyclical of 1943, the *Divino Afflante Spiritu*. The Confraternity Old Testament has taken advantage of certain encouragements to critical scholarship in the encyclical and has used the Hebrew, not the Latin, as its basis. Further, it is a fresh translation, not a revision of Challoner, and employs a thoroughly modern idiom, even "thou" being abandoned. Thus, at the very time Knox was readying his Old Testament for the printer, American Roman Catholic scholars were beginning a project which was vastly different in its approach, and, in its use of Hebrew rather than the Vulgate as the primary source, surely superior on historical grounds.

It is not quite true, however, that Roman Catholic translators were confined to a Latin base for their work until Pope Pius' "liberating" encyclical of 1943. The "Westminster Version"[5] was, with permission, based on the Greek and Hebrew. Work on its New Testament part went on over a period from 1913 to 1935, the results published in small fascicles, and the Old Testament (still in process) was begun in 1934. Father Cuthbert Lattey, S.J. (1877–1954), a man who also aided in the Confraternity New Testament, was the general editor. There was also a translation into modern English, U.S. style, from the Greek New Testament, completed in the 1940's by James A. Kleist, S.J., and Joseph Lilly, C.M.[6] To the list must be added the work of Francis Aloysius Spencer, an Episcopalian who became a Paulist Father and then a Dominican. He published the gospels as translated from Latin in 1898, as translated from Greek in 1901, and finished the entire New Testament from Greek before his death in 1913. Spencer's completed New Testament was finally seen through the press in 1937, and it was reprinted five times during the war years when Knox was at work on his translation. Thus the fact of the matter is that when Knox the translator appeared on the scene, there had already been stirrings among Roman Catholics toward better vernacular renderings, either by amending Rheims-Douay or starting afresh, even from the original languages. Knox, true to his conservative nature, was to follow a middle way between the extremes possible, as he took up the task for which his life and training had so well prepared him. He chose to translate afresh but into "timeless English," not "modern speech"; he did not just adapt Rheims-Douay, but he did not go back to the original languages fully either, choosing to work from the Latin.

The highlights of the career of Ronald Arbuthnott Knox— the middle name, shared with his father, derives from the family into which the sister of his grandfather's wife married, and it seems to have been rather consistently misspelled on medals and awards which Ronald Knox received—can be related with dispatch, since a splendid biography exists by no less a literary figure than Evelyn Waugh, himself another convert.[7] But some of the sidelights pertinent to Knox's work as a biblical translator deserve special emphasis.

The future translator was born in 1888 at Kibworth rectory, Leicestershire, not too far from Lutterworth where Wyclif had been priest. He was the youngest of six children and the fourth son. His father, who had been a fellow of Merton College, Oxford, and was, at the time of Ronald's birth, a country rector, later became Bishop of Manchester. A grandfather had also been a Church of England bishop at Lahore, India. Hence young Ronald was well connected ecclesiastically. He grew up in an Evangelical Anglican home, for his father, Edmund Knox, was one of the prominent leaders of the Evangelical or Protestant wing of nineteenth-century Anglicanism, being especially known for his summer missionary preaching at the seaside resort center of Blackpool, the English Atlantic City. Culture and learning abounded in the family—at six, Ronnie was signing letters to his father in a combination of Latin and Greek—but so did a sense for games and jest. Wit characterized all the life of Ronald Knox, and it is probably worth recording that a brother became one of the editors of *Punch*.

During the years from 1900 to 1906 at Eton, a school Knox loved, Anglo-Catholic companionships and interests began to replace the Evangelical upbringing at home. Was there an element of rebellion against his father in the change? A later comment has often been quoted: "I felt I had to have some religion, and I couldn't stand Father's." He was attracted to rigorous asceticism, once subsisting on bread and water for six weeks when a friend was fatally ill with typhoid, and then practicing the discipline of prayer fifteen minutes a day with hands held above his head. At seventeen he vowed celibacy, so as to escape the comfort of a happy marriage and have "power to attend upon the Lord without impediment."

At Balliol College, Oxford, which he entered the next year (and liked less than Eton), Knox continued a brilliant academic career with "first honours" in classics, philosophy, and history. He took prizes for his Latin verse and also achieved a reputation as a satirist. Skill in debate earned him that much-sought Oxford post, election as president of the Union, and he had the distinction of being quoted by *The Times* of London while still an undergraduate.[8] The shift toward the Catholic wing of the Church of England continued. Pusey House, a center of the "High Church" Oxford Movement, was his spiritual home; he attended High Mass and confession at the Cowley Fathers and had Friday teas with the "spikes" or Anglo-Catholics, as a contemporary's letter shows. On one point, however, he agreed with his father's views, and that was in his absolute opposition to all liberal-sounding biblical criticism. In one of his best known bits of satire, paraphrasing Dryden's *Absalom and Achitophel*, Ronnie Knox lashed out in 1912 against source criticism with a poem mischievously called, *Absolute and Abitofhell:*

> Twelve Prophets our unlearned forefathers knew,
> We are scarce satisfied with twenty-two;
> A single Psalmist was enough for them,
> Our list of authors rivals A and M;
> They were content MARK, MATTHEW, LUKE and JOHN
> Should bless th' old-fashion'd Beds they lay upon:
> But we, for ev'ry one of theirs have two,
> And trust the Watchfulness of Blessed Q.[9]

He added a frontal assault with a book called *Some Loose Stones* the next year. Its title was a crack at a theological symposium called *Foundations,* which had set forth "Christian belief in terms of modern thought" and included essays by a number of Oxford divines, among them B. H. Streeter and A. E. J. Rawlinson, New Testament scholars, and William Temple, later Arch-

bishop of Canterbury—who, incidentally, answered Knox's poem
with a post card in the same jocular vein.

Upon graduation, Ronald Knox was appointed a fellow and
lecturer in classics at Trinity College, Oxford, in 1910. He also
began to prepare for ordination in the Church of England. The
decision to enter holy orders had matured over the undergraduate years and was a natural thing. Knox never attended a seminary
or theological college, however, for the Bishop of Oxford dispensed him from the usual requirement and also from the customary year spent in a parish as a deacon. He was left to prepare
for ordination on his own, with spiritual guides of his own
choosing, and spent his diaconate year at Oxford. Thus in these
years of preparation he was lecturing on Homer and Virgil,
tutoring the brother of an Eton friend (whom he also sought to
"make a Catholic"), and going into retreat at an Anglican
Benedictine monastery on the isle of Caldey off the coast of
Wales. This strange community, which Knox later referred to
as a "make-believe . . . fairy-story island," "Hollywood Cin-
ema" in its style, lay on an island outside the jurisdiction of
Anglican bishops, and had been created by a self-taught monk
of uncertain ecclesiastical status. The whole community transferred its allegiance to Rome in 1913, and later moved to Prink-
nash, where the order today makes a famous type of pottery.
Knox spent several Long Vacations at Caldey, and it must be
reckoned a formative influence. Theologically and biblically he
continued to oppose the threat to the Christian faith he saw in
German text critics and the "historical Jesus" of Albert
Schweitzer.

In 1912, at the age of twenty-four, Ronald Knox was ordained
a priest and appointed to the post of chaplain at Trinity College.
He continued to teach also. The war years he spent officially in
his Oxford post but actually on leave of absence to teach in a
boys' school at Shrewsbury. Many of Knox's former students
and friends were killed in the war. He himself seems to have had
no inclination toward service in the armed forces, though he

once toyed with a plan whereby he might become a chaplain behind German lines to British prisoners of war. It was in this period of World War I that he had a famous conversation, variously recalled by the two participants, with the Jesuit father C. C. Martindale, another convert to the Church of Rome, who was to become both an adviser and a critic of Knox's Bible translation. To Martindale, Knox broached the question openly, "Will you receive me into the Church?" and he was somewhat taken back with the apparent answer, "Not like that," for Martindale wanted him to realize that *not* being "C of E" did not necessarily imply being "RC."[10] The full story of Knox's eventual reception into the Roman Catholic Church in 1917 is told from his own point of view in *A Spiritual Aeneid*.[11] It would seem that the question of valid ecclesiastical authority was a significant factor. Ordination as a Roman Catholic priest came in 1919.

Knox's years as a Roman Catholic fall into three phases: as a seminary teacher, as university chaplain at Oxford, and as a writer and translator. Thus, he never served in a parochial situation, nor did he ever join any monastic order. From 1919 to 1926, he taught Latin and New Testament at St. Edmund's College, Ware, a town halfway between London and Cambridge. He taught both schoolboys and seminarians, and endeared himself to the students both by his clever teaching—he was famed for creating mnemonic devices and once invented a diceboard game to teach the travels of St. Paul—and by his interest in the students—once he is said to have deserted "high table" (for the faculty) and to have sat with the students to protest the poor food. The post of Professor of New Testament in the seminary was assigned to him in 1922. While this meant composition of lectures in a new field and brought sufficient knowledge to write a later commentary on all twenty-seven books of the New Testament, one doubts that Knox can be reckoned a serious *Neutestamentler*, certainly not in the sense that translators like Moffatt or Goodspeed were.

In 1926 Father Knox was appointed Roman Catholic chaplain

at Oxford, a position he held till 1939. Thus ended the comparative "exile" at Ware, the furthest from Oxford and Eton he had ever lived for any length of time. In Oxford Knox had a house of his own as a base from which to practice what he delightfully termed "chaplaincraft." The Catholic undergraduates in these years totaled about 170 annually, and to these he ministered. Converts were not his aim. The times were not easy ones for work with university students, but Knox's ministry left its mark on more than a few. To augment his income and provide for more of the proper amenities at tea with the students, Knox wrote a number of books during this period, not only collections of sermons and essays both theological and literary, but also the six well-known detective stories and *A Book of Acrostics*. His literary work earned him over £900 in some years.

A London newspaper which once reported that Ronald Knox's "chief interest in life is detective novels" was, of course, wrong, but there was an enduring interest here, and there is surely no other Bible translator who penned so many mystery tales. As early as 1911 Knox had written a paper on "Studies in the Literature of Sherlock Holmes," intended as a satire on the methods of German critical biblical scholarship. Much later in life there appeared an essay on "Father Brown," the character created by another Roman Catholic convert of great literary ability, G. K. Chesterton. Still another essay set forth proper rules for detective stories, and these rules were adopted as the oath for a society of writers which included Chesterton, Dorothy Sayres, and Agatha Christie. The first of Knox's own novels, *The Viaduct Murder*, was published in 1925 while he was still at St. Edmund's College. One wag later asked if the title page of his New Testament would bear the line, "By the author of *The Viaduct Murder*." The other books were *The Three Taps* (1927, subtitled "A Detective Story without a Moral," since Knox believed that such books ought be neither didactic nor psychological, but exercises in intellectual agility); *The Footsteps at the Lock* (1928); *The Body in the Silo* (originally published as

Settled Out of Court, 1933); *Still Dead* (1934), and *Double Cross Purposes* (1937). Granted that Miles Bredon, Knox's hero, who is a private investigator for The Indescribable Insurance Company, is not quite Hercule Poirot, and that few other novelists would lift their plot from *The Merry Wives of Windsor* or provide footnotes in the concluding chapter referring to earlier pages where clues were given, the detective stories by Ronald Knox are good enough so that at least two have recently been reprinted in paperback.[12] There are no theological overtones as in Chesterton, but it is not true, as rumored, that Knox always made the murderer a Catholic. What we do have is a keen, precise mind at play, but even here there are rules that circumscribe the game for author and readers.

The third period in Knox's Catholic years, when he was freed from teaching and chaplain's duties to write and to translate, is of most interest for our purposes, since this was the time when the Bible translation materialized. The first recorded hints of a desire to translate the Vulgate appeared in 1937. How much earlier there had entered into Knox's mind a sense of vocation to put Scriptures into English—and the whole Bible at that—is impossible to say. In 1938 any ideas of turning biblical translator were placed in jeopardy when Knox was offered the presidency of St. Edmund's College and along with it the prospects of a bishopric. He declined the offer, however, and went ahead with plans for literary work, interspersed with weekend preaching. Even the war clouds in 1939 and Hitler's invasion of Poland did not alter them. Father Knox resigned as chaplain at Oxford effective in June, 1939. He was then appointed private chaplain to the family of Lord and Lady Acton at Aldenham, in Shropshire. Here he had previously spent several vacations and had written what some consider his best book, *Let Dons Delight,*[13] a series of sketches of conversation in the Senior Commonroom of "St Simon Magnus College," Oxford, every fifty years from the time of the Spanish Armada to the Munich Agreement of 1938, showing his contention that education falls apart into separated disciplines unless there is the integrating factor of theology and faith. Here at Aldenham Knox was to work on the Bible translation all through the war years, until 1947. The final stages were completed at another country estate, that of Lord and Lady Oxford, at Mells, south of Bath, near the Roman Catholic Abbey at Downside.

A commission to translate the Vulgate New Testament was officially bestowed on Ronald Knox by the hierarchy of England and Wales in 1939. This meant that the Roman Catholic bishops (with one dissenting and with several wondering where the money was going to come from) authorized the translation and agreed to an annual stipend of £200 a year to support the translator, in exchange for the copyright. Even so, at first the bishops staked the undertaking only for the New Testament. Provision for the Old Testament, which Knox seems to have intended doing from the outset, was added later, in 1944. It is a fact that the hierarchy attained possession of a lucrative copyright. Evelyn Waugh estimates that by 1957 the Knox translation had brought in some £50,000 on the investment, and he adds that once "Ronald remarked drily, but without bitterness, that no word of thanks was ever said to him for this substantial benefaction."[14] A more recent writer, Arnold Lunn, a convert of Knox in 1933, holds that Waugh has been misinformed and is overly severe on the hierarchy at this point and that the record needs correction.[15] The fact of the matter seems to be that, however much the Knox translation may subsequently have benefited the hierarchy financially, some bishops were initially opposed to the project, and Knox's work had difficult going. This experience he shared with many other translators, along with the fact that he did not benefit personally from translation.

The years at Aldenham, while devoted to the translation, were not limited to that. A girls' school in London, run by the Assumptionist Nuns, was evacuated to the estate of the Acton family, and Father Knox took on the duty of chaplain, at no salary but with the stipulation that he need never *sing* Mass[16] nor perform ceremonies except distribution of ashes at the beginning of Lent. Out of the sermons preached to the school-girls came several of his later books, including *The Creed in Slow Motion*.[17] He also did some teaching and outside preaching in this period, and worked on the book subsequently published as *Enthusiasm*,[18] a study of the extremes of fervor and skepticism in religion of the seventeenth and eighteenth centuries. In some ways the historical view expressed here typifies Knox himself, who prized a middle way between excesses.

Life was Spartan for the translator in this period, even though he was cut off from any direct involvement with the war. He was seldom away from Aldenham. His biographer speaks of "few hints of pleasure" and of "a grim catalogue of professional duties"[19] in his schedule. Lunn again feels that Evelyn Waugh has overstressed a point here,[20] but something of the same un-happiness which multiplied itself at Aldenham seems to have marked even Ronald Knox's years at Oxford or his time on a Mediterranean cruise—on Lunn's own say-so. Perhaps, in view of the chore of translating, all this was just as well. Gregarious-ness and the opportunity to roam the countryside are no help to the man engaged in Englishing the Bible. Knox's own attitude to his task is suggested by the title he gave to a talk over Radio Eireann after he finished the job. He spoke of it as "Nine Years' Hard," i.e., nine years of hard labor as a sentence, from 1940–48.[21]

The mechanics of the translating were amazingly simple. Knox worked by himself in a small room at Lord Acton's house. Waugh describes the books piled on the window ledges and the table crowded with files, typewriter (an instrument which Knox found aided the precision of his writing ever since his days as an Oxford don), and even the dishes from his meals. Knox has observed that he often spent more time searching the Oxford *New English Dictionary* for the right word in translation than a Latin lexicon for the meaning of the original, so we must imag-ine his room as filled with English reference works as with biblical commentaries.[22]

Discussion with other scholars was rarely possible, though

much of Knox's correspondence in this period was with biblical experts. A committee was set up to advise on the work, including old colleagues at St. Edmund's; the Dominican, Father Hugh Pope, author of a detailed study on Bible translations in English; the Jesuit Martindale (already mentioned); and the Abbot of Downside, Christopher Butler. The last mentioned is one of the most articulate Roman Catholic spokesmen in Britain today, and in biblical studies has been the champion of Matthean priority over Mark. In the long run this committee seems not to have helped or influenced Knox too much, but during the first year of the project there were severe criticisms of Knox's renderings, especially by Father Martindale. He opposed any attempt to be radically different from Rheims-Douay, disliked the notion of "timeless English," criticized a "pseudo-archaist" style in the Old Testament, and felt that Knox paid too little attention to previous translation work. He was also surprised that an author who, in *Let Dons Delight*, had subtly expressed the different outlook of each speaker by the way he wrote, failed utterly to distinguish the style of various New Testament authors.

Because of such charges, there was considerable debate in 1940 over whether the hierarchy, in commissioning "a new version," had really meant a *fresh* translation or simply a *revision* of Rheims-Douay. The Knox translation almost suffered a Dunkirk. Conservative officials who wanted no new translation indicated their opposition to what Knox was turning out. The translator in turn threatened in 1941 to discontinue the project for the hierarchy. Knox actually offered to return the stipend given and suggested that he might publish at his own risk a translation for private use with the *imprimatur* of some individual bishop. However, what has been described as "a real snorter" of a letter from the Archbishop of Westminster cleared the way for Knox's project to continue.[23] Further, the odd coincidence that Father Martindale had gone to Denmark and been interned there during the Nazi invasion removed the foremost critic from the advisory committee, and Knox was able to go on his way.

Revelation, the last book in the New Testament, was finished on September 30, 1942. A "trial edition" of 1,500 copies was then printed. It was not sold through normal channels but was simply announced in January, 1943, as available for those who would apply for it in writing. This arrangement had been arrived at after long discussion with the bishops over whether the translation should be authorized for public use or not. The eventual agreement stipulated that the Knox New Testament should be only for "private use" for the time being, and that no copies were to be displayed or sold by booksellers. It is amazing that in wartime Britain over 9,500 applications were received. The publication appeared after further delay in April of 1944. Finally official permission for it came in early 1945, and that same year a "definitive edition" of the New Testament, with some five hundred minute changes, was printed.

Meanwhile work on the Old Testament had been going on at the rate of about twenty-four verses a day. The task was finished in 1948, two years earlier than Knox had expected, with the preface dated on September 30, St. Jerome's Day, of that year. The translator celebrated with an essay, "Farewell to Machabees,"[24] where he cites the words with which Jerome's translation of II Maccabees ends; they provide an appropriate conclusion, reading in his own rendering: "if the book be too nicely polished at every point, it grows wearisome. So here we will have done with it." The Old Testament was published in two separate volumes, 1948 (Genesis-Esther) and 1950 (Job-II Maccabees), with diocesan *imprimatur* from the Cardinal Archbishop of Westminster for private use.[25]

When Ronald Knox began his "nine years' hard," he had, of course, a number of qualities of inestimable import for a translator as part of his makeup, in addition to his skills with Latin and English and Greek. (Curiously, he took up Hebrew for the first time only during the Easter vacation of 1939—though, doubly curiously, the first words he set down for the Bible translation were Genesis 1:1 rather than any part of the New

Testament he had been commissioned at that time to do!) We may note that Knox was an author and translator of hymns. He also translated a *Manual of Prayers* for extra-liturgical services (which, however, the opposition of certain ecclesiastics caused to be withdrawn from publication after printing because its phrases were held to be too daring—a fate which might have befallen his New Testament!). And he had considerable experience and reputation as a preacher. All of these areas of experience rate as positive influences for the translator.

Knox as preacher has been analyzed in a recent essay by Horton Davies.[26] His habit, noted there, of polishing and developing sermons after they were preached and before they were printed, seems not without parallel to Knox's work in biblical translation and his concern for polished expression. To catalog him as a liturgical, ecclesiastical preacher seems again to parallel his understanding of the Bible translation, for while certain bishops may have had doubts about authorizing the Knox translation for more than private use, he seems to have been regularly aware of public, liturgical usage of the Bible. In fact, before he had finished the Old Testament, he had published the gospels and epistles read at Mass during the church year with a commentary of his own—which is surely the Bible in a liturgical setting.[27]

When Davies notes the wit in Knox's sermons—"the merry Monsignor," he calls him—we can add that some humor, good-natured or satirical, appears in almost all that he wrote. Even in the Bible translation, for all the seriousness of the subject matter and the grimness of the years in which the translation was carried out, there is at least a joyousness, if not laughter at times. Davies feels the comment in one sermon a little too wittily gruesome, that Easter as a season "is rich . . . in martyrs" because "in Spring, perhaps, you got the best bookings for the amphitheatre."[28] But who can forget the famed limerick, lampooning the philosophical notion of Bishop Berkeley that things exist only when observed by an observer?

> There once was a man who said: "God
> Must think it exceedingly odd
> If he finds that this tree
> Continues to be
> When there's no one about in the Quad."

Oral tradition has attached to it an answering poem by an unknown author:

> Dear Sir, Your astonishment's odd,
> I am always about in the Quad;
> And that's why the tree
> Will continue to be
> Since observed by Yours faithfully, GOD.

Knox, after all, was a man of imagination as well as wit, as is attested by a radio broadcast given at Edinburgh in 1926, when he created an effect on listeners not unlike that which Orson Welles stirred up in the United States in the thirties with his fictional account of men from Mars landing in New Jersey. Knox put on a "Broadcast from the Barricades," replete with sound effects, pretending to be a newsman describing a crowd in London sacking the National Gallery, with one "Sir Theophilus Gooch" being roasted alive in Trafalgar Square. The B.B.C. received many an anxious call and Knox an ecclesiastical reprimand.[29]

How would such a man handle Scripture? Perhaps it is too much to expect some of his native humor to appear in so formal a thing as a Bible translation. However, the phrase at II Thessalonians 3:11, about people who neglect "their own business to mind other people's," rates a plus, and the chapter dripping with irony and invective at II Corinthians 11 is superlatively done. Perhaps the Old Testament, where Knox is a bit freer and more himself, reflects even better a boisterous, contagious joyfulness at times.[30]

The best examples of the humor which Knox brought to his task can be found, however, in the remarks made in some of his essays on translating. He had a passion against traditional "Bible English," whether of the Rheims-Douay or King James varieties. Some of his choicest barbs devastatingly deflate that pompous "pseudo-Semitic," Elizabethan phraseology which many people defend as the proper idiom for a Bible or the worship of God. Parodying the King James rendering of Mark 7:3, he asks, " 'For the Nazis, and all the Germans, except they say *Heil Hitler!* meet not in the street, holding their lives valuable'; is that English idiom?"[31] Or again: "We should have thought it odd if we had read in *The Times* 'General Montgomery's right hand has smitten Rommel in the hinder parts'; but if we get that sort of thing in the Bible we take it, unlike Rommel, sitting down. 'Mr. Churchill then opened his mouth and spoke'—is that English? No, it is Hebrew idiom clothed in English words."[32] It would be going too far to suggest that the Knox translation should be read as the work of a man of Franciscan gaiety. He was too much an Oxford don, too urbane for that sort of naïveté; Evelyn Waugh points out too much basic unhappiness and frustration. But at the least the reader ought to appreciate the innate wit, perhaps more delightfully expressed than by any other Bible translator in history.

Against this personal background, the Knox translation of the Bible can now be characterized and assessed. Ronald Knox was quite clear on his goal: he aimed at a rendering of the Vulgate, with references to the Hebrew and Greek, into "timeless English," which Roman Catholics might read in private and, hopefully, on public occasions too as an official version. He had no illusions, though, about the difficulties or the need to convince would-be readers of the value of the work. Among Roman Catholics, the audience at which such a translation aimed primarily, the prospects were none too happy; Knox once wrote,

> We are in an odd situation. Nobody reads the Bible, Popes and Bishops are always telling us we ought to read the Bible, and when you produce a translation of the Bible, the only thing people complain about is your rendering of the diminutive snippets that are

read out in Church on Sundays. 'Of course,' they add, 'the book is all right for *private reading*'—in a tone that implies that such a practice is both rare and unimportant.[33]

Of the clergy he expected little more than from the laity.

In my experience, the laity's attitude towards the Bible is one of blank indifference, varied now and again by one of puzzled hostility. The clergy, no doubt, search the Scriptures more eagerly. And yet, when I used to go round preaching a good deal, and would ask the P.P. [parish priest] for a Bible to verify my text from, there was generally an ominous pause of twenty minutes or so before he returned, banging the leaves of the sacred volume and visibly blowing on the top. The new wine of the gospel, you felt, was kept in strangely cobwebby bottles.[34]

We must remember that all this was prior to the encyclical of 1943 encouraging "use of Scripture in instruction of the faithful" and prior to the Bible study movement in Roman Catholicism of recent years. Knox's endeavor was pioneering in some ways for English Roman Catholics.

He himself continued to be a traditionalist, however, we have already noted, in that he based his work not on the original languages directly, but on the traditional "Clementine Vulgate" of 1592. Knox himself was aware of certain drawbacks involved. At Acts 17:6 the Greek original says that Paul and the Christians have "turned the world upside down," and many Latin manuscripts also have the word "world" (*orbem*). However, some Latin manuscripts, by the corruption of one letter, read *urbem* instead; the Clementine Vulgate has this, and so Knox must render, "are turning the state [*urbem*, literally "city"] upside down." Even the Confraternity Version deserts the Clementine text here at what is obviously an internal Latin corruption. Similarly at Matthew 11:10 Knox must render rather awkwardly the words about John the Baptist,

Behold, I am sending before thy face that angel (*angelum*) of mine, who is to prepare thy way before thee.

Rightly the Confraternity Version makes it "that messenger of mine." Knox has written, somewhat wistfully, "I confess that I should have preferred to render *angelos* "messenger" if the Latin had not precluded it."[35]

Having committed himself to use of the Latin, Knox does give evidence of having regularly consulted the Greek or Hebrew which lies behind it. Often in a note he calls attention to problems. A good example is Acts 17:18, alliteratively rendered, "What can his drift be, this dabbler?" The note explains that the Greek term *spermologos*, which the Stoic and Epicurean philosophers apply to Paul, meant "a bird which picks up seeds" and hence a lounger who picks up thoughts here and there and makes a philosophy of them; we are told further that the Latin failed to grasp this and made up a word, *seminiverbius*, "the seed-word man." Monsignor Knox knew the problems but loyally chose the 1592 Vulgate text. One wonders, if he were doing it again today, whether he would repeat the choice.

What he translated from can to this extent be criticized. What of the "timeless English" into which he seeks to put his rendering? His opposition to Elizabethan English as the medium for Bible translation today has already been noted. "Nothing," he wrote, "will induce me to let king David pray for the renewing of a right spirit within his bowels."[36] Rheims-Douay phraseology he called at times "gibberish." But what, on a more positive level, did he make his goal? Two brief quotations from Knox indicate what he had in mind:

> The man who sits down to translate the Bible slips, as a rule, into the idiom of his grandfathers. . . . My own idea has been to secure, as far as possible, that Englishmen of 2150, if my version is still obtainable then, shall not find it hopelessly 'dated'.[37]

> . . . what you want is neither sixteenth-century English nor twentieth-century English, but timeless English. . . . no phrase, and so far as possible no turn of sentence, which would not have passed as decent literary English in the seventeenth century, and would not pass as decent literary English to-day.[38]

This goal has often been highly praised. But the merits of many individual renderings apart, one cannot help but wonder if "timeless English" is not a chimera; must not English always be that of a particular age or land or man? An English that is "normal" over the decades from 1650 to 2150 is liable to be rather routine and drab. A studied impression is that Knox pleases because he is both at times a bit archaic and at times almost "slangy." Is that "timeless English"?

Opinions on the matter will vary, but it was on this point, this notion of "timeless English," that C. C. Martindale was most critical, and Arnold Lunn tends to agree. Knox, Lunn thinks, "never attains to the beauty of the Authorized Version at its best," and what is more he often lost the simplicity of the Greek.[39]

Perhaps part of our difficulty in assessing the translation lies in the fact that we are always comparing Knox with some earlier translation—a practice he protests. He himself fought a battle to win the right to do more than revise Rheims-Douay. Yet the question he was asked again and again, he reported, was:

> 'Why did you *alter* such and such a passage?' Why did I *alter* it— when you say you are going to translate the Bible, it is assumed that you do not mean to do anything of the kind. It is assumed that you mean to revise the existing translation, with parts of which we are all familiar; altering a word here and there, like a compositor correcting proofs with a pair of tweezers. The more you plagiarize from the work of previous interpreters, the better you public will be pleased. . . . really translating [the Bible means] approaching it as if nobody had ever translated it before.[40]

Strangely, some seem to like the Knox translation precisely because it reminds them of King James phraseology!

Knox, on occasion, achieves striking, novel renderings, as with the colors for the four horsemen at Revelation 6:1–8. The first three horses are, respectively, white, fiery-red, and black. That ridden by death, according to the Authorized and Rheims Versions, is "pale." But, says Monsignor Knox, "My objection to

the word 'pale' is that it does not denote colour; was it pale blue
or pale pink or what? The whole heraldry of the chapter demands four different colours, white, red, black, and—what?"[41]
The word used in the Greek literally means "green," and J. B.
Phillips has been bold enough to call death's horse "sickly green
in color." Knox comments, "I don't think my committee would
have stood for a green horse. But my motive for avoiding it was
a perfectly simple one—*I was translating the Vulgate*." And the
Vulgate says the horse was *pallidus*. Knox felt "bound to follow
it . . . with regret."[42] However, his literary feeling was strong
enough to keep him from making the horse just "pale." Aware
that the Greek word had been used in medical treatises to mean
"yellow" or "bilious-looking," he made death ride a "cream-
white" charger. This may be overtranslation, but it surely grips
the reader's attention.

At times, Knox seems too periphrastic, using many words to
explain what the original said in few. For example, "You know"
(Acts 20:18) becomes "It is within your knowledge." "I pity
the multitude" becomes "I am moved with pity for the multitude." "Herod will search for the child" might suggest the king
"poking about in the shrubbery," so Knox translates, "Herod
will soon be making search for the child."[43]

Like most modern translators, Knox employs logical para-
graphing but has dispensed with all quotation marks. Their absence scarcely makes the English "timeless," only more confusing.
The failure to use conventional English spellings for many proper
names can likewise be called an obstacle to many readers. Knox
transliterates the Latin transliterations of the Greek or Hebrew
originals, and so among the prophets are "Osee," "Abdias," and
"Aggaeus."[44]

Archaic verb endings as in "seeketh" or "findeth" are generally dropped. However, "thou" is retained, not just in prayers
to God but elsewhere too. This second singular form is a con-
venient one to make a distinction from "ye," the only way in
English unless we adopt "you-all" or a slang plural, "youse."

But is it timeless or archaic today? Among the less than modern expressions are such phrases as "he must needs pass that way" (Luke 19:4), and "the livery you wear" (Col. 3:12). In the Old Testament there are expressions like "guerdon" (Jer. 38:2), "baldric" (Isa. 11:4), and "sepulture" (Isa. 14:20). Sometimes these words are quite effective. But can they be called "timeless"? Their very effectiveness in a given passage may stem from the antique, to us medieval, effect they conjure up.

In familiar verses, like the Pater Noster and Ave Maria, "timelessness" is achieved by leaving the familiar wordings alone or little touched. Some critics have argued that Knox was not radical enough at these points. To say "Hallowed be thy name" or "Hail Mary" is a contradiction, they hold, in a quest for timeless English. Who says, "Restored be thy health," or "Hail Churchill"? Perhaps our final decision on whether to put such familiar passages into current language or to keep much of the old, rests in part on whether or not we are impressed with a need for keeping a tradition of language for its liturgical associations, to which we have long been accustomed.

On some occasions the Knox translation changed words that seem perfectly clear in the older versions to less usual terms. At Matthew 10:21 we read, "children will rise up against their parents and will compass their deaths"—this is Msgr. Knox speaking. Surely the traditional rendering was clearer when it said, "the children shall . . . cause them to be put to death." Consider also Luke 17:7, "Go and fall to at once." The verb there means literally "recline (at table)" and therefore "sit down (to meat)." To "fall to (it)" suggests beginning something or coming to blows, and can strike one here as simultaneously too archaic, too slangy, and too obscure.

Perhaps the most serious charge against Knox in this matter of archaic language is his tendency to fall into Latinisms. He was, of course, a thorough Latinist and was working from the Vulgate. Therefore it was a temptation sometimes simply to transliterate the Latin. Unfortunately, however, the term thus arrived at may not always be the happiest one in our language. Matthew 7:13 is a case in point. Knox translates, "It is a broad gate and a wide road that leads on to perdition." K.J.V., Douay, and the Confraternity rendering all say "that leads to destruction." Why the change? One guess is that it is an almost unconscious Latinism—the Vulgate reads *ad perditionem;* see also Phil. 3:19 and Acts 8:20 in the same vein. In I Corinthians 13 the Latin *charitas* was doubtless a factor in Knox's choice of "charity" over "love." On the other hand, some Latinisms fit in quite naturally. At II Timothy 2:17, Knox translates, "their influence eats in like a cancer," following the Latin *ut cancer;* compare the R.S.V., "their talk will eat its way like gangrene," following the Greek *hos gangraina.*

Knox likes to omit conjunctions so that his style is quite terse at times. "Barabbas, they said, not this man" (John 18:40). Counterbalancing this is a tendency, already noted, to expand on what the original says. The K.J.V. is certainly graphic and brief in phrases like, "Behold the man!" and "I thirst." In Knox they have become, "See, here is the man!" and "I am thirsty." Even the terse command, "Lazarus, come forth," becomes "Lazarus, come out here."[45] It is true that Knox is trying to bring out here the fullest meaning of the original, but the simplicity of the earlier renderings had much to commend them.

Both terseness and expansion appear most clearly in the Old Testament. Perhaps the Hebrew encourages this, or more properly the Hebrew-based Latin. Perhaps the committee's hand was gone and Knox could be more himself. It may be that the subject matter lends itself better. At any rate, parts of the Old Testament exhibit almost a roughness of style—not poetry, for Knox disdained poetic lines, even in the Psalms—but rugged prose that is a challenge to read or parse. Consider Isaiah 11:4, "here is judgement will give the poor redress, here is award will right the wrongs of the defenceless." Or Jeremiah 38:5, "king is none may withstand you." Our first impulse is to suspect a printer's error, for not only conjunctions but also relative pronouns have disappeared!

Knox also loves inverted sentences—sometimes aping the He-brew, sometimes the Latin word order, and sometimes just for effective English. For example, Jeremiah 36:14, "come thither he must"; 36:15 "so read it he did." Or Isaiah 7:14, "Sign you ask none, but sign the Lord will give you."

There is a tendency to be almost too colloquial at times. Jeremiah 38:28, "for, sure enough, Jerusalem was taken," sounds rather "folksy." Perhaps Knox lets alliteration creep in more than he ought. In Jeremiah he has "weal or woe" (42:6, 44:27) and "heed and hearing" (44:5). In Isaiah we meet the combinations, "scholar . . . simpleton" (29:12), "webs a-weaving," and in a single verse, "gape and gaze . . . hum and haw . . . bemused . . . besotted" (29:9).

There are some splendid phrases, however, where Knox reaches the acme of style or at least attains word combinations to prick up the ear. Isaiah 9:5 gives a magnificent picture of the messianic age, when

> All the trophies of the old tumultuous forays, all the panoply stained with blood, will be burnt up now, will go to feed the flames—

even if the Hebrew differs somewhat. The New Testament has memorable turns of speech like "Christ's nursery" (I Cor. 3:1), or the statement that God has acted "so as to abash the wise" (I Cor. 1:27). More than occasionally there are exegetical sug-gestions different from what is customary—e.g., when Goliath is described as "bastard born," rather than as simply a "cham-pion" of the Philistines (I Kings [= I Sam., in Jewish and Protes-tant canons] 17:4).

There is little in the translation itself which shows Roman Catholic tendencies. In the footnotes, however, the translator sometimes explains the text in ways that conform to the tradi-tions of his church. At Matthew 1:25, where Douay had read, Joseph "knew her not till she brought forth her firstborn son," Knox has the Latin say "he had not known her when she bore a son" and explains that the phrase "does not impugn the perpetual virginity of our Lady." At 12:47 the verse occurs, "Here are thy mother and thy brethren standing without." Knox translates literally; only in a note does he add, "Since it is impossible for anyone who holds the Catholic tradition to suppose that our Lord had brothers by blood, the most common opinion is that these 'brethren' were his cousins."

Polemics, then, there is little of in the translation. Criticisms can more legitimately be made on (1) the choice of the Vulgate base; (2) the rather "anticritical" outlook of the translator—Knox, like his Anglican father and like much of the Roman Catholic Church in the nineteenth and early twentieth centuries, was in many ways opposed to the historical-critical method which has come to mean so much in modern biblical studies; he chose in its stead the "patristic, ecclesiastical norm" of tradition—and (3) certain features of "timeless English." The average reader is probably less aware of the "what" and "how" than of the actual translation results in English. Here it can be judged a curiosity that Knox declined to print poetry as such, and his reasons as even more curious: because, he said, the average English reader doesn't understand poetry, and because it takes an extra tenth of space![46] What will linger longest, though, for the average reader is a recollection of "timeless English" and its amalgamation of the antique and the modern. The Christmas story is at places almost harshly modern. "All must go and give in their names." Yet the baby Jesus is still wrapped in "swaddling-clothes," and Mary is described as "his espoused wife," though she is said to be "in her pregnancy." Is this latter phrase any improvement over the traditional renderings? Even Goodspeed, whose primary concern is hardly literary or timeless English, puts it less bluntly; he speaks of Mary, "who was engaged to him and who was soon to become a mother."

For readers who like to measure a translation by how it handles what they know and love best, the Knox version offers an abundant testing ground in the Psalms. For Knox has rendered them twice, once from the Latin of the Clementine Vulgate and the second time from the "new Latin translation" of the Hebrew text published by the Pontifical Biblical Institute with approval from Pius XII in 1945.[47] Both are printed in his Bible edition. Both are based on the Latin, but the latter is closer to the Hebrew text as viewed by modern scholarship. Psalm 22 (23 in most reckonings)[48] runs thus:

> The Lord is my shepherd; how can I lack anything? He gives me a resting-place where there is pasture, and leads me out by cool waters, to make me live anew. As in honour pledged, by sure paths he leads me; what though I walk with the shadow of death all around me? Hurt I fear none, while thou art with me; thy rod, thy crook are my comfort. What though my enemies trouble me? Full in their view thou dost spread a banquet before me; richly thou dost anoint my head with oil, generous the cup that steals away my senses! All my life thy goodness pursues me; through the long years, the Lord's house shall be my dwelling-place.

and from the "new Latin":

> The Lord is my shepherd; how can I lack anything? He gives me a resting-place where there is green pasture, leads me out to the cool water's brink, refreshed and content. As in honour pledged, by sure paths he leads me; dark be the valley about my path, hurt I fear none while he is with me; thy rod, thy crook are my comfort. Envious my foes watch, while thou dost spread a banquet for me; richly thou dost anoint my head with oil, well filled my cup. All my life thy loving favour pursues me; through the long years the Lord's house shall be my dwelling-place.

There is poetic diction, but not poetic structure. The similarities and differences compelled by the two Latin texts employed serve to show the importance of the underlying text from which a translator works. What difference would it have made if, throughout, Knox would have had the equivalent of "new Latin" text, or the original Hebrew or Greek?

Until his death, on August 24, 1957, Knox continued to speak of his translation. He wrote essays about the undertaking and a

three-volume commentary on his New Testament.[49] There has
been a posthumous publication of the New Testament translation in the "Knox-Cox" arrangement. Here, in volumes originally prepared for discussion groups of the New Zealand
Catholic Youth Movement, Ronald Cox, C.M., has placed the
Knox translation on one page and, facing it, on the other, Cox's
comments.[50] Interestingly the Pauline epistles have been arranged,
not in canonical sequence, but in the order in which it was presumed they were originally written, and each letter is placed in
the framework of Acts at its proper point! Such a rearrangement
of the canonical sequence was also found in *The Twentieth
Century New Testament,* though, ironically, the paperback
reprint of it from Moody Press has put the *Twentieth Century*
version back in canonical order. Recent editors have also arranged
the Knox translation of the gospels into a harmony.[51]

The final public oration which Ronald Knox ever gave, in
June, 1957, concerned Bible translation.[52] He was invited to
present the Romanes Lecture at Oxford, a famed series in which
Gladstone, Theodore Roosevelt, Churchill, Gilbert Murray, and
Galsworthy had all spoken. Knox literally left a sick bed for the
trip to Oxford, and a doctor sat nearby the rostrum of the
Sheldonian Theatre. But Knox spoke with all his old fire, urging
translation that is literary as well as literal. He flayed the over-
inflated reputation of the K.J.V.—"the God of Abraham and the
God of Isaac and the God of Jacob" is not English but a Semitic
ghost in the grammar which can only suggest to us three gods,
as if one were talking of "the train to Bletchley and the train
to Rugby and the train to Crewe," three trains—he agreed with
C. S. Lewis that "Bible English" ought not be imitated, and he
complained that religion, e.g., the Oxford Movement, usually
had low standards for translations. When he called for the use of
modern English, though with some words out of fashion, he was
describing, one may assume, his own endeavor at "timeless English." The lecture closed with a hope for a yet more brilliant
future in Bible translation, "a second Elizabethan age of English

translation."[53] That that hope has begun to be fulfilled in the movement toward tomorrow must rejoice Knox the Christian, even though these new developments may thrust aside his own translation.

Evelyn Waugh once went so far as to claim that in time, as Bible-reading declines among non-Catholics, the only Englishmen who know their Bibles will be Catholics, and they will know it in the Knox version, which will be the best-known Bible in English. One doubts, even from the present limited vantage point, that that will be true. *Aggiornamento* and "a new Elizabethan age" have come too quickly. The opinion of Robert Dentan in a *New York Times* review may be more to the point, that the real place of the Knox version "is not on the lectern or at the altar but in the library."[54] Knox himself wanted no revision of his translation for fifty years, and by 1998 situations and tastes may well change. An "interfaith" Bible is by then a distinct possibility, based on the original language, shared by Christians both Protestant and Catholic. Besides, who could stylistically revise what Knox has done? Style was his trademark.

The story is told of the last words of Ronald Knox. "For three days he lay in a coma, but once Lady Eldon saw a stir of consciousness and asked whether he would like her to read to him from his own New Testament. He answered very faintly, but distinctly: 'No'; and then after a long pause in which he seemed to have lapsed again into unconsciousness, there came from the death-bed, just audibly, in the idiom of his youth: 'Awfully jolly of you to suggest it, though.' "[55]

How like this prince among the royalty of translators. To him Father Martin D'Arcy applied, as a funeral text, the words of Ecclesiasticus 38:39–39:1—in Knox's own translation, of course: "But the wise man will be learning the lore of former times, the prophets will be their study. Theirs it is to support this unchanging world of God's creation; craftsmanship is their title to live; . . . lending themselves freely and making their study in the law of the most High."[56]

Epilogue:
Toward Tomorrow

T HE PROCESSION OF TRANSLATORS MOVES ON. THE DRAMA OF
Bible transmission continues. New chapters in the romance of
Scriptures and scholars will follow. Can we foresee what any of
these will be? Within limits, yes, though we must always leave
room for the unexpected—and for the One who does "a new
thing" and who "makes all things new" (Isa. 43:19, Rev. 21:5).

It is obvious, first of all, that the usual motives for Bible translation will continue. The educational factor operates in planning
an R.S.V. or N.E.B. just as in the time of *The Letter of Aristeas.*
The liturgical element appears as often as thought is given to the
use of Scripture in worship. Portions of the Confraternity Version Old Testament, for example, were rushed to completion in
1964 specially for use in the vernacular Roman Catholic Mass.
Surely the evangelistic motivation still flourishes, for the modern
missionary movement has accelerated Bible translation tremen-
dously, from the average over the first fifteen centuries of one
new language every forty years, to three new languages a year
by William Carey's day at the rise of the modern missionary
movement, to the present pace of a new dialect each month.

The literary side of translation may appear the weakest influence today, for there are not many men like Ronald Knox.
But few translations totally ignore style. Many employ a literary
panel to achieve felicity of phrase. The poet Robert Graves has
recently offered some samples of what he thinks Bible translation
should be like.[1] Thus, the literary side is far from dead, especially

214

if we remember that "literary" ought not be equated solely with Jacobean English. Perhaps our fetish for "Bible English" and the "hieratic language" of the K.J.V., against which Knox protested,[2] is the real menace to literary achievement. C. S. Lewis has warned that "literary delight" is only a by-product, and that to read the Bible simply as literature is not to read it as *the Bible* at all.[3]

To this list of motives ought be added that of "eschatological compulsion"—the feeling of some Christians that "the gospel must first be published among all nations" (Mark 13:10, K.J.V.) before "the End" can come, and that therefore Bible translation into every language under the sun is part of God's "Great Plan." And another factor must be added to the list—that modern publishers may commission a translation project, as the "Anchor Bible" was commissioned. Both of these factors are not to be found in the time of Aristeas.

Next, it requires no crystal ball to note that (2) a number of translations now in progress will continue to completion. These include the Roman Catholic Confraternity Version, now virtually complete; the New English Bible, of British Protestants; the "New Jewish Version," of which the Torah (Genesis-Deuteronomy) has already appeared, and the interfaith "Anchor Bible."

Equally plain is that (3) further study of existing manuscripts, new discoveries, and thorough analysis of the total evidence will lead to yet more detailed and accurate Hebrew and Greek texts, on which the translations of tomorrow will be based. Currently text criticism is in a fluid state. The Dead Sea Scrolls and Greek papyrus finds, like those at the Bodmer Library, Geneva, are forcing re-evaluation of many theories forged in the nineteenth century when data was more meager. More ample editions of the Hebrew text are now being prepared, and at least three projects are under way to produce more accurate Greek New Testaments.

One of these latter efforts, by Professor G. D. Kilpatrick, of Oxford, is predicated on the assumption that all manuscripts went through a fair amount of correcting and "prettying up" during the crucial second century A.D., and so Kilpatrick does not hesitate to accept as original a reading found only in a tiny minority of manuscripts. Even more important is a vast "International Greek New Testament Project," which aims at nothing less than a "new Tischendorf"—a text which will report all the evidence now known as fully and as accurately as the "Manuscript Detective" did for his day.

(4) Of the theological trends today, the one which looms largest for the future of biblical translation appears to be "the New Hermeneutic," a massive attempt to pull together biblical criticism, church history, and Christian existence under the word of God, so that "the whole theological enterprise" is embraced "as a movement of language from the word of God attested in Scripture to the preached sermon in which God speaks anew."[4] Any movement concerned with bringing life to the biblical text so that it speaks today has potential significance for Bible translation—even though the initial essays of the New Hermeneutic movement give little promise of help here and often exhibit a turgid, esoteric style. Meanwhile the efforts of the Bible Societies in examining developments in psychology, anthropology, and linguistics to aid translators[5] are a step toward a better hermeneutic, the art and science of interpreting. What the New Hermeneutic adds is the Reformation's theological concern.

(5) Translations by private individuals will continue, but not, in all probability, with the frequency of the past. The time is over of the deluge of "modern speech versions," like Moffatt and Goodspeed, inspired by the papyrus discoveries and by a desire to break away from the K.J.V.-E.R.V. bondage. That battle is won, and with the victory there has come a lessening of interest among scholars for each to try his hand at translation. Of course, individual translators there will always be. But publishing costs now exclude much experimentation, and a venture like *The Twentieth Century New Testament*, with its few hundred pounds of capital, would not get far at today's prices. Individuals

recently bringing out translations of the Scriptures—men like
J. B. Phillips, William Beck, Olaf Norlie, or John Beardslee—
are in many ways "late blossomings" of the earlier "Moffatt-
Goodspeed era." The younger scholars do not seem inclined to
include a Bible translation in their plans (though they may take
part in a group venture); is this a sign of the times, or of
maturity, because scholars today realize the problems involved
in putting a translation on paper?

(6) An unprecedented step involves "interfaith Bibles." In
the nineteenth century it was a daring step when a Unitarian was
included among the E.R.V. revisers, and objections were raised;
likewise in the 1950's, when a Jewish scholar assisted with the
R.S.V. Old Testament. Now the "Anchor Bible" project numbers
seven Catholic, five Jewish, and fifteen Protestant translators in
its ranks, and when their thirty-eight volumes are finished sometime after 1970—in time for "our astronauts to take with them
to the moon," one of the project's editors has quipped[6]—the
various translations may be combined in a single volume. Meanwhile, the R.S.V., with minor changes, has been published in
early 1965 with *imprimatur* for use by Roman Catholics, and
cooperative translation projects involving Protestants and Catholics are at various stages in Holland, Germany, France, Ceylon,
the Congo, Samoa, and other lands. A common Bible for all
Christians is no idle dream. One German Roman Catholic, out-
lining desirable features for such a future translation, recently
listed among these the need to employ the original text as a
basis; the necessity of guidance from true insight into the Scriptures arising out of "charismatic experience"; a style suited to
the modern man; team effort, and testing through a "trial edition."[7] Each point has precedent in Protestant endeavor from
Luther on.

(7) Lastly, there will doubtless be specific changes in the
Bibles of the future from phrases and verses to which we are
now accustomed. Some of these changes will lie in the area of
text, though perhaps the significant steps here have already been

taken. The task may now be to explain *why* R.S.V. and N.E.B. have already departed from K.J.V. I would regard it as important that readers of the future not only be confronted with important variants but that they also come to realize why certain omissions or additions were made by scribes. At Luke 23:34, for example, in connection with Jesus' words from the cross,

"Father, forgive them; for they know not what they do,"

honesty demands such a note as that in the R.S.V., "Other ancient authorities omit the sentence." Admittedly the verse bristles with problems; does the "them" refer to the Jews, or the Roman soldiers, or men generally? But the next step, I feel, is to help readers appreciate why certain scribes in the second century omitted these words. Very probably the theory of Rendel Harris[8] is correct, that such copyists thought the verse referred to the Jews and that God *could* not forgive them (for, unlike the Gentiles, they were not "without excuse") or that God *had* not forgiven, as witness the double destruction of Jerusalem in A.D. 70 and 135. Therefore these scribes omitted the verse.

Other changes will arise from our increased knowledge of grammar, word meaning, even punctuation, and the evangelist's intent. Will the Bibles of the future say that a disciple is to forgive his sinning brother "seventy-seven times," not "seventy times seven" (Matt. 18:22), or that Jesus entered Jerusalem on a horse instead of a donkey (according to Matt. 21:2)? It is possible that they will hint that the crown of thorns or "thorn-twigs" (Phillips) was a device of mockery, not torture. Perhaps they will even indicate the ambiguity of that scene at John 19:13, where the Greek allows, and the evangelist's theology suggests, that Pilate caused *Jesus* to sit down on the judgment seat, rather than that Pilate himself sat down there. The point would be that for a moment at Pilate's court we catch a glimpse of what will turn out to be the ultimate truth: Jesus is the future Judge, Pilate on trial before him! No one can be sure whether precisely these changes will come, but development and change will occur, and there will be further dramatic chapters in the story of the Scriptures.

New editions of the original text have been mentioned. Currently Israeli scholars at Hebrew University, Jerusalem, are at work on a definitive Bible based on the famed "Aleppo Codex." This manuscript was copied between A.D. 900 and 950. Long regarded as a model, it has reposed at various times in Jerusalem, Cairo, and Aleppo, and is now at Jerusalem again, its history proving that romantic adventures for manuscripts are by no means a thing of the past. The great scholar Aaron Ben Asher went over this codex himself in the tenth century and fixed its text. A wealthy Karaite Jew from Basra gave it to the Karaite community in Jerusalem where it was kept under the care of two princes, to be brought forth for reading at the festivals of Passover, Pentecost, and Tabernacles; at times serious students might also examine it. The codex was among the booty taken by the Crusader army under the adventurer-prince, Baldwin, that "second Judas Maccabeus" who became king of Jerusalem, when the city fell in 1099. But the manuscript was returned to the owners in 1106—an event prompting a thanksgiving service in the synagogue.

Sometime thereafter the book was taken to Cairo, where Maimonides saw and admired it in the latter half of the twelfth century. By the middle of the fifteenth century the codex was moved again, this time to the synagogue of the Sephardic Jews in Aleppo, where it remained until modern times, available for consultation on debated points but not for protracted study. Rudolf Kittel and Paul Kahle, for example, could not obtain permission to photograph its pages for use in preparing their 1937 Hebrew Bible. Newspaper headlines in 1948 reported that the Aleppo manuscript was destroyed when the synagogue was burned in fighting there. Its destruction has subsequently been noted in several books. But in a manner not yet fully made public, the codex was rescued from the burning building and eventually, in a way not disclosed, found its way to Israel, where scholarly study is at last analyzing its readings and notes for a printed text. Future translators will employ its evidence, and some day we shall know the full story of the Aleppo Codex.

Who knows what other treasures await scholarly recovery? Or what insights lie ahead? Of this we can be sure: there is yet more light. *Dies diem docet,* one generation learns from another, and the Lord has yet more light to break forth from his word.

Appendix:
Bible Translation Projects for the Future

In order to identify more fully some of the projects alluded to in the Epilogue, a brief annotated listing is here provided.

Of translations now in progress, the Roman Catholic revision of the Rheims-Douay-Challoner Bible is being prepared under the auspices of the Episcopal Committee of the Confraternity of Christian Doctrine (Paterson, New Jersey, 1941–   ; the Old Testament part amounts to a fresh translation). The N.E.B. New Testament appeared in 1961 (Oxford and Cambridge University Presses); panels are at work on the Old Testament and Apocrypha, with 1966 as the earliest possible target date. Of the "New Jewish Version"—officially *A New Translation of the Holy Scriptures according to the Masoretic Text*—the first part, *The Torah: The Five Books of Moses*, appeared in 1963 (Philadelphia: The Jewish Publication Society of America). *The Anchor Bible* is published by Doubleday and Company; Vol. 1, *Genesis*, by E. A. Speiser, and 37, *The Epistles of James, Peter, and Jude*, by Bo Reicke, were the first two sections available (Garden City, 1964). Vol. 21, *Jeremiah*, by John Bright, and 15, *Job*, by Marvin H. Pope, appeared early in 1965.

Standard critical texts are those in Hebrew of Kittel-Kahle and in Greek of Nestle-Aland (Stuttgart: Württemberg Bibelanstalt). G. D. Kilpatrick is editing The British and Foreign Bible Society's third edition of the New Testament under the title of *A Greek-English Diaglot* (London, 1958–   ). The International Greek New

Testament Project is now cosponsored by Candler School of Theology, Emory University, Atlanta, and Duke University Divinity School. Two volumes on Mark and Matthew had been done by S. C. E. Legg for a predecessor group in England in 1935 and 1940; it is hoped that Luke will appear soon. A third Greek testament project, by an international committee of scholars for the American and Associated Bible Societies (Scotland, Germany), will publish its text by early 1966; this judicious volume will probably have wide use.

Among individual translators, J. B. Phillips, after completing the New Testament, has now tackled the Old Testament, with *Four Prophets* (New York: Macmillan, 1963). William Beck's *The New Testament in the Language of Today* (St. Louis: Concordia) first appeared in 1963; *Norlie's Simplified New Testament in Plain English* (Grand Rapids: Zondervan), in 1961; Beardslee's *Mark, A Translation with Notes* ("Occasional Paper" published by the Theological Seminary, New Brunswick, N.J.) in 1962. Note also the idiomatic rendering begun by Robert G. Bratcher for the American Bible Society with *The Right Time: Mark's Story About Jesus* (New York, 1964).

A detailed report on "Common Bible Projects" is given in *Herder Correspondence,* Vol. 1 (1964, special issue), pp. 3–5.

Notes

Chapter One

[1] F. C. Grant, *Translating the Bible* (New York: Seabury Press, Inc., 1961), pp. 163, 16 f.

Chapter Two

[1] *The Encyclopaedia Britannica*, Eleventh Edition (New York: 1911), Vol. XVII, p. 692.

[2] *The First Epistle of Paul to the Corinthians* ("Moffatt New Testament Commentary"; New York: Harper and Brothers Publishers, 1938), p. 46. There is a similar note in the Moffatt New Testament translation. The error in certain early printings of the Moffatt New Testament at I Cor. 4:6 where the words "myself and Barnabas" appear for "myself and Apollos" is a slip of the pen made in modern times, based on no ancient evidence or hints at all. It is an example of how the most careful of scholars can nod, a very salutary example which teaches us to be patient with manuscript errors in antiquity.

Chapter Three

[1] See E. G. Schwiebert, *Luther and His Times: the Reformation from a New Perspective* (St. Louis: Concordia Publishing House, 1950), p. 281. Schwiebert's book is a mine of information about the period.

[2] *Ibid.,* p. 531, and Hans Volz in *The Cambridge History of the Bible: The West from the Reformation to the Present Day,* S. L. Greenslade, ed. (New York: Cambridge University Press, 1963), p. 95. Schwiebert cites an estimate that within two months 5,000 copies were sold.

[3] Details on university enrollment at Wittenberg are given in Schwiebert, *op. cit.,* pp. 603–12.

[4] L. J. Trinterud, "A Reappraisal of William Tyndale's Debt to Martin Luther," *Church History,* 31,1 (March, 1962), pp. 24–45; the phrase quoted occurs on p. 26. For a recent examination of Luther's influence on Coverdale, see H. Bluhm, "Luther and the First Printed English Bible: Epistle to the Galatians," *Anglican Theological Review,* 40, 4 (October, 1958), pp. 264–94.

[5] R. Bring, *How God Speaks to Us: The Dynamics of the Living Word* (Philadelphia: Muhlenberg Press, 1962), p. 22.

[6] As quoted by Roland H. Bainton, "The Bible in the Reformation," in *The Cambridge History of the Bible, op. cit.,* p. 20.

[7] Luther's account has often been translated and is widely quoted. The original is found in the Weimar edition of his *Werke,* Vol. 54 (1928), pp. 185 f. The translation quoted here is that of E. Harris Harbison, in *Great Problems in European Civilization,* K. M. Setton and H. R. Winkler, eds. (Englewood Cliffs, New Jersey: Prentice-Hall, Inc., 1954), pp. 252 f.

[8] Willem Jan Kooiman, *Luther and the Bible* (Philadelphia: Muhlenberg Press, 1961), p. 208.

[9] W. Schwarz, *Principles and Problems of Biblical Translation: Some Reformation Controversies and Their Background* (New York: Cambridge University Press, 1955). See also his articles, "Studies in Luther's Attitude towards Humanism" and "Examples of Luther's Biblical Translation," in *The Journal of Theological Studies,* 6 (1955), pp. 66–76 and 199–209.

[10] The words in the King James Version at Acts 9: 5–6, *"it is* hard for thee to kick against the pricks. And he trembling and astonished said, Lord, what wilt thou have me to do? And the Lord *said* unto him, . . ."* stand in no Greek manuscript but were inserted by Erasmus on the basis of the Latin into his Greek New Testament, whence they came into English translations. They derive ultimately from Acts 22:10*a* and 26:14*b.*

[11] In addition to the book reviews in periodicals noted in *New Testament Abstracts,* 2,2 (Winter, 1958), pp. 189 f., see also E. Harris Harbison, *The Christian Scholar in the Age of the Reformation* (New York: Charles Scribner's Sons, 1956), pp. 103–35, where detailed material is cited on Luther's attitude toward Erasmus and Jerome.

[12] In the *Table Talk,* as recorded by Veit Dietrich, No. 312, summer or fall, 1532; in the Weimar edition of Luther's *Werke,* Vol. 69, *Tischreden 1. Band* (1912), p. 128.

[13] The phrase is Bainton's, in *The Cambridge History of the Bible, op. cit.,* p. 24.

[14] *Encomium Eloquentiae (Corpus Reformatorum,* Vol. 2, col. 64), as quoted in Schwarz, *op. cit.,* p. 195.

[15] *The Four Gospels: A New Translation from the Greek* (London and Baltimore: Penguin Books, 1952).

[16] A transcript of the broadcast is printed in E. H. Robertson, *The New Translations of the Bible* ("Studies in Ministry and Worship," 12; London: SCM, and Naperville: Alec R. Allenson, 1959), pp. 119–32. The quotations are found on pp. 121, 124, and 132. The last two sentences also occur in the Introduction to Rieu's *Four Gospels, op. cit.,* pp. xxxii–xxxiii.

Chapter Four

[1] *Fathers and Heretics* (London: SPCK, 1948), p. 43.

[2] Kurt Aland, *Kirchengeschichte in Lebensbildern, 1. Teil: Die Frühzeit* (Berlin: Verlag "Die Kirche," 1953), p. 125.

³ Most information about Origen is given in Eusebius' *Ecclesiastical History*, Book Six, 1. 1 ff.

⁴ "Among them [the heretics] are those who make their way into households and capture weak women, burdened with sins and swayed by various impulses, who will listen to anybody and can never arrive at a knowledge of the truth."

⁵ The charges made against Jesus by the Jews in our canonical Luke at 23:2, 5, "We found this man perverting our nation and forbidding us to give tribute to Caesar, and saying that he himself is Christ a king. . . . He stirs up the people, teaching throughout all Judea, from Galilee even to this place," have been rewritten in Marcion and some Old Latin manuscripts to read, "We found this man perverting our nation *and abolishing the Law and the prophets* [contrast Matt. 5:17], and forbidding us to give tribute to Caesar *and misleading the women and children,* and saying that he himself is Christ a king. . . . He stirs up the people, teaching throughout all Judea, from Galilee even to this place, *and turns our sons and wives from us, for they are not baptized as we, nor do they purify themselves."* The additions (indicated by italics) presumably represent charges made against Marcion by the orthodox; he sought to suggest that already Jesus had been charged by the Jews with such things as people alleged against the Marcionites. Note that this obvious second-century change has infiltrated certain (orthodox) Old Latin manuscripts.

⁶ Hans Lietzmann, *The Founding of the Church Universal* (*The Beginnings of the Christian Church,* Vol. II, tr. by B. L. Woolf; New York: Charles Scribner's Sons, 1938), p. 417. Paperback reprint, *A History of the Early Church* (Cleveland and New York: Meridian Books, World Publishing Company, 1961), Vol. II, p. 316.

⁷ *Fathers and Heretics, op. cit.,* p. 64.

⁸ It is usually held that this first revision of the Psalms was immediately put into use by Damasus, and that it is the form that was used in the Roman liturgy until about 1570, and that is still employed at St. Peter's in Rome, in Milan, and at St. Mark's in Venice. It seems to me more likely, following the arguments of De Bruyne, that nothing of Jerome's first translation of the Psalms is extant, and that the *Psalterium Romanum,* the version used as noted above, is by someone else. *See* B. J. Roberts, *The Old Testament Text and Versions* (Cardiff: University of Wales Press, 1951), pp. 247 ff.

⁹ A detailed account is provided of this and other aspects of his life in C. L. Hulbert-Powell, *John James Wettstein 1693-1754* (London: SPCK, 1937).

¹⁰ *Kommentar zum Neuen Testament aus Talmud und Midrasch,* by Hermann L. Strack and Paul Billerbeck (4 vols. in 5 parts, Munich: Beck, 1922-28), with two supplementary index volumes in 1956 and 1961. Strack was the famed professor at Berlin who was listed as coeditor, but Billerbeck, a pastor at Frankfurt-am-Oder, has increasingly been recognized as the real workman.

[11] See W. C. van Unnik, "Corpus Hellenisticum Novi Testamenti," *Journal of Biblical Literature*, 83 (1964), pp. 17–33.

Chapter Five

[1] Edmund C. Burnett, "Thomson, Charles," in the *Dictionary of American Biography*, Dumas Malone, ed. (New York: Charles Scribner's Sons, 1936), Vol. 18, p. 481.

[2] Lewis R. Harley, *The Life of Charles Thomson* (Philadelphia: George W. Jacobs and Co., 1900), pp. 32 f., quoting *The Friend: A Religious and Literary Journal*, Vol. 1, p. 230. This *Life* is an expansion of Harley's *Charles Thomson, Patriot and Scholar* (Norristown, Pennsylvania: Historical Society of Montgomery County, 1897). See also Sarah Dickson Lowrie's published address to the Philadelphia Athenaeum in 1953, "Lest We Forget."

[3] Historical Society of Pennsylvania, the Hand Papers, Vol. 1, p. 2. Much of the Thomson material hereafter referred to is available in his manuscripts at the Historical Society and also at the library of the American Philosophical Society in Philadelphia; a portion of his correspondence with Franklin, Jefferson, and others is printed in *Collections of the New-York Historical Society for the Year 1878* (New York, 1879), pp. 1–286.

[4] Harley, *Life, op. cit.*, p. 161, quoting John F. Watson, *Annals of Philadelphia and Pennsylvania* (Philadelphia: Elijah Thomas, 1857), 1, 568.

[5] Vincent F. Pottle, "Charles Thomson's Translation of the Greek Bible," unpublished paper read at the Oriental Club of Philadelphia, 1942. I am appreciative that the late Father Pottle, formerly Dean of the Philadelphia Divinity School, allowed me to make use of his research at several points.

[6] Vol. 54, no. 15, 179, quoted in Pottle, *op. cit.*, pp. 2–3.

[7] Letter to the Reverend Samuel Miller, Jan. 6, 1801, quoted in a newspaper clipping from the *National Gazette*, May 18, 1839.

[8] Harley, *Charles Thomson, Patriot and Scholar, op. cit.*, p. 36, citing Joseph H. Jones, *Life of Ashbel Green* (New York: Robert Carter and Brothers, 1849).

[9] "Charles Thomson's New Testament," *The Pennsylvania Magazine of History and Biography*, Vol. 15 (1891), p. 329. The reference is to John F. Watson, "Collections of the Historical Society of Pennsylvania," Philadelphia, 1853, p. 90. Some of Thomson's papers were saved quite by chance when an Irish junkman had the sense to take them to the Historical Society in the 1870's because he knew the author had "signed the Paper" in 1776.

[10] J. A. Munroe, "The Philadelawareans," *ibid.*, Vol. 69 (1945), p. 141.

[11] *Ibid.*, Vol. 15 (1891), p. 499.

[12] Letter to the Reverend Samuel Miller, Jan. 6, 1801, quoted in Harley, *Charles Thomson, Patriot and Scholar, op. cit.*, pp. 33 f.

[13] Kendrick Grobel, "Charles Thomson, First American New Testament Translator—an Appraisal," *Journal of Bible and Religion*, 11 (1943), p. 147.

14 Dr. Edward Harwood, *A Liberal Translation of the New Testament,* 1768. Harwood attempted to ape the style of Samuel Johnson and the elaborate language then being used in translations of classical texts. He aimed at elegance, propriety, and perspicuity and achieved pomposity. Typical is his translation of Peter's words at the Transfiguration: "Oh, Sir! what a delectable residence we might establish here!"

15 Alexander Geddes, a Roman Catholic priest from Aberdeenshire in northern Scotland. He settled in London and, supported by a patron, began a translation of the Bible with explanatory notes. The first volume, to which Thomson refers, appeared in 1792. Geddes was one of the few scholars in the English-speaking world of the day in touch with radical German biblical criticism. In many ways he anticipated later theories on oral tradition. His views about the origins of the Pentateuch roused opposition among both Protestants and Roman Catholics. Geddes died in 1802 without completing his translation. On Geddes, see further pp. 186 f.

16 *Pennsylvania Magazine, op. cit.,* Vol. 13 (1889), p. 458.

17 *Life, op. cit.,* pp. 164 f.

18 So Grobel, *op. cit.,* p. 145, referring to Charles W. Upham, *Life of Timothy Pickering* (Boston: Little, Brown and Company, 1873), 2, 436.

19 Watson, *Annals, op. cit.,* 1, 568, and Harley, *Life, op. cit.,* p. 161.

20 L. C. L. Brenton, *The Septuagint Version of the Old Testament, according to the Vatican text, translated into English: with the principal various readings from the Alexandrine copy* . . . (London: S. Bagster, 1844), two volumes.

21 *Ibid.,* p. xi.

22 *Hades* . . . (London: Skeffington and Son, 1904).

23 Pells's views are set forth in a book, *The Church's Ancient Bible* (Hove, England: published by the author, no date), and in advance sheets and advertisements for Pells's reprints of the Thomson Septuagint in 1904 and 1907.

24 *Ibid.,* pp. 84, 87, 88.

25 *Ibid.,* p. 89.

26 *The Septuagint Bible, The Oldest Version of the Old Testament in the Translation of Charles Thomson, Secretary of the Continental Congress of the United States of America, 1774–1789,* as Edited, Revised and Enlarged by C. A. Muses (Indian Hills, Colorado: Falcon's Wing Press, 1954).

27 E.g., the remarks of Harry Orlinsky in the *Journal of Biblical Literature,* 75,2 (June, 1956), pp. 155 f., to which Muses responded in *JBL* 76,1 (March, 1957), p. 84; or J. P. Smith, in *Biblica,* 37 (1956), pp. 497–500; or *Journal of Bible and Religion,* 24 (1956), pp. 133 f.

28 P. 429, as quoted in Harley, *Life, op. cit.,* p. 177.

29 *A Manual of Biblical Bibliography* (London: T. Cadell, 1839), p. 263. The last-mentioned quality, use of the dialog form in the Pauline epistles, has been compared by Grobel, *op. cit.,* p. 148, to the conclusion in Rudolf

Bultmann's doctoral dissertation—that Paul's letters employ the diatribe form. Thomson had certain literary insight and liked to arrange Old Testament passages into dialogs between the Lord and a prophet. Thomas H. Horne, whose opinion has been quoted above, is an interesting person in his own right. The grandfather of the Old Testament scholar T. K. Cheyne, Horne achieved a reputation as a bibliographer and for his widely read commentaries on the Scriptures. His judgment carries some weight.

[30] Quoted in Harley, *Life, op. cit.,* pp. 178 f.

Chapter Six

[1] Ernest A. Payne, *Henry Wheeler Robinson, Scholar, Teacher, Principal: A Memoir* (London: Nisbet, 1946), p. 92.

[2] See H. P. Rickman, "From Detection to Theology (The work of Dorothy Sayres)," *The Hibbert Journal,* 60,2 (July, 1962), pp. 290–96.

[3] Chicago: Willett, Clark and Company, 1935.

[4] Reprinted, London: Arthur Barker, Ltd., 1955, and Ithaca: Cornell University Press, 1956.

[5] Erhard Lauch, "Nichts gegen Tischendorf," *Bekenntnis zur Kirche: Festgabe für Ernst Sommerlath zum 70. Geburtstag* (Berlin; Evangelische Verlagsanstalt, 1960), pp. 15–24.

[6] Ihor Ševčenko, "New Documents on Constantine Tischendorf and the *Codex Sinaiticus," Scriptorium: International Review of Manuscript Studies* (Brussels), 18 (1964), pp. 55–80. Professor Ševčenko's conclusion is that as a scholar Tischendorf's acumen was impeccable—Porfirij Uspenskij saw Codex Sinaiticus in 1845 and 1850 but failed to realize its importance; Tischendorf grasped its significance immediately—but as a negotiator, Tischendorf can be termed "honorable" only after the final settlement in 1869; between 1859 and that date Professor Ševčenko terms him honorable "only retroactively" (p. 80).

[7] Christian Tindall, *Contributions to the Statistical Study of the Codex Sinaiticus* (Edinburgh: Oliver and Boyd, 1961).

[8] London: Epworth Press, 1939.

Chapter Seven

[1] Chicago: Moody Press, 1961. *The Twentieth Century New Testament* was originally published in a "Tentative Edition" of three parts, London: Mowbray House, and New York: Fleming H. Revell, 1898, 1900, 1901; then in a one-volume format, 1901; and finally in a "Permanent" or "Revised Edition" in 1904 by Revell, and London: Horace Marshall (later, The Sunday School Union).

[2] "The Making of the Twentieth Century New Testament," *Bulletin of the John Rylands Library, Manchester,* 38,1 (September, 1955), pp. 58–81.

[3] *Ibid.,* p. 61.

[4] *The New Schaff-Herzog Encyclopedia of Religious Knowledge*, ed. Samuel Macauley Jackson (New York: Funk and Wagnalls, 1912), Vol. 12, p. 554.

[5] R. F. Weymouth, *The New Testament in Modern Speech*, fifth edition, revised by J. A. Robertson (Boston: Pilgrim Press, 1943), p. 118. However, this note does not occur in the third edition, 1909, edited by Hampden-Cook; but the idea appears there on pp. 559 and 688.

[6] *The New Testament in Modern Speech; An idiomatic translation into every-day English from the text of 'the Resultant Greek Testament'* (London: J. Clarke and Co., 1903). Subsequent editions in 1904, 1909, 1924, 1929, and 1952.

[7] J. Rendel Harris, *Side-Lights on New Testament Research* (London: Kingsgate Press, and James Clarke and Co., 1908), p. 9.

[8] James Hope Moulton (1863–1917) began, in 1906, under the influence of Deissmann, a *Grammar of New Testament Greek*, and in 1914 a series of volumes, *Vocabulary of the Greek Testament, illustrated from the Papyri*. The latter work was completed in 1930, but the *Grammar* has been under a seeming "spell of doom." Moulton's pupil, W. F. Howard, finished Volume II of the *Grammar* in 1929, but died before he could plan much of Volume III. H. G. Meecham took over the task but died in 1955. Nigel Turner then "broke the spell," as he said, by living to publish Volume III in 1963. The Moulton family has made great contributions to Bible translation for a century. The father of J. H. Moulton, William Fiddian Moulton (1835–98), headmaster of The Leys School, Cambridge, was one of the revisers of the 1881 New Testament, and produced along with A. S. Geden a famous Greek concordance which every New Testament scholar uses. His brother, Richard G. Moulton, a professor of English at the University of Chicago, edited the famous *Modern Reader's Bible* in 1895. In the present generation a son, H. K. Moulton, is secretary of The British and Foreign Bible Society. See also *James Hope Moulton 11th October 1863—7th April 1917* (London: Epworth, 1963).

[9] *Amicitiae Corolla: A Volume of Essays Presented to James Rendel Harris, D. Litt. on the Occasion of His Eightieth Birthday*, edited by H. G. Wood (London: University of London Press, 1933), p. xiii, translation by L. R. M. Strachan.

[10] Harris, *op. cit.*, pp. 7–28.

[11] *Op. cit.*, p. 68.

[12] John Hamilton Skilton, *The Translation of the New Testament into English, 1881–1950: Studies in Language and Style*, unpublished Ph.D. dissertation, University of Pennsylvania, 1961, especially pp. 360–64. (Available in microfilm-Xerox, University Microfilms, Ann Arbor, Michigan.)

[13] *The New Testament in the Language of Today* (St. Louis: Concordia, 1963).

[14] *Op. cit.*, p. 81.

Chapter Eight

[1] *Time,* 59, 6 (Feb. 11, 1952), 41. An obituary article appears in 70, 10 (Sept. 2, 1957), 36–38.

[2] For a thorough study by Roman Catholic scholars of the entire sweep of English Bibles, from Anglo-Saxon versions to 1950, see *English Versions of the Bible,* by Hugh Pope, O.P., revised and amplified by Sebastian Bullough, O.P. (St. Louis and London: B. Herder, 1952). Father Pope was a member of the advisory committee for the Knox translation; Knox dedicated Volume II of his *New Testament Commentary* to Father Bullough. Unfortunately, the treatment of the Knox version, appended by Father Bullough, is very brief, pp. 502–504, cf. 495, 497.

[3] Ronald Knox once commented of the Douay version that it "was written in the language of exiles, which became, with time, an exiled language" (*The Trials of a Translator* [New York: Sheed and Ward, 1949], p. 75).

[4] *Time,* 70,10 (Sept. 2, 1957), 38. Knox's general conservatism is indicated in another anecdote. When requested to perform a baptism in English, he replied, "The baby doesn't understand English, and the Devil knows Latin" (E. Waugh, *Monsignor Ronald Knox* [Boston: Little, Brown and Company, 1959], p. 111).

[5] *The New Testament in the Westminster Version of the Sacred Scriptures,* Cuthbert Lattey, S. J., and Joseph Keating, S. J., eds. (published in separate fascicles, the New Testament 1913–35, the Old Testament, 1934–   ; [London: Sands; and New York: Longmans, Green]. For details on the several editions, see Pope, *op. cit.,* pp. 500 f.).

[6] *The New Testament Rendered from the Original Greek with Explanatory Notes,* by James A. Kleist, S. J., and Joseph L. Lilly, C. M. (Milwaukee: Bruce Publishing Company, 1954). Father Kleist, a classics scholar who died in 1949, had published a translation of Mark as early as 1936; his foreword to his rendering of the Four Gospels is dated 1948. Father Lilly, who translated the rest of the New Testament, died in 1952. Their work is thus contemporary with Knox's undertaking, but reflects much more the modern, critical Bible study movement among Roman Catholic scholars and the spirit of *Divino Afflante Spiritu.*

[7] *Monsignor Ronald Knox, Fellow of Trinity College, Oxford, and Protonotary Apostolic to His Holiness Pope Pius XII, compiled from the original sources,* by Evelyn Waugh (Boston: Little, Brown and Company, 1959).

[8] The quotation, from a speech at the Union, ran, "The honourable gentlemen have turned their backs upon their country and now have the effrontery to say they have their country behind them," Waugh, *op. cit.,* p. 90, citing N. Micklem, *The Box and the Puppets* (London: G. Bles, 1957), pp. 34 f. One of Knox's speeches consisted entirely of limericks.

[9] Originally in *The Oxford Magazine,* November, 1912, reprinted in

London: Society of SS. Peter and Paul, 1913 (?), then in *Essays in Satire*
(London: Sheed and Ward, 1928), 81 ff., and in *In Three Tongues* (London: Chapman and Hall, 1959), pp. 112 ff; quoted by permission of Mr.
Evelyn Waugh and Sheed and Ward, Ltd. On Knox's attitude toward
much of critical biblical scholarship in this period, cf. Waugh, *op. cit.,*
p. 107, or some of his essays satirizing the critical method, e.g., "proving"
that Queen Victoria wrote Tennyson's *In Memoriam;* a favorite is "The
Identity of Pseudo-Bunyan," in *Essays in Satire, op. cit.*

10 See Waugh, *op. cit.,* pp. 146 f.

11 London: Longmans and Co., 1918, later reprinted.

12 *The Three Taps* and *The Footsteps at the Lock* (reprinted, London:
Methuen, 1951 and 1950 respectively; and Baltimore: Penguin Books, 1960
and 1963).

13 London: Sheed and Ward, 1939.

14 *Op. cit.,* p. 273.

15 From *Thirteen for Christ* edited by Melville Harcourt, © Sheed and
Ward Inc., 1963, p. 156.

16 I.e., he *said* Mass, Waugh, *op. cit.,* p. 277. Horton Davies says that
"Monsignor Knox spoke like an angel, but sang like a rook" (*Varieties
of English Preaching 1900–1960* [Englewood Cliffs: Prentice-Hall, Inc.,
1963], p. 128). Significantly, Knox's book, *The Mass in Slow Motion*
(London: Sheed and Ward, 1948) consists of meditations on *Low* Mass; he
wrote there, ". . . it is a long time since I had to sing High Mass, and
when I did, the only thought I can remember entertaining, was a vivid
hope that I might die before we got to the Preface" (p. x). From *The Mass
in Slow Motion* by Ronald Knox, Copyright 1948 Sheed and Ward Inc.

17 London and New York: Sheed and Ward, 1949.

18 Oxford: Clarendon Press, 1950.

19 Waugh, *op. cit.,* pp. 282 f.

20 *Thirteen for Christ, op. cit.,* 156 ff.

21 Printed in *The Trials of a Translator, op. cit.,* pp. 106–13.

22 See Waugh, *op. cit.,* p. 284, and also *The Trials of a Translator, op.
cit.,* p. 19.

23 *Ibid.,* p. 290.

24 Reprinted in *The Trials of a Translator, op. cit.,* pp. 24–45.

25 The publisher for the several volumes and editions of the Knox Bible
has been Sheed and Ward in both the United States and Britain.

26 "Liturgical Preaching: Monsignor Ronald Knox," in *Varieties of
English Preaching, op. cit.,* pp. 116–37.

27 *The Epistles and Gospels for Sundays and Holydays: Translation
and Commentary* by Ronald Knox, copyright 1946 Sheed and Ward Inc.,
New York.

28 From *Bridegroom and Bride* by Ronald Knox, © 1957 Sheed and
Ward Inc., New York, p. 69, as quoted in *Varieties of English Preaching,
op. cit.,* p. 137, n. 1.

[29] Waugh, *op. cit.,* pp. 190–92.

[30] See Charles M. Cooper, "Msgr. Knox's Old Testament in English," *The Lutheran Quarterly,* 3,4 (Nov., 1951), pp. 366–82.

[31] *The Trials of a Translator, op. cit.,* p. 76.

[32] *Ibid.,* pp. 8 f.

[33] *Ibid.,* pp. 34 f.

[34] *Ibid.,* pp. 21 f.

[35] *The Epistles and Gospels for Sundays and Holydays, op. cit.,* p. 16; cf. *The Trials of a Translator, op. cit.,* p. 104.

[36] *The Trials of a Translator, op. cit.,* p. 102.

[37] *Ibid.,* pp. 89 f. Knox did not desire his translation to be revised and refurbished at some later date; rather, scrap it, and start afresh; See Waugh, *op. cit.,* p. 312.

[38] *Ibid.,* p. 19.

[39] *Thirteen for Christ, op. cit.,* p. 165.

[40] *The Trials of a Translator, op. cit.,* pp. 106 f.

[41] *The Trials of a Translator, op. cit.,* p. 103.

[42] *Ibid.,* p. 104.

[43] *Ibid.,* pp. 87 ff. The critic "Glaucon" referred to there reminds one of some of the members on Knox's advisory committee; cf. Waugh, *op. cit.,* pp. 285 ff.

[44] *The Westminster Version of the Sacred Scriptures* in its Old Testament (1934–   ) had abandoned Vulgate names for those common in English since the King James Version.

[45] John 11:43 in Knox's "trial edition" and in the edition published by Sheed and Ward, New York. However, the "final edition" had an even longer paraphrase, "Come out, Lazarus, to my side"; see *The Trials of a Translator,* pp. 102 f. There are also other little variations in the "trial" and "final" editions, such as whether "lads" or "friends" is used at John 21:5.

[46] *Ibid.,* pp. 39 f.; see also Cooper, *op. cit.,* pp. 367, 373.

[47] This, the third Latin rendering of the Psalms attributed to Jerome, was completed A.D. 392 and represents the form closest to the Hebrew of the three; see Charles M. Cooper, "Jerome's 'Hebrew Psalter' and the New Latin Version," *Journal of Biblical Literature,* 69, 3 (Sept., 1950), pp. 233–44.

[48] Psalm 10 of the Hebrew has been attached to Psalm 9 in the Latin. Psalm 147 of the Hebrew has been divided into two psalms (146 and 147) in the Latin. Thus, the numbering in the Vulgate from 10 to 147 equals 11 to 147 in the Hebrew. Knox follows the Latin system; the King James Version, R.S.V., etc., follow the Hebrew.

[49] *A New Testament Commentary for English Readers, Vol. I, The Gospels* (London: Burns, Oates and Washbourne, 1953, and New York: Sheed and Ward, 1952); *Vol. II, The Acts of the Apostles, St. Paul's Letters to the Churches* (1954); *Vol. III, The Later Epistles, The Apocalypse*

(1956). A summary of reviews is given in *New Testament Abstracts,* 2,2 (Winter, 1958), pp. 184 f.

[50] *The Gospel Story* (New York: Sheed and Ward, 1958); *It Is Paul Who Writes* (New York: Sheed and Ward, 1959). Knox dedicated *The Trials of a Translator* to Cox, with these words (in Latin); "To the Reverend Father Ronald Cox, a friend totally separated by the distance of a world, but in name and study how astonishingly near!"

[51] *A Harmony of the Gospels in the Knox Translation,* L. Johnston and A. Pickering, eds. (New York: Sheed and Ward, 1963).

[52] "On English Translation," reprinted in *Literary Distractions* by Ronald Knox, © Evelyn Waugh 1958, published by Sheed and Ward Inc., New York, pp. 36–58.

[53] *Ibid.,* p. 58.

[54] *The New York Times,* April 29, 1956, p. 10.

[55] Waugh, *op. cit.,* p. 333.

[56] *Ibid.,* pp. 333 f. ". . . love of former times" in Waugh is a misprint; Knox wrote "lore." D'Arcy has "their study" in place of "his study" in the Knox translation, probably to make a connection with the plural form "their" in the next sentence. A glance at the Knox Bible will further show that Father D'Arcy has rearranged the verses in the sequence 39:1, 38:39, and that Father Knox felt that the last half of verse 39 (after the three dots) goes with 39:1, about those who study the word of God, in contrast to the picture of manual laborers in chapter 38 through verse 39*a*. The R.S.V. renders,

> [manual laborers] keep stable the fabric of the world,
>   and their prayer is in the practice of their trade.
> On the other hand he who devotes himself
>   to the study of the law of the Most High
> will seek out the wisdom of all the ancients,
>   and will be concerned with prophecies.

Thus, even in such seemingly appropriate verses, there remains a problem of text to try the translator and preacher.

Epilogue: Toward Tomorrow

[1] In his review of the N.E.B. New Testament in *The Observer* (London), March 19, 1961, pp. 21 f., reprinted in *Atlas, The Magazine of the World Press,* 1,3 (May, 1961), pp. 70–73.

[2] See pp. 202, 204, and 212 in this text, and *Literary Distractions, op. cit.,* p. 38.

[3] *The Literary Impact of the Authorized Version,* "Facet Books—Biblical Series," 4 (Philadelphia: Fortress Press, 1963), pp. 31–34.

[4] *The New Hermeneutic* (J. M. Robinson and J. B. Cobb, Jr., eds.; "New Frontiers in Theology," Vol. II; New York: Harper and Row, 1964), p. 4. This volume provides a good introduction to the movement.

[5] E.g., Eugene A. Nida, *Toward a Science of Translating* (Leiden: Brill, 1964), and the other volumes in the series "Helps for Translators," prepared under the auspices of the United Bible Societies.

[6] David Noel Freedman, as quoted in *Time*, 84, 17 (Oct. 23, 1964), 87.

[7] H. Schlier, "Erwägungen zu einer deutscher Einheitsübersetzung der Heiligen Schrift," *Biblische Zeitschrift*, 8 (1964), pp. 1–21.

[8] According to B. H. Streeter, *The Four Gospels* (London: Macmillan, 1956 ed.), p. 138; but cf. J. Rendel Harris, *Side-Lights on New Testament Research, op. cit.*, pp. 96–103.

Scriptural Index

Old Testament

New Testament

GENERAL INDEX

Adams, John, 124

Agricola, Michael, 73

Akiba: 33–37, 60, 141, 146;
  attitude to Bar-Cocheba, 35 f.
  early life, 33 f.
  martyrdom, 36
  relations with Rome, 34 f.
  study of the Law, 34, 36

Aland, Kurt, 95, 121; 224, n. 2.
     See also "Nestle-Aland
     text."

Alexandria, 8–19, 49, 95–100

Alison, Dr. Francis, 123 f., 129

Allegheny College, 126, 133

allegory, 101

Ambrose of Milan, 93

Ambrose (Origen's patron), 98,
  100

American Bible Society, 217, 222

American Philosophical Society, 4,
  137; 226, n. 3

am ha-arez, 34

Ammonius Saccas, 97

Anchor Bible, 215, 217, 221

anti-Semitism, 28, 96

Apocrypha, 14, 27, 66–68, 111,
  131

Apollos, 48–51; 223, Chap. 2, n. 2

Aquila: 34, 37–40, 44, 60, 91,
  103, 110, 146
  as a translator, 37–39
  background, 37
  conversions, 37
  hermeneutics of, 38 f.
  use and value of his work, 40

"Aristeas legend," 143

Aristeas, The Letter of, 8–22, 74,
  84, 86 f., 214 f.

Augsburg Confession, 53, 57,
  67 f.

Augustine, 86–88, 94, 104 f.

Aurogallus, M., 68 f.

Authorized Version: see "King
  James Version."

Bainton, Roland H., 224, n. 6, 13

Baljon, 52

Ballentine, F. S., 178

Bar-Cocheba (Kosebah, Coziba),
  Simon, 22, 29, 35 f., 140

Barnabas, 180; 223, Chap. 2, n. 2

Barth, Karl, 6, 42

Basel, 62, 74, 84, 115 f., 118 f.

Bazett, the Rev. Henry, 169 f.,
  178

Beardslee, John, 217, 222

Beck, William, 182, 217, 222;
  229, n. 13

Ben Asher, Aaron, 219

Ben Asher Text, 26

Ben Chayim, Jacob, 26

Bentley, Richard, 117 f.

Beza, Theodore, 149

"Bible English," 20, cf. 70, 202–
  204; see also "Elizabethan
  English."

Billerbeck, Paul, 120; 225, n. 10

Bluhm, H., 223, n. 4

Bodmer Library papyri, Geneva,
  215

Bora, Katherine von, 67, 69

Boulton, Thomas Sibley, 173

237